PSYCHOLOGY AND PRODUCTIVITY

PSYCHOLOGY AND PRODUCTIVITY

Edited by

Paul Whitney
Washington State University
Pullman, Washington

and

Robert B. Ochsman
University of Arkansas at Little Rock
Little Rock, Arkansas

PLENUM PRESS • NEW YORK AND LONDON

Library of Congress Cataloging in Publication Data

Psychology and productivity / edited by Paul Whitney and Robert B. Ochsman.
    p.   cm.
  Includes bibliographical references and index.
  ISBN 0-306-42937-3
  1. Labor productivity—Psychological aspects—Congresses. 2. Labor productivity—
Research—United States—Congresses. 3. White collar workers—United States—
Congresses. 4. Psychology, Industrial—United States—Congresses. I. Whitney, Paul. II.
Ochsman, Robert B.
  HD57.P78   1988   88-17895
  158.7—dc19   CIP

Proceedings of a symposium on Psychology and Productivity: Bringing Together Research
and Practice, held August 3–4, 1987, in Little Rock, Arkansas

© 1988 Plenum Press, New York
A Division of Plenum Publishing Corporation
233 Spring Street, New York, N.Y. 10013

PREFACE

This volume is based on the symposium "Psychology and Productivity: Bringing Together Research and Practice" held at the University of Arkansas at Little Rock in August 1987. The conference was made possible by the Marie Wilson Howell's bequest to the UALR Psychology Department.

The symposium participants (and others invited to contribute to this volume) came from three different perspectives. There were basic researchers with a broad range of theoretical interests, applied researchers with an industrial-organizational orientation, and practitioners who apply psychological principles in business settings. The conference was organized into three sessions, each consisting of presentations and discussions from one of the perspectives. This book follows the same format.

It was our hope that the symposium would serve as a forum for communication across different areas that can contribute to understanding and improving white collar productivity. We hope that this volume helps to continue, on a broader scale, the communication established at the symposium.

Paul Whitney
Robert B. Ochsman

CONTENTS

INTRODUCTION AND OVERVIEW

Prognostication will always be a tricky business. Yet, for the foreseeable future, issues of American productivity and competitiveness are likely to be dominant themes in our news, our elections, and our boardrooms. It would be a mistake, however, to assume that concerns about productivity are just trendy topics. Many of the issues are not new. Obviously, business managers have a long history of interest in the factors that lead to higher productivity. Social scientists, too, have a longstanding interest in productivity, especially if we consider it in comprehensive, human terms. As Norbert Weiner (1950) explained,

> It is simpler to organize a factory or a galley which uses human beings for a fraction of their worth than it is to provide a world in which they can grow to their full stature (p. 16).

The challenge put forth by Weiner is an extraordinary one. It is also one that the field of psychology should be able to help society address. One of the attractions for psychologists may be that productivity represents an old problem, but one that changes as society evolves. Complex challenges of this sort are relished by the quixotic science of psychology.

How might psychologists help address present day problems of productivity? The seminal idea for the conference that generated this book was that this question must be faced by examining a broad range of perspectives, methods, and findings within psychology. Although there are diverse, and sometimes divergent, perspectives represented here, the chapters are bound together by a concern for how sound empirical research in psychology can be applied toward improving productivity.

Because of recent changes in the American economy, we focused our attention on white collar productivity. As Thurow (1986) pointed out, a social scientist who is concerned only with input and output on the factory floor is concentrating on the sector with the fewest problems. Between 1978 and 1985 there was a 6% reduction in blue collar jobs and at the same time there was an 18% gain in business output. So what is wrong with our productivity? During this same period, white collar payrolls went up 21%. White collar workers now outnumber their blue collar counterparts by close to two to one. It is not difficult to see where the "bottleneck" in productivity lies.

The concerns that have been expressed most often when considering white collar productivity center around three areas: managerial and organizational policy, the impact of technology (especially computers), and how to measure the effectiveness of programs designed to increase productivity. For example, a number of authors have considered whether the disappointing pace of gains in American productivity could be improved by adopting management styles more like those of our foreign competitors (cf. Lehrer, 1983). Thurow (1986), among others, raises the question of why the considerable investment in new business software and hardware has not brought with it clear-cut increases in productivity (see also Fitch, 1983). Of course, an issue basic to all other issues in productivity is the problem of measurement. Unfortunately, there appears to be a great deal of misunderstanding regarding the measurement of productivity (Thor, 1983).

Questions about management, technological impact, and measurement are addressed here, as well. However, the contributors to this book have considered these issues specifically in the context of how we can bring research and practice together in developing solutions. The researcher-practitioner division has a long and troublesome history in many areas of psychology. Establishing links across this division is not easy, but it is almost certainly necessary with a problem as complex as productivity. It is encouraging that, despite the considerable differences in training and professional settings among the authors, several areas of common (and complementary) interest appear in the book. To help the reader appreciate the unifying themes, I will preview each of the chapters in terms of their relevance to the general issues of management, technology, and measurement.

In Part I, the chapters center on basic research in human factors, cognition, and artificial intelligence (AI). Many of the future interactions between business and psychology will be influenced by developments in these areas.

The importance of such basic research to understanding the problems of implementing new technologies is clearly shown in Thomas Cocklin's chapter. He provides a clear rationale for the necessity of taking human information processing characteristics into account in system design. The problems encountered by new users of complex computer systems are, by now, notorious and much of the seemingly failed promise of computer enhancement of productivity can be traced to ignoring the body of work that Cocklin discusses.

In the next chapter, Diana L. W. Whitney and I consider how research on the psychology of language can give insights into a problem of increasing importance to white collar workers--the production of clear, coherent text. Here again, new technologies may be of great benefit. However, we are currently limited by the scarcity of empirical data on the writing process. We outline a program of research that combines both basic and applied elements with the ultimate goal of developing computer aids to the production of technical prose.

George Kellas, Greg Simpson, and Richard Ferraro present new data on cognitive processes in the elderly. Their work challenges the assumption that mental functions steadily decline in later years. In fact, the authors identify a subpopulation of elderly subjects who outperform college students on a language processing task. Given the rate of growth of the older segments of our population, organizations soon will be required to become responsive to questions of productivity and aging. The research reported by Kellas and his colleagues has general, and important, implications for conceptualizing the whole issue of individual differences in the mental abilities of older people.

To conclude Part I, Sally and Walter Sedelow address the future of technological effects on productivity by providing an overview of current trends in AI. Clearly, many of the trends taking place in AI have profound implications for the workplace. This is particularly true in considering the future of "expert systems" that interact with professionals in a variety of scientific and technical fields. As the authors point out, there are many pitfalls on the way to realization of the dramatic potential for AI applications. Although we tend to think of new technologies as displacing the factory worker, one impact of expert systems will be demoralization of some white collar workers as automated systems make certain jobs obsolete. The chapter also contains discussions of more subtle problems that can slow the growth of productivity. In particular, ideological factors that discourage long-range conceptual development and exploratory projects may become a most serious threat to America's competitiveness.

In Part II, the contributors take a close look at current research in industrial-organizational psychology and point out what directions seem most promising. All five chapters consider how psychologists could increase the positive impact of their research on problems of productivity.

Wayne Cascio first outlines the scope of issues relevant to productivity and its measurement. He then considers what sort of changes in productivity behavioral science interventions are likely to bring about. Cascio makes a clear case that selection and training programs, long a mainstay of I/O psychologists' repertoire, can have a major impact on productivity. However, he faults the field for a failure to demonstrate the effects of interventions in terms that will attract the notice of the consumers of behavioral science programs.

Richard Guzzo's chapter deals with both productivity measurement and managerial practice. Guzzo's specific concern is the effect of financial incentives on productivity and he has found that the effects of incentive programs are anything but straightforward. A given incentive program can increase, fail to change, or even decrease productivity. So much for the contention that psychological research merely confirms common sense! Guzzo makes a number of concrete suggestions for ways that future research can clear up what is presently a rather clouded issue.

Robert Hogan, Susan Raza, and James Driskell point out an important gap in the research on organizations. Perhaps it is the independent streak that characterizes the American psyche, but for whatever reasons, researchers have seriously neglected the issue of team effectiveness. Hogan and his colleagues present data on how individual personalities and organizational context jointly determine the effectiveness of work teams. Based on their data, the authors provide a number of suggestions for how organizations can improve team performance.

Mio and Goishi's chapter is concerned with the effectiveness of employee assistance programs. In particular, they consider the interesting problem of trying to reach troubled white collar workers. Here the problems of measuring productivity can result in failure to reach troubled employees with interventions that could be of great benefit to the person and the company.

Reilly and Clevenger take a hard empirical look at the relationship between stress and performance in nursing. Nurses are an interesting population to consider because they, in many ways, seem representative of problems facing many human service workers. Of particular interest in Reilly and Clevenger's chapter is their thorough evaluation of the status of the concept of "burn out". While they note that there is preliminary evidence that a variety of interventions may be of help in reducing the incidence of burnout, much research remains to be done to improve relevant measurement techniques.

In Part III, the chapters are directly relevant to the issue of implementing research in applied settings. All three authors have extensive experience with the problems of implementation.

Clark Wilson's chapter exemplifies the concern that I/O psychologists have for issues of measurement. His discussion begins with very basic issues in learning theory. He then considers the implications of learning theory for the measurement of leadership abilities.

Robert Ochsman and Roger Webb provide a broad view of a key issue in organizational performance: employee training. They show how many of the important considerations are made salient by taking a systems approach. One of the advantages of taking a systems view is that it becomes easier to see the relationships between basic and applied research. For example, Ochsman and Webb discuss the importance of understanding how particular system elements (managers, trainees, computers) interact--a problem considered in somewhat similar terms in Cocklin's chapter.

Finally, Virginia Boehm specifies the factors that determine whether a particular body of research gets implemented. Her discussion contains many valuable suggestions for those who try to do psychologically based interventions in business settings. In many respects, Boehm's chapter complements Cascio's by discussing ways that psychologists can work more effectively with managers.

In summary, the work presented in the various chapters shows quite clearly that psychological research can have important applications to problems in the areas of managerial practice, technological change, and productivity measurement. The chapters also make it clear that a great deal more work is needed if psychologists are to increase their ability to address problems of white collar productivity. Future problems will be addressed more successfully if we do a better job of bringing together research and practice.

REFERENCES

Fitch, D. S. (1982). Increasing productivity in the microcomputer age. Reading, MA: Addison-Wesley

Lehrer, R. N. (1983). A conceptual framework. In R. N. Lehrer (Ed.), White collar productivity (pp. 6-24). New York: McGraw-Hill.

Thor, C. G. (1983). Productivity measurement in white collar groups. In R. N. Lehrer (Ed.), White collar productivity (pp. 29-42). New York: McGraw-Hill.

Thurow, L. C. (1986) [Review of The positive sum strategy: Harnessing technology for economic growth]. Scientific American, 255(3), 24-31.

Wiener, N. (1950). The human use of human beings: Cybernetics and society. Boston: Houghton Mifflin.

SOME ISSUES IN BASIC RESEARCH

SOFTWARE USABILITY AND PRODUCTIVITY

Thomas G. Cocklin

Hewlett-Packard
Ft. Collins, Colorado

INTRODUCTION

Computers play an integral role in our lives. Computer systems perform a wide variety of tasks automatically that were once done manually. They have literally changed the way people do business, teach their children lessons, heal themselves, and keep themselves informed on a daily basis. Computers control monetary flow, speed the judicial process, decipher our past and shape our future.

The CEO of a major personal computer manufacturer reports that engineers using their computers have "cut time, manpower requirements, and error rates significantly" (Sculley, 1987, p. 236). He adds that "...the data suggest that they [the engineers] could produce the project with 43 percent less cost. They [the management] also estimated that the competitiveness of their company rose 46% and the quality of their work increased 52%." These fantastic increases in productivity, voiced despite the lack of supporting empirical evidence, are still noteworthy. But do computers make users more productive? And if they do, are users satisfied with the method or the outcome?

PRODUCTIVITY: A USER-CENTERED DEFINITION

Productivity as a measure of useful output gained over time has been viewed from many different perspectives. Economic theories measuring cost-effectiveness have been mathematically derived (Williams, 1983). Also, return-on-investment metrics as they relate to costs and benefits have been developed (Primrose, Creamer, & Leonard, 1985), as have task-specific productivity metrics (Groover & Zimmer, 1984). However, the following discussion will be concerned with productivity from a user's perspective. From this perspective, productivity is a measure of performance that goes beyond allocation of time and resources. Essentially, it is the quality and magnitude of accomplishment relative to the needed amount of effort. So, encapsulated within this definition are not only time and the expenditure of resources but also job completion with some sense of satisfaction.

In the computer domain, questions of productivity often involve comparisons between performing a task by computer and performing it manually. The list of computer-aided tasks which were once done by hand or with specialized equipment is endless. For example, the abundance of word processing equipment in the market place seems to stem from the fact that users are more productive and are more satisfied with them than with non-error correcting typewriters. However, the point remains that when computer systems and their software are not effective tools, it is the user that is thought of as being ineffective. Over time, the hapless user is imprisoned, not by the task but by the computer system that lies between the user's intentions and an acceptable outcome.

Rubinstein and Hersh (1984) maintain that productivity "reflects how well the computer system matches user needs" (p. 11). Productivity and performance are interchangeable in terms of the number of human-machine interactions, the time spent waiting by users, the number of errors produced, the degree of user satisfaction, and the system's complexity level. Ultimately they maintain that, "using a computer should be easier than not using a computer." This may seem to be an idealistic and somewhat trivial statement considering the state of some computer systems today. However, it is also fairly profound considering the time it takes to prepare, install, configure, learn, and ultimately use these systems to complete jobs previously accomplished fairly well by hand.

Computers as Tools

Computer systems act as functional helpers between users and their tasks. Software programmers develop a system by forming and instantiating a conceptual model of a particular task domain through their understanding of how the task is carried out manually. This conceptual model then, hopefully, corresponds to the users' mental model—a mental representation of the starting problem, the problem space, the task rules, and the end goals. Computer systems help users execute the steps needed to complete the task by supplying work space, providing the appropriate tools, and offering guidance in the form of feedback. If the system executes the tasks in accordance with the users' directives, then all is well. However, if the system misdirects task execution by not understanding the user or by not providing the correct tools, then the conceptual model of the system is not matched with the mental model of the user. When this occurs, productivity is lost because users are compromised by the way the system translates the users' activities. In this case, users are left doing two jobs: understanding how to make the system accomplish the task and trying to complete the task itself. This effectively doubles the users' efforts and decreases productivity by moving users further from the goal of effective task completion.

Consider the following analogy. Normally, asking someone to do something requires an understanding of the task to be accomplished, a knowledge of the listener's language, and the ability to speak the message clearly. We have a mental model of the task, how it should be done, and approximately what the end results should be. We also know what tools to use in order to complete the task. The mental model, in this case, represents our perspective of the task within the context of our language.

The listener, too, forms a conceptual model of the task requirements that may or may not totally correspond with the mental model of the asker. The development of the conceptual model on the listener's part stems from the listener's own knowledge of the task, understanding of the language, and ability to clearly hear the asker. If the asker does not use appropriate language to describe the task or uses phrases with foreign meanings, then the listener may misinterpret the request. Frustrated, the asker is then faced with two tasks, first to recognize the misinterpretation, and second, to recommunicate the directive in a way that more closely matches the listener's conceptual model of the task. The moral is that the users' intent does not necessarily guarantee a predictable outcome. Any failure on the listener's, or analogously on the system's part, to communicate with the user or to complete an action will lead to less than suitable results.

It has been noted that if a computer system helps the user actively participate in accomplishing a task, then the system's role as intermediary disappears (Laurel, 1986). The system becomes transparent, perfectly involving the user with the task at hand. The user is never faced with the double task of working the system and accomplishing the goal because the system never interferes with the users' intentions (Maas, 1983; Thimbley, 1984). But in some sense, the user is always separated from being directly involved in the task. In the computer domain, users view their tasks through the system, which reflects the task at hand (see Figure 1). The system reflects the task to a user with information processing and storage capabilities and limitations. The users have a mental model of the task demands, the sequences involved, and the resources to allocate. Achieving an effective outcome and producing correct and interesting results are primary goals to users regardless of their shortcomings or the system's shortcomings.

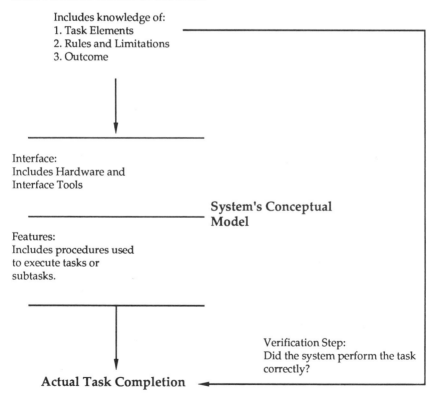

Figure 1. The relationship between the user's mental model and the conceptual model implemented on the system. Notice verification is needed to insure that actual outcome matches the user's intent.

The task is reflected by the system's interface. The interface component is what the user sees and interacts with. It represents the functions and features that are executed to perform desired actions, anything from drawing lines to simulating tornadoes. But the system does not always accurately reflect the users' mental model of the task. The possibility of distortion occurs because the users' mental model of the task does not have a one-to-one mapping with what was implemented in the system.

The important thing to note is that the task is accomplished directly by the system and only indirectly by the user. If the manner or means of the accomplishment matches users' expectations and conditions, and if those accomplishments are of an acceptable quality, then the system reflects reality. If the system represents a view of the tasks as convex or wide-angled, it may inhibit the user from acting at the level of detail needed to accomplish any particular subtask well. On the other hand, if the system's representation of the task is concave and too detail-oriented, then subtasks may be too finely delineated and too specialized. Thus, the user may not be able to see the forest for the trees as individual tasks become a blur of badly represented subtasks without any logical connection.

It is important to discuss the users in more detail in order to understand how mental models are developed and used. It is also important to discuss a way of structuring the system's conceptual model so that it remains transparent and yet helps users clearly focus on their objectives.

The User

In discussing the user, it may be helpful to present a brief overview of a human information processing framework and discuss some of its important elements since these are what constitute mental models. Also discussed is how each element contributes to the formation of the users' mental model. These elements are (a) Information Processing (needed for all tasks), (b) Attention (needed for all tasks), (c) Decision Making (specific to tasks where choice is required), and (d) Problem Solving (specific to developing hypothesis about complex stimuli).

Human Information Processing: A Review

Information Processing includes perception, cognition, and memory (as reviewed in Majchrzak, Chang, Barfield, Eberts, & Salvendy, 1987). The perceptual system, as the sensory front end, is our initial contact with the environment. It captures information and begins to filter the relevant from the irrelevant through the use of a sensory buffer. This buffer guards the cognitive system from sensory overload through a process of information consolidation. After information is consolidated, it is integrated into another buffer, termed short-term or working memory. There, information is further refined as irrelevant information and is discarded by cognitive processes which act upon it. These include semantic (general) and episodic (personal) knowledge, decision processes, and linguistic and spatial processors. Information is then prioritized (based upon attentional demands) and either stored in long-term memory or forgotten after a short time. Response control involves the process in reverse, with needed information passing from long-term memory to short-term memory which then sets up the appropriate channels for verbal or motor responses.

Memory can be quantitatively described in terms of the type of information to be stored, the amount of information, and how long memory for items persists before they decay (Card, Moran, & Newell, 1983). For instance, the short-term memory buffer, that placeholder that is used to make decisions and solve problems, can hold from 5 to 9 chunks of information for approximately 30 seconds before the information is forgotten (unless further attended to in some way). Short-term memory is more efficient than visual buffers in that it stores information in a consolidated form or a chunk.

Chunks are sets of relevant information usually grouped by the user through practice, experience, or as a function of decision making. For example, data is irrelevant until processed in terms we can understand. After processing has been completed by those cognitive forces that help us make sense of the incoming information, all the information is reduced and grouped into smaller and more meaningful units of information which are analog representations of the real stimuli.

The number of chunks stored in short-term memory is inversely proportional to the time it takes for them to decay. That is, as the number of chunks of information held in short-term memory becomes smaller, the length of time before decay occurs increases. Factors other than amount of information can also influence the speed of decay (Card et al., 1983). These factors include the similarity of various chunks of information and how the chunk was encoded (echoic or visual).

Better conceptual models can be developed by knowing human perceptual, cognitive, and memory capabilities because these processes are the building blocks of mental model development. Knowing the working parameters of each process can help in the prediction of users' reactions to different interface elements while performing many different tasks. The processing range, both capacity and decay rate, has been used as a basis of estimating task time when interacting with different components in the user interface (Card et al., 1983), how users' motor response is influenced by different items in different settings (Schweickert & Fisher, 1987), and cognitive task analysis models (see Rasmussen, 1986). When these processes are considered in concert with how features are implemented on the system, then users can work within their own capabilities and the system becomes better more transparent to the user. While this may not increase productivity, at least the system does not interfere with how the user completes the task.

Also, considering the human information processing scheme helps to promote the development of a better system conceptual model. While systems have vastly more memory than humans for certain types of information and can process and display certain types of information faster, they must be constrained to conform to human information processing limits. Otherwise, information may be displayed too quickly or in the wrong representations, which may leave users solving problems about how the system works instead of solving task problems.

Attention: Allocating Resources

Attention is important in several parts of the information processing system. It acts as the "glue" holding different processes together. Users must attend to information long enough to get visual information into short-term memory, otherwise perceptual decay and masking will occur. After information is consolidated and integrated in short-term memory, it can be maintained longer if attended to.

Wickens (1980, 1984) formulated a model of attention based on three distinct but parallel processing resource pools. While previous research was based on the concept that attention consisted of a single processing resource pool, Wickens (1980) defined three distinct resource dimensions that work interactively. He proposed a modality-specific resource which allocates attentional energy to both auditory and visual encoding. He proposed another stage-defined resource that allocates attentional energy depending upon which process is acting on the incoming information at the time, and a third resource which allocates energy based on whether information is encoded spatially or linguistically.

Having different resource pools for different information types means that information can be processed simultaneously from two different modes as long as any one resource is not depleted. Resource allocation becomes more dynamic in that shared processing pools are not depleted as rapidly as any single resource.

Again, understanding the characteristics of how humans allocate attention helps in the development of better conceptual models. Because users can attend in parallel to different types of information, the interface, as the implementation of the conceptual model, can better impart information if both graphical and textual formats are used. Also, supplying acoustic feedback along with visual information reduces resource loading when users attend to critical information. For example, an audio beep and a visual warning, presented together, will be processed as separate and distinct inputs. In critical situations, using redundant but separate sources of information may mean the difference between destroying or not destroying an aircraft.

Decision Making

Many tasks not only require users to attend and store information but to act on that information by making decisions or solve problems. So, an important part of the information processing system is the ability to make decisions. Three different types of decision processes have been identified within the human information processing scheme (Wickens, 1984, as reviewed in Majchrzak et al., 1987). The decision-making types are choice, prediction, and diagnosis. We will consider two types here, choice and diagnosis.

In choice decisions, users sample data about two different hypotheses to determine which is better, or more important. The key elements of this kind of decision depend on the type of decision to be made and the probability that the outcome will yield the correct results. Users develop hypotheses based on the fact that some number of positive or negative events will occur and base a prediction on which event is most likely to occur.

People make less than optimal decisions when forced to make decisions sequentially, like having to pick certain elements from a screen one at a time. A common phenomenon, known as anchoring, occurs when operators give unrealistic weights to some of the first elements sampled (Tversky & Kahneman, 1974). In addition, users are conservative when wrestling with prior probabilities and do not make better decisions even if there are more than two sources of information to choose from (Dawes, 1979).

In a diagnostic task like correcting an error, there may be many different considerations to be made in order to find a solution to a particular task. This works much the same way as choice decisions in the anchoring that occurs, and users have the tendency to selectively attend to confirmatory information and ignore information which disproves the hypothesis. Also, users are only able to maintain three hypotheses, on average, in memory at a time. This is congruent with the storage limitations in Card et al.'s (1983) Model Human Processor.

Productivity problems of choice decision and hypothesis testing can be handled by integrating information. Thus, important chunks of information are displayed together instead requiring the user to find them on the display or within a hidden menu structure. This, in turn, eliminates the effect of anchoring and recency which gives the user equal access to each type of information in turn. With this in mind, the conceptual model "appears" to promote a more effective use of the users' mental model. Users "feel" that the right amount of important choices are readily available to them at any particular place in the decision-making process. Other choices may be accessible later as they become more important to the task solution.

Ultimately, productivity of diagnostic decisions can be optimized by allowing users to determine the prior probability of successes or failures. These probabilities can then be built into the system—a decision "helper" in the form of "intelligent" systems. Here the system's conceptual model may literally change as users find new ways of solving problems.

Problem Solving

Problem solving usually involves systematically breaking a task into subtasks and then solving each subtask until the desired objective is realized. Certain methods and operations are applied to each subtask via a selection rule in order to solve each subtask. In that regard, a map of solutions can be developed by tasks and subtasks into goals and then performance can be analyzed through the users' actions, and visual and verbal protocols. The task structure can then be divided in categories ranging from the highest conceptual level to the lowest level of response. Waern (1985) analyzed these categories as Goals, Conditions, and Methods and used a system of production rules in order to understand how people used prior knowledge to solve problems about a single task.

She described a word processing scenario in which the word being searched for was not present. She explained this situation may be different from scanning a paper document in that in this scenario the reader could not see all of the text. Thus, there were two conditions to be searched through, the current screen and the rest of the text. She used comparators to translate search possibilities in order to better understand how problems were solved.

By understanding and developing models for how users perform basic decision making and problem solving tasks, predictions can be made to maximize task operations. Card et al. (1983) using the Goal, Operator, Method, and Selection rules (GOMS) model of task time have shown that, through the analysis of the problem-solving behavior of users and the corresponding goal structure, the system's conceptual model can be optimized around the user's problem solving abilities. In this way, productivity can be increased as the user's time and effort decrease.

Norman (1983, as reviewed in Majchrzak et al., 1987) synthesized the evidence drawn from the human information processing structure and observed that a user's mental model is often less than perfect. He found that, unlike a system's conceptual model, a user's mental model:

1. was incomplete. It knew only a small subset of available commands as a function of human information processing limitations.
2. was unstable. Forgetting occurred through disuse.
3. had no firm boundaries between systems. Users confused systems easily. Transfer of training across systems that were somewhat similar was more difficult than across systems that were truly unique. Similarity led users to expect all features of the system to be the same.
4. was unscientific. Superstitious behavior was used to solve problems. Users often did not develop many successful hypotheses about how to interact with the system and instead used a trial-and-error approach.
5. was parsimonious in that extra steps were taken in lieu of using foresight. They used stereotypical command sequences instead of using the most effective commands possible.

Understanding this, how can the conceptual model of a system be built to realistically represent a task structure that users understand? While the human mental processing scheme has not changed much in the last few thousand years, computer systems have. They have become more flexible in the way information is input and output and it is important to understand how information can be best represented by the system so as to affect the development of a good conceptual model and ultimately effective user productivity.

THE COMPUTER SYSTEM

The computer system is represented by two components for this discussion. First, features are the underlying code or set of instructions that control the system's actions. Features are the sequence of steps or rules the system follows after commands are executed by the user. But in the user's eyes, features are the keys to solving problems, large and small. They can be anything from a simple sorting routine to a feature that controls a robotic arm on the space shuttle. For features to be successfully utilized, they must be represented to users in accordance with how they are used within the total task domain.

The interface is a representation of features of the system and contains physical elements used by operators to communicate with the system. The hardware elements, such as the display, keyboards, and other input devices, are included as part of these elements. The interface also represents the conceptual framework of the task structure, in the way the conceptual model of the task is developed and implemented in the system (Thimbley, 1984).

The conceptual model, then, is represented through the interrelationship between feature and interface. If features match those required from the user to solve problems mentally then the system seems to be perfectly matched to the task. However, if features are less than successfully represented by the interface, then users must struggle with understanding the interface as well as understanding how to solve the task. There are a couple of situations that can create a mismatch between the user's mental model and what the system delivers:
1. If the feature set is incomplete, then the system cannot be used to solve the problem for which it was intended. The best interface representation will not help users with badly implemented or incomplete feature sets.
2. Even if all of features required to solve a problem exist in robust form, the interface must accurately represent the feature set on the system. The conceptual model of the system and its functionality must be represented in a way that is clear, concise and learnable.

Interface Economics

The need is to develop systems by using tools that clearly represent the system's conceptual model to the user and allow the user to reliably infer about one part of the system from another. A system should be a cohesive unit and implicitly represent the user's mental model.

At the height of usability and productivity is the notion of system transparency (Maas, 1983). Maas explains that effective communication is fundamental to how the user interacts with the system. Systems that are transparent:

1. Do not hide functionality and mechanism. Users have the ability to "look inside" the system to see how it is performing and why.

2. Do not obscure the user's view of problems that need to be solved. This is described by Maas as a "clear window to the problem space." Interfaces that do not hide their functionality from the user support this notion of a clear window.
3. Are well-structured, consistent and comprehensive interfaces. This relates back to the user's model. They completely represent the feature set accurately throughout various stages of use.
4. Conform to a user's prior knowledge or intuition. Systems should be built around the user's perception of the task and should take the role of helper and not dictator.

In order to develop systems that are transparent, conventions and tools need to be developed that apply to the mental model. Maas' guidelines do nicely to support this approach:

1. Dialog conventions should appear natural to the user. Use engineering terms in an engineering environment.
2. Avoid artificial expressions. Systems should use realistic terms that describe events from the user's perspective.
3. Allow system's questions-and-answers to prompt users in places of incomplete parametric specification. Systems may be able to offer valuable information about optional parameters needed during the completion of a task that the user may not know or remember. Here, the system should help users to restrict their attention to only the most optimal choices.
4. Allow for multiple communication channels. Users should have a choice of different display and dialog techniques, as well as input methods.
5. Develop consistent user interfaces. Above all else, the system programmer should develop tools that accurately describe the conceptual model of the system to users.

This last point is extremely important and in many instances means the difference between mastering a system and being frustrated. To create cohesive and consistent systems, they should be developed with the effective use of three basic elements; metaphor, dialog, and tools.

The User Interaction Metaphor

First, systems should be defined around a well-developed metaphorical scheme (Carroll & Thomas, 1982). Next, a cohesive dialog structure should be developed that governs how users communicate their intent to the system (Hammond & Barnard, 1984). Last, tools should be created that assist users in completing the translation of their thoughts into realistic actions. When these elements work together, the system in the user's mind becomes a transparent transmitter of intent into action. Poorly-designed systems are said to be "user-hostile" because users are left to develop their own metaphorical scheme, are left to reinterpret communications from the system, or are left with inadequate tools. These three elements are explained in further detail below.

Carroll et al. (1982), in defining the metaphor principle, state that "People develop new cognitive structures by using metaphors to cognitive structures they have already learned" (p. 109). They explain that learning systems not only requires an understanding of the relationship between one part of the system and another but also requires the user to integrate those complex structures with previous experience. Accordingly, Carrol et al. contend that people must process new information in short-term memory by referencing their existing knowledge framework. These frameworks may or may not be relevant but are never thrown out (see Lawler, 1981).

To be truly useful, the system metaphor must be congruent to the users' mental model, to users' attitudes, and convey a sense of "naturalness".

Systems that are designed around a careless or incomplete metaphor can cause serious learning and usability problems. Most importantly, naive users will be deprived of the chance of translating the conceptual model into their previous nonsystem experience and expert users will learn not to trust a system that is incomplete or ambiguous.

Some of the more successful systems use an "office" metaphor. This is a conceptual model that is easily integrated into the office users' previous experience. Using this system requires users to manipulate "objects" which are usually set on a "desktop." An example of an "object" can either be representations of the file structure (data files, folders, directories) or features themselves. In this way, data objects can be placed in objects which represent folders or they can be acted on by other objects which represent commands. This metaphor has been extended to consider virtual space considerations, which allow users to better organize their "desktop" within various "rooms" (Henderson & Card, 1986).

Dialog: Communicating with the System

After developing a consistent metaphor, it is important to discuss how to develop the most optimal communication link between users and their systems. Information exchange between the system and the user can be considered in terms of style, structure, and content (Hammond & Barnard, 1984). Each of these dialog areas has great impact on learnability and usability of systems.

Style, as represented by different control types such as menus selections, parametric input and direct manipulation, is bound to users-system interaction and is important to the user's perception of "control." An example of a complex system with a less than clear dialog style is the UNIX operating system (a product of ATT Bell Laboratories). This system is one of the most powerful and elegant operating systems in use today. It has become a standard across many different industries and is the basis for many software applications. It supports multi-tasking, multi-processing environments and has numerous other features. Users, however, are forced to use rote memory to complete tasks in UNIX because there is no consistent way to communicate with the system. For example, the command CUT allows users to pull out specific fields while SORT allows the user to rearrange data based on specific fields. CUT uses a "-d" option for specifying the field delimiter while SORT uses a "-t." This prevents the user from developing a role for field specification and requires them to memorize arbitrary and dangerously similar command sequences.

The point is that the feature set of UNIX is hidden and all but lost to but a few experts who can command the system. As though learning a foreign language, users must literally work through a period of practicing translation of syntax. The users must also memorize nouns, verbs, modifiers, and participles and build sentence-like structures in order to communicate with their systems. As discussed before, for users to correctly interpret the conceptual model of the system, the system itself should impart information in a way that is consistent and comprehensible to the user. The system should not be opaque.

Structure, as the representation of how features are ordered, is important because the users' model task is usually ordered by importance. If dialog structure seems random, then users are left prioritizing features on their own, with complete disregard for how the task structure is represented by the system. These "work-arounds" are time-consuming and are usually last-ditch efforts by the user to make sense of the system.

Content, as the vocabulary of the features themselves, is important but also difficult to define. A label describing a feature may convey different meanings to different users depending on the context of the task, users' experience, and cognitive demands. In order to develop effective labels, developers have to understand the precise task demands, what information is available to users at the time, the amount of user experience, as well as the style of interaction. Features do not exist in a vacuum and must be considered along with others, as well as the metaphor upon which they are built. So, the labels that represent features must also follow the logical language of the task. With these considerations in mind, content and structure play an important role in implementing a conceptual model and ultimately building a system that is learnable and usable.

Direct manipulation systems use the aforementioned dialog elements effectively in establishing an understanding between the user's intents and the system's capabilities. According to Verplank (1986), systems developed around the direct manipulation process establish and reinforce a consistent user's model (also see Hutchins, Holland, & Norman, 1983, for an excellent review). The system elements Verplank (1986) discussed include:

1. The user of a set of concrete and visible objects. Abstract and invisible ones that are less likely to be integrated into long-term memory should be avoided.
2. A simplifying set of user actions applied uniformly. These are a set of commands that exploit recognition instead of recall and require decisions between best alternatives instead of creating alternatives from scratch. For instance:
     Copying instead of creating.
     Choosing instead of filling.
     Recognizing instead of generating.
     Editing instead of programming.
3. Rapid feedback as opposed to batch mode. Users work interactively with the system and see the direct result of their actions via immediate feedback.

Interface Tools

Other interface tools, besides direct manipulation, have been developed to create a more effective link between the user's intent and features implemented in the system. These tools, in a general sense, become an extension of the dialog style in that they represent system features. Effective tools are developed by incorporating critical aspects of human understanding and cognitive processes into the interface and they have proven successful in improving productivity in certain cases. These tools are menus, question-and-answer prompts, and parametric input.

Menus are usually a list of commands prioritized by task function, importance, or other logical arrangement, and displayed for the user in sequence. They are normally used when features can be classed together categorically within the confines of a certain set of tasks. Users can rapidly find items since menus are normally a short, scannable list. Their use speeds task execution time. Another reason why menus increase user performance is that users need only recognize commands they need as opposed to having to recall them from memory. This leads to faster processing and response times (Anderson, 1980), which also helps increase user output.

There are disadvantages to menus under some circumstances. Users have some problems when using menus with a large list of elements because user search time may increase dramatically, overshadowing the benefits of recognition (Card et al., 1983). Also, expert users having learned the system well, may be slowed by accessing menus over other forms of system communication.

Another form of interactive communication with the user is the question-and-answer display method. In this technique, the computer queries users for possible responses in a question-and-answer format. This technique can be used in "intelligent" software, which anticipates the users' next request based on a previous one. While this type of input may lead to increased input errors, users can still concentrate on the task with help from the system. Also, this type of display technique is effective when the parameters of input are known or easily retrieved. It is also an effective mode for system experts or applications that require rote responses.

The last input tool considered here is parametric input. Parametric input is made directly by typing commands from the keyboard. The computer does not prompt the user for specific information as in the question-and-answer format. When systems are structured primarily around this input, users have to remember and recall many commands, their parameters, and any abbreviations associated with them. Like the question-and-answer format, the benefits of command recognition processing are lost. Also, learning time is slowed and transfer of training between systems may be hindered by command sets that are similar but not identical.

However, parametric input can be very fast and extremely flexible in the hands of an expert. Experienced users feel they have greater control and flexibility using this type of input (Shneiderman, 1987). Used in combination with other input modes, expert users may proceed more rapidly using parametric input while novices learn the system's language by using other methods of input (e.g., menus, question-and-answer).

Another factor that affects productivity is the hardware used to input information into the system. Input devices such as keyboards and mice are used to input information, to draw, and to point to objects on a screen. Task context and system constraints may determine which input device is optimal. For example, CAD designers normally use pointing devices twice as long as keyboards for input (Majchrzak et al., 1987). Word processors on the other hand use a keyboard extensively and use pointing devices less often. However, the data are still unclear as to the benefits of some input devices over others.

Greenstein and Arnaut (1986) reviewed the literature comparing 10 different input devices for positioning tasks. They found that how input devices were implemented often had no bearing on how the conceptual model was implemented on the system. One of the most salient conclusions that can be drawn from these data is that users seemed more accurate with light pens than with any other pointing device. This is notable because light pens do not often appear in the market place. This is mostly due to the cost of the device and the amount of process overhead required to control lightpens.

No single interface tool in isolation can accurately implement a robust conceptual model. Through the effective combination of metaphor, dialog, and interface tools, systems can be built that best represent the users' mental model. These elements help users be more productive because they allow users to draw on their previous real-world experience, they compensate for our limited processing capacity, and they exploit our attentional talents. According to Maas (1983), if these dialog schemes and tools are developed well enough, responsibility for operating the system is overshadowed by our goal to be more productive. The system becomes part of the task solution and not another problem to be solved.

CONCLUSIONS

The very nature of productivity emphasizes getting tasks completed in an efficient manner with a certain amount of satisfaction. We want computer systems to make us more effective in doing the tasks we know and sometimes rely on them to help us do tasks that, to this point, have been impossible. Computer systems can improve our abilities to perform a function but as we have seen, they can be implemented so as to hinder our abilities to perform those tasks optimally.

Computer systems can outperform humans in a variety of ways, ranging from mathematical calculations to data output. Users, even when processing different types of information in parallel, must consolidate, integrate, and store only small bits of information at a time. The bottleneck effect of short-term memory may make us ineffective data processors but it allows us the opportunity to make decisions or to solve problems. This ability to integrate our knowledge and experience with current incoming information in order to shape a response gives us a unique advantage over a binary, two-dimensional computer system. The system, as a mirror, reflects only the users' actions and should otherwise be invisible. This perspective can be used to create a better reflection of the tasks in the systems. Systems improve understanding through the use of analogies and metaphor. Interfaces can be developed that allow users to directly act on objects, which creates, in itself, a closer relationship between the task and the user. Also, tools can be developed with human information processing capabilities in mind. These tools, used in context with the correct metaphor and interface, give users a clearer view of their task.

Users need to keep this in mind when developing, buying, or using software to perform a job. Systems that have been developed around the users' mental model but remain "transparent" to the user are the ones most desired. These systems are usually developed around a user-centered philosophy that incorporates an understanding of users, their tasks, and the context within which systems are used (Norman, 1986). Through the effective use of user-centered design, systems can be created that release users from the burden of "operating" computers.

Owning up to these development criteria is the greatest challenge for system designers. By using a user-centered approach, systems can be implemented that are effectively tuned to users and their tasks. Systems developed around priorities which do not include usability criteria of users' model of purpose (e.g., performance, price, or even support) are missing the key ingredients needed to support productive users. These systems support themselves for a while because their use and self-maintenance becomes a self-fulfilling "white elephant." However, as the market indicates, users want more effective tools and not toys (Bannon, 1986).

Productivity goes beyond task performance; it also refers to user satisfaction. Users have dictated trends in the market toward usable systems even at the risk of performance decrements (1987 Software User Survey). Users know their capabilities and want systems to compliment them. Those systems that are matched to the user's needs, and not vice versa, will find a successful niche in a productive market. Ultimately, those systems that do not compliment a wide range of users in their quest for productive solutions will fail, regardless of their history, size, or price.

SUMMARY

Productivity, as effective output relative to the amount of effort, is an important issue when viewed from the computer user's perspective. Gains in productivity can realized by understanding the users' information processing strengths and weakness. System elements can be developed and enhanced that create an accurate reflection of the user's task. These elements include: (1) the creation of a metaphor that accurately embodies the user's task structure; (2) the effective development of communication through a dialog style, structure, and content; and (3) the creation of interface tools that are uniquely matched to the task. Systems that are tuned to user-centered design are gaining ground in the marketplace. Systems that do not employ this user-centered philosophy, so as to maintain a coordination between user intent and user actions, may make the user unproductive.

ACKNOWLEDGEMENTS

The author wishes to thank Mark Stempski, Evelyn Williams, and Greg Foltz for their critical review of this paper. Please send all inquires to Thomas Cocklin, Hewlett-Packard, 3404 E. Harmony Road, Fort Collins, CO 80525.

REFERENCES

1987 Software User Survey. (1987). Software news. Westborough, MA: Sentry Publishing.

Anderson, J. R. (1980). Cognitive psychology and its implications. San Francisco, CA: Freeman Press.

Bannon, L. J. (1986). Issues in design: Some notes. In D. A. Norman & S. W. Draper (Eds.), User centered system design (pp. 25-29). Hillsdale, NJ: Lawrence-Erlbaum Associates.

Card, S. K., Moran, T. P., & Newell, A. (1983). The psychology of human-computer interaction. Hillsdale, NJ: Lawrence Erlbaum Associates.

Carroll, J. M., & Thomas J. C. (1982). Metaphor and the cognitive representation of computing systems. IEEE Transactions on Systems, Man, and Cybernetics, SMC-12(2), 107-116.

Dawes, R. M. (1979). The robust beauty of improper linear models in decision making. American Psychologist, 34, 571-582.

Greenstein, J. S., & Arnaut, L. Y. (1986). Human factors aspects of manual computer input devices. In G. Salvendy (Ed.), Handbook of human factors/ergonomics. New York: John Wiley and Sons.

Groover, M. P., & Zimmers, E. W. (1984). CAD/CAM: Computer-aided design and manufacturing. Englewood Cliffs, NJ: Prentice-Hall.

Henderson, Jr., D. A., & Card, S. K. (1987). Rooms: The use of multiple virtual workspaces to reduce space contention in a window-based graphical user interface. ACM Transactions on Graphics, 5(3), 211-243.

Hutchins, E. L., Holland, J. D., & Norman, D. A. (1983). Direct manipulation interfaces. In D. A. Norman & S. W. Draper (Eds.), User centered system design (pp. 87-124). Hillsdale, NJ: Lawrence Erlbaum Associates.

Laurel, B. K. (1986). Interface as memesis. In D. A. Norman & S. W. Draper (Eds.), User centered system design (pp. 67-85). Hillsdale, NJ: Lawrence Erlbaum Associates.

Lawler, R. W. (1981). The progressive construction of mind. Cognitive Science, 5, 1-30.

Maas, S. (1983). Why system transparency? In T. R. G. Green, S. J. Payne, & G. C. van der Veer, (Eds.), The psychology of computer use (pp. 19-28). London: Academic Press.

Majchrzak, A., Chang, T-C. Barfield, W., Eberts, R., & Salvendy, G. (1987). Human aspects of computer-aided design. Philadelphia, PA: Taylor and Francis.

Norman, D. A. (1986). Cognitive engineering. In D. A. Norman & S. W. Draper (Eds.), User centered system design (pp. 31-61). Hillsdale, NJ: Lawrence Erlbaum Associates.

Norman, D. S. (1983). Some observations on mental models. In D. Gentner & A. L. Stevens (Eds.), Mental models (pp. 7-14). Hillsdale, NJ: Lawrence Erlbaum Associates.

Primrose, P. L., Creamer, G. D., & Leonard, R. (1985). Identifying and quantifying the company-wide benefits of CAD within the structure of a comprehensive investment program. Computer-Aided Design, 17(1), 3-8.

Rasmussen, J. (1986). Information processing and human-machine interaction: Series volume 12. New York: North-Holland.

Rubinstein, R., & Hersh, H. (1984). The human factor: Designing computer systems for people. City: Digital Press.

Schweichert, R., & Fisher, D. L. (1987). Stochastic network models. In G. Salvendy (Ed.), Handbook of human factors (pp. 1204-1205). New York: John Wiley and Sons.

Sculley, J. (1987, October). Professionals and their computers. Personal Computing, 11(10), 236.

Shneiderman, B. (1987). Designing the user interface: Strategies for effective human-computer interaction. Reading, MA: Addison-Wesley.

Thimbley, H. (1984). User interface design: Generative user engineering principles. In A. Monk (Ed.), Fundamentals of human-computer interaction (pp. 165-18). London: Academic Press.

Tversky, A., & Kahneman, D. (1974). Judgment under uncertainty: Heuristics and biases. Science, 185, 1124-1131.

Verplank, B. (1986). Design graphical user interfaces. ACM-SIGCHI Tutorial 1, Boston, MA.

Waern, Y. (1985). Learning computerized tasks as related to prior task knowledge. International Journal of Man-Machine Studies, 22, 441-455.

Wickens, C. D. (1980). The structure of attentional resources. In R. Nickerson (Ed.), Attention and performance VIII (pp. 239-257). Hillsdale, NJ: Lawrence Erlbaum.

Wickens, C. D. (1984). Engineering psychology and human performance. Columbus, OH: Merrill.

Williams, J. C. (1983). Cost effectiveness of operator features in equipment design. Applied Ergonomics, 14(2), 103-107.

PSYCHOLINGUISTICS AT WORK IN THE INFORMATION AGE

Paul Whitney and Diana L. W. Whitney

Washington State University
Pullman, Washington

INTRODUCTION

". . .Much of the professional reputation of this company rides on how we
present ourselves in our technical reports."
                              -engineering consultant

". . .The reader should not be forced to wonder what the writer intended to
say."
                              -marketing representative

". . .People who can't write don't last very long around here. We can't
afford them..."
                              -scientific consulting firm executive

These comments, from a survey by Faigley and Miller (1982), depict a
growing awareness of the importance of appropriate writing skills to the
commercial success of business and individual professionals within business.
The connection between productivity and effectiveness in written communication
is supported by numerous observations. For example, in recent years we have
witnessed a surge in the number of "communications managers" employed by
Fortune 500 companies (Harris & Bryant, 1986). These specialized managers
have primary responsibility for the writing quality of internal and external
publications. The demand for this new type of business executive by successful organizations suggests that quality of writing is indeed important to
commercial success.

Another indication of the importance of writing to today's professionals
is the amount of writing time required by white collar occupations. Faigley
and Miller (1982) report that persons in professional and technical occupations
devote an average of 29% of their total work time to writing activities.
That is, many professionals and technical workers spend the equivalent of
1 out of every 4 work days just writing!

It is important to note that such writing intensive occupations no
longer represent a minor segment of the work force. In 1981 Paul Strassman,
an expert on employment trends, predicted that 55 million people would be
employed in the "information sector" by 1990. This number represents nearly
one-third of the adult population of the United States. That the term
"information age" aptly characterizes today's working environment is hardly
questionable. Ironically, documentation for and about the new information
technology is an often mentioned example of writing that is poor in

23

readability (e.g., Weiss, 1985) and presumably of poor quality. This, of course, can have serious consequences. For example, Nickerson (1986) has reported that inadequate documentation and training aids are a major reason for worker rejection of computer tools (and the resultant wasted expenditure for such tools).

Even more striking are numerous findings indicating that deficiency in writing ability is a frequent complaint about workers in professional positions--particularly new hirees (e.g. Faigley & Miller, 1982; Rader & Wunsch, 1980; Stine & Skarzenski, 1979). For example, 78% of Faigley and Miller's (1982) respondents indicated that "bad writing" was a problem in their places of employment. The respondents reported that such writing deficiencies commonly resulted in misunderstandings, increased workload, wasted time, and lowered public perceptions of their companies' competence.

A major conclusion to be drawn from findings such as those noted above is that, increasingly, writing is an important component of the process and product of doing business. That is, not only are many professionals required to write in the performance of their jobs but also the product of many business endeavors is itself a written product. Clearly, improving the efficiency and quality of writing is important to productivity in many areas.

Our purpose in this chapter is to show how recent psycholinguistic research on the writing process is important to understanding and correcting writing difficulties. In the next two sections of this chapter we provide a broad survey of recent research on the information processes involved in writing. We then discuss how an information processing analysis of writing can be applied to the improvement of writing and examine various computer-assisted composing aids currently on the market. We conclude the chapter with an illustration of how psycholinguistic research can lead to useful applications by presenting some exploratory work on schema-based computer-assisted composing.

HUMAN COGNITION AS AN INFORMATION PROCESSING SYSTEM

Human cognitive functioning is often conceptualized in terms of a sophisticated system that receives, stores, manipulates, and utilizes various types of information. This view became popularized as cognitive scientists found that the computer serves as a useful metaphor for human information processing (Lachman, Lachman, & Butterfield, 1979). It is important to bear in mind that we do not argue that human thought and computer operations are isomorphic, merely that, in the abstract, they both represent realizations of information processing systems. All information processing systems share some common attributes. One way of conceptualizing these attributes is presented in Table 1.

As Table 1 implies, successful information processing depends upon both possession of the requisite information processing components and the appropriate coordination of these components during performance. Another way of stating this idea is that successful information processing requires effective symbol manipulation. Further, several types of symbol structures (knowledge) are used in cognitive processing. For example, much of our knowledge is declarative, i.e. factual. We also possess procedural knowledge about how to perform processing operations. In addition, we employ metaknowledge, which is the knowledge used to control and coordinate processing. These distinctions are useful (although not necessarily mutually exclusive) categories representing the variety of knowledge types (symbols) that information processing systems manipulate (cf. Norman, 1981; Stillings et al., 1987). We will illustrate the role played by these knowledge

Table 1. Elements of an Information Processing System

---

   1) receptors for receiving information
   2) effectors for performing actions on the world
   3) a set of basic processing operations for
      a) recoding data into symbol structures (sets of related
         symbols)
      b) manipulating symbols
   4) memory for storing and retaining symbol structures
   5) buffer to hold small amounts of information for
      manipulation and to synchronize internal and external events
   6) an interpreter that determines sequence and timing of
      execution of basic operations (i.e. a means of guiding how
      finite resources are used)

Note: Adapted from Newell and Simon (1972); Norman (1981).

types more explicitly in the next section. The important point here is that
we must draw on various knowledge structures at the appropriate time in
order to accomplish our information processing goals.

     However, there is an important limitation inherent to both human and
nonhuman information processing systems that must be considered: Information
processing systems are limited in capacity. The final attribute listed in
Table 1 indicates that information processing systems need a means of
guiding and distributing our finite cognitive resources. This aspect of
human information processing systems is integral to understanding difficulties
in the performance of many cognitive activities (such as writing). Much
current basic research in cognitive psychology is concerned with this issue
of resource capacity. For example numerous researchers (e.g. Posner, 1978)
have looked at the issue of how attention is allocated to the various
elements of a task during performance. The central problem here is one of
coordinating knowledge use given the limitations we have in the amount of
information we can maintain and manipulate in our working memory "buffer"
(see, for example, Klatsky, 1984).

     In general, then, failures in performance can result from the lack of
particular kinds of knowledge or from limitations on our ability to access
the needed knowledge at the appropriate time. The next section discusses
ideas and research findings related to a view of writing as a complex
information processing activity.

INFORMATION PROCESSING AND WRITING

     The overt activities involved in the composition of a written "product"
are fairly easy to specify. In most writing situations there is a linear
development as the writer moves from prewriting activities to composing a
first and subsequent drafts (Sommers, 1979). However, each of these production phases involve several sets of underlying or mediating processes.
These processes guide and direct the overt writing activities seen during
the production phases and are the primary focus of an information processing
analysis of writing.

     The actual processes that take place in each production phase are only
beginning to be understood. However, from interview studies and analysis of
verbal protocols collected during composing, it is clear that the processes
do not form a fixed series of stages. Rather, each writing production phase

can involve several sets of processes applied recursively (Hayes & Flower, 1980; Murray, 1978).

It is useful and, we feel, appropriate to discuss the mediating processes of writing within the general taxonomy of collecting, planning, translating, and reviewing (Benton, Kraft, Glover, & Plake, 1984; Hayes & Flower, 1980; Kellogg, 1987). Collecting involves searching for and reading information relevant to the writing task. These activities are obviously used mainly during prewriting activities. However, we are more concerned here with the three categories of processes most often associated with the act of composing (planning, translating, and reviewing). Planning consists of organizing ideas and setting goals. Translating involves transforming mental representations into sentence constructions. Reviewing consists of reading, evaluating, and editing the text.

Now, consider what demands these writing processes are likely to place on our information processing system. In planning, writers must draw on declarative, procedural, and metaknowledge in order to organize the text. For example, writers must coordinate factual knowledge and knowledge about text conventions with knowledge about the specific writing context (e.g. genre patterns, audience, individual abilities, etc.). Protocols, obtained by having writers "think out loud" as they compose, indicate that writers use several types of strategies and information to develop a hierarchically organized set of goals (Flower & Hayes, 1980; Graesser, Hopkinson, Lewis, & Bruflodt, 1984). Thus we would expect that planning activities would place a heavy burden on our finite processing resources and the working memory buffer. Psycholinguistic research on planning processes appear to support this expectation. For example, Gould (1980) found that executives spend two-thirds of their composition time in planning. In addition, Collins and Williamson (1984) found that a major cause of poor writing was difficulty with adapting writing plans to fit the constraints imposed by particular writing tasks.

The information processing demands of translation should be less than those of planning because, of all the processes used in writing, translation benefits most from the extensive experience people have with spoken language (Kellogg, 1987). Of course, problems do arise, particularly when writers form multiclause sentences. For example, Dauite (1984) found that syntactic errors often occur as grammatical information fades from working memory thus causing a mismatch between earlier and later portions of a sentence. (The authors obtained anecdotal support for Dauite's conclusions while producing several of the sentences found in this chapter!)

The cognitive demands of reviewing would seem to be comparable to the demands of planning. During reviewing there is information physically present so less knowledge must be kept in an active state. However, several levels of analysis are required to adequately review text (e.g. semantic, syntactic, stylistic, etc.). Unfortunately, evaluations of text are not well practiced by most writers (Nold, 1981). In fact, a major problem for many writers may be metaknowledge failure that leads to their making reviewing less demanding than it should be. That is, inexperienced writers view the process of revising as simply "polishing the words". More experienced writers understand that reviewing entails complex activities such as evaluating the organization of ideas and the appropriateness of tone and style (Sommers, 1980).

In summary, writing is a highly demanding activity. This seems to be particularly true of the planning and reviewing phases. Direct evidence on this matter was recently obtained by Kellogg (1987). Subjects were trained to classify their composing activity as planning, translating, or reviewing. At variable intervals, the subject's writing (of persuasive essays) was interrupted by a tone. The subjects had to respond to the tone as quickly as possible and report what type of composing process they were using. Reaction time in responding to the tone was used as an index of cognitive effort devoted to particular writing processes. Specifically, the cognitive effort associated with each phase of writing was defined in terms of the cost to reaction time to the tone. Cost was measured in comparison to a baseline condition in which the subjects were not writing. This type of dual task methodology has been used extensively to assess the allocation of cognitive resources (e.g., Britton & Tesser, 1982; Kellas, Simpson, & Ferraro, this volume; Posner & Boies, 1971). The results indicated that planning and reviewing were higher in cognitive load (effort) than was translating. Interestingly, the overall amount of interference with tone detection in Kellogg's study was comparable to the interference obtained in other studies when the primary task is playing chess (Kellogg, 1986). Writing is an extremely resource demanding activity!

APPLICATIONS

Over the past 10 years, a _process_ view of writing has become very popular. This approach emphasizes the teaching of skills—what to do as you write—rather than the teaching of a static set of rules (e.g., Flower, 1985; Scardamalia & Bereiter, 1983). As exemplified by the previous section, one of the ramifications of the process orientation has been to open up the study of writing to interdisciplinary collaboration, particularly among researchers in rhetoric, liguistics, and psychology. These fields have, at the same time, been greatly affected by advances in computer science and artificial intelligence. Not surprisingly then, there is now considerable interest in computer applications to studying and teaching writing (e.g., Collins & Sommers, 1985; Hillocks, 1984).

Our purpose, in this section, is to briefly discuss the kinds of computer products that have been developed to assist writers and, based on our analysis of the writing process, indicate what new kinds of computer tools might be of help in improving writing efficiency. We report some work we have in progress as an illustration of one such promising approach to computer assisted composing.

We limit our focus here to assistance with the planning process, particularly to smoothing the transition from planning to translation. One reason for focusing on planning is because of its resource demanding nature (as discussed above). A somewhat more practical reason for concentrating on planning is that fewer writing aids are available to assist in this process (Kellogg, 1986; Strickland, 1985). Bibliographic searching systems to aid collecting are in wide use. In addition, most word processing programs include some help with reviewing text. These reviewing aids range from programs that check spelling and punctuation to sophisticated programs that provide feedback on diction, readability, and style. An example of the latter type is the well known WRITER'S WORKBENCH (Macdonald, Frase, Gingrich, & Keenan, 1982).

There is much less software available to help the user plan a first draft. The programs that are available tend to be based around general problem solving strategies. An example is INVENT, developed by Burns (1984). It asks the writer a series of questions based on established heuristics. One set of questions comes from the analogy of the document as a dramatic act. The writer is probed for information about scenes, acts, agents, purposes, and agencies (Rueckert, 1963). Another planning aid is found in the WRITER'S HELPER package (Wresch, 1984). This program probes the writer for a list of ideas and then helps in developing a hierarchical structure depicting the relationship between concepts.

It is possible that the currently available programs can be of great benefit to many writers, but at present there is very little empirical evidence for their effectiveness (see Sommers, 1985; Kellogg, 1986). Clearly, research is needed on how such tools interact with the writer's purpose and style of composing. A related concern, recently expressed by Kellogg (1986), is that we need more than validation studies concerning whom the extant programs benefit. It is possible that, as a class, general purpose writing aids may yield limited benefits. Most current theories of composing in writing rely heavily on the notion of plans generated from schemata (e.g., Bracewell, Frederikson, & Frederikson, 1982; Cooper & Matsuhashi, 1983). However, the assumption underlying current planning aids is that writers can be effectively guided by general problem solving heuristics. Thus, a potential limitation of such broad, general purpose, planning aids is that they ignore the role that context dependent schemata (such as text conventions and genre patterns) play in planning.

As noted earlier, the coordination of multiple knowledge structures is one of the factors that make planning difficult. It is important to bear in mind that different knowledge structures will be relevant in different writing contexts. The importance of being able to employ the appropriate schemata (knowledge structure) for a given context is highlighted by Collins and Williamson's (1984) finding that writing difficulties are associated with adapting to task-dependent constraints. It is also notable that business executives frequently express concern that personnel be trained in specific business and technical formats (see Faigley & Miller, 1982).

There are thus several reasons to believe that writing aids might be most useful if they make the appropriate schemata transparent to the writer at the appropriate point in composing. Of course, this means that such a writing aid will have a narrower range of applicability than those currently in use. However, we believe that the narrower scope will bring concomittant benefits.

The idea for the specific writing aid that we are developing arose in the context of teaching experimental psychology students to write a report of their own empirical research. The applied goal of this project is to develop a computer tutorial system that will ease the processing demands on novice writers by interactively prompting them with information and questions that aid in the drafting of an appropriately organized manuscript.

It is in considering what kinds of information to provide that our project takes on theoretical significance. Our intent in the current phase of the research is to describe the rhetorical schemata from which experienced writers generate reports of experiments in psychology. A later phase of this line of research will integrate the schematic structures into a software package to aid composition. Besides the practical "product" to be developed, the present research promises to provide a general methodology for developing similar kinds of writing aids in other domains. Thus, this project has potential for application well beyond the specific knowledge domain we are investigating.

The rationale for our approach is based on two facts. First, while most composing theories rely on the concept of schemata, little work has been done to actually specify the contents of the postulated knowledge structures. Two notable exceptions are the work of Graesser (1981) and that of Mandler and her colleagues (e.g., Mandler & Goodman, 1982; Mandler & Johnson, 1977). However, most of this work is on the schemata involved in the comprehension and production of simple narratives and stories, respectively. Second, we do not know how detailed the computer prompting can be without first examining how much variation there is in the text structures of this genre. Perhaps the greatest value of this research will be in providing a model of how to go about characterizing the knowledge structures in fairly constrained areas of writing. Clearly, much of the writing in science and business calls for acquiring and adhering to particular logical and stylistic formats (Danielson, 1985).

The goal behind the portion of the research undertaken so far is the specification of the schemata used to write research reports in psychology. Of course, the highest levels of the schemata involved are easy to specify. Virtually all reports contain sections corresponding to an introduction, method, results, and discussion. Our focus is on the underlying schemata involved in each section. We are pursuing the description of these schema by using the prose analysis system developed by Meyer (1975). Meyer's system is an obvious choice because of its connections with work in linguistics and rhetoric (cf., Meyer, 1985). Meyer classifies the macro-propositions (gist) of a text into five groups of logical relationships: collection, causation, response, comparison, and description (See Table 2).

In essence, Meyer has developed a detailed system for classifying connections between text elements and mapping out the hierarchical structure of the logical relationships within the text.

Our main focus is on what types of relationships provide an overall characterization of each section of a report and on what relationships tend to be nested within the dominant organizing scheme of each section. The reports we are using come from a text that has reprinted particularly good examples of experimental reports from several areas of psychology (see Solso & Johnson, 1984). We begin by breaking up the report sections into separate idea units. Independent raters then classify the idea units according to Meyer's system. The product of these efforts is a tree diagram with the branches depicting the logical relationships between idea units.

This work has only begun but we already have indications that this approach will yield insights that might not be gained by simply basing the composing aid on the proselytizing and advice found in textbooks. We have analyzed the introductions to three articles. All three have a response

TABLE 2. Meyer's Text Schemata (and some subtypes)

---

1) Collection: ideas or events grouped on the basis of some commonality (no subtypes; consists of several elements)

2) Causation: one idea is the antecedent and the other is the consequent (covariance: equally weighted arguments; explanation: antecedents are subordinate to consequent)

3) Response: problem-solution construction (sometimes a problem only construction)

4) Comparison: similarities and differences between two or more topics (alternative: involves options with equal weight; adversative: a favored alternative contrasted with a less favored one)

5) Description: provides more information about a topic (specific: go from abstract to concrete; manner: describe how event is performed; equivalent: restate information in a new way)

Source: Meyer, 1985.

structure as their most inclusive level. Problem development comprises the first several paragraphs and solution development is performed in the last few paragraphs. Interestingly, all three articles have a description-equivalent section in the first few lines of the paragraph that begins the solution development. This description always restates the problem being investigated. We have yet to analyze enough texts to determine if regular patterns emerge within the problem development portion of the article. It is possible that particular patterns of logical development are characteristic of different types of articles (e.g., theory testing, theory development, resolving methodological questions, etc.).

A GENERAL PERSPECTIVE

The nature of science, business, the humanities, and other areas is such that productivity and effective communication are interlinked. In many situations, the ineffectiveness of written communication can be a major stumbling block. Given the nature of the writing process, we believe that careful analysis of the logic structure of high quality text from a given domain will prove to be an effective base from which to design prompts to direct the composer. Of course, confirmation of this belief must take the form of empirical tests of the usefulness of composing tools designed in this way. The methodology for comparing different writing aids is an area that needs further development (cf. Nickerson, 1986).

Furthermore, those in research and development of writing aids might face resistance from those who are to benefit from new products. One source of concern is the general fear of technologically sophisticated instrumentation. Of course, it is not necessary to implement schema-based composing aids as computer tools. However, it would seem that computers are ideal devices for getting the right information (or questions) to a person at the right time, that is, while composing. As documentation improves and computers become more common in educational settings, general resistance should decline.

A concern more specific to computer assisted writing is the idea that creativity will be stifled. These fears are not well founded. Certainly, it is undesirable to provide a format so rigid that creative expression is impossible. However, the goal of computer tools to aid writing is to provide useful information and strategies that promote clear writing. This need not conflict with creativity. In the case of the type of system we are developing, the idea is to communicate to novice writers the implicit assumptions shared by readers and writers in a given domain. The format should leave considerable room for creative thought.

The concerns about writing tools and similar areas of computer assisted performance may persist because of a misunderstanding about the difference between expert systems in artificial intelligence (see Sedelow & Sedelow, this volume) and "procognitive" systems of the kind we would like to develop. The term procognitive system comes from Licklider (1965). He stated that the purpose of such a system is to "get the user of the fund of knowledge into something more like an executive's or commander's position" (p. 31). The idea is to have information easily accessible and in a form that will augment the performance of the user. However, in contrast to expert systems, the thinking, reasoning, and discoveries are the user's, not the system's.

The major limiting factor on the development of such systems is the lack of "knowledge engineers," i.e. people who can discover what knowledge is important in skilled performance and how to make that information more widely accessible (Nickerson, 1986). This brings us back to a central question of this book: How can basic researchers contribute to solving problems of productivity? For basic researchers in cognitive science, the answer is that we have the training to be knowledge engineers for procognitive systems. Clearly, the time has arrived to apply ourselves more earnestly in this direction.

REFERENCES

Benton, S. L., Kraft, R. G., Glover, J. A., & Plake, B. S. (1984). Cognitive capacity differences among writers. Journal of Educational Psychology, 76, 820-834.

Bracewell, R., Frederickson, C. & Frederickson, J. D. (1982). Cognitive processes in composing and comprehending discourse. Educational Psychologist, 17, 146-164.

Britton, B. K., & Tesser, A. (1982). Effects of prior knowledge on use of cognitive capacity in three complex cognitive tasks. Journal of Verbal Learning and Verbal Behavior, 21, 421-436.

Burns, H. (1984). Recollections of first-generation computer-assisted prewriting. In W. Wresch (Ed.), The computer in composition instruction (pp 19-30). Urbana, IL: National Council of Teachers of English.

Collins, J. L., & Sommers, E. A. (Eds.). (1985). Writing on-line. Upper Montclair, NJ: Boyton/Cook.

Collins, J. L., & Williamson, M. M. (1984). Assigned rhetorical context and semantic abbreviation in writing. In R. Beach & L. S. Bridwell (Eds.), New directions in composition research. New York: Guilford Press.

Cooper, C. R., & Matsuhashi, A. (1983). A theory of the writing process. In M. Martlew (Ed.), The psychology of written language (pp. 3-39). Chichester, England: John Wiley & Sons.

Danielson, W. A. (1985). The writer and the computer. Computers and the Humanities, 19, 85-88.

Dauite, C. A. (1984). Performance limits on writers. In R. Beach & L. S. Bridwell (Eds.), New directions in composition research (pp. 205-224). New York: Guilford Press.

Faigley, L., & Miller, T. P. (1982). What we learn from writing on the job. College English, 44, 557-572.

Flower, L. S. (1985). Problem solving strategies for writing. New York: Harcourt Brace Jovanovich.

Flower, L. S., & Hayes, J. R. (1980). The dynamics of composing: Making plans and juggling constraints. In L. W. Gregg & E. R. Steinberg (Eds.), Cognitive processes in writing (pp. 31-50). Hillsdale, NJ: Erlbaum.

Gould, J. D. (1980). Experiments on composing letters: Some facts, some myths, and some observations. In L. W. Gregg & E. R. Steinberg (Eds.), Cognitive processes in writing (pp. 97-128). Hillsdale, NJ: Erlbaum.

Graesser, A. C. (1981). Prose comprehension beyond the word. New York: Springer-Verlag.

Graesser, A. C., Hopkinson, P. L., Lewis, E. W., & Bruflodt, H. A. (1984). The impact of different information sources on idea generation: Writing off the top of our heads. Written Communications, 1, 341-364.

Harris, T. E., & Bryant, J. (1986). The corporate communication manager. The Journal of Business Communication, 23, 19-29.

Hayes, J. R., & Flower, L. S. (1980). Identifying the organization of writing processes. In L. W. Gregg & E. R. Steinberg (Eds.), Cognitive processes in writing (pp. 31-50). Hillsdale, NJ: Erlbaum.

Hillocks, G. (1984). What works in teaching composition: A meta-analysis of experimental treatment studies. American Journal of Education, 93, 133-170.

Kellogg, R. T. (1986). Designing idea processors for document composition. Behavior Research Methods, Instruments, & Computers, 18, 118-128.

Kellogg, R. T. (1987). Effects of topic knowledge on the allocation of processing time and cognitive effort to writing processes. Memory & Cognition, 15, 256-266.

Klatzky, R. L. (1984). Memory and awareness. New York: W. H. Freeman.

Lachman, R., Lachman, J. L., & Butterfield, E. C. (1979). Cognitive psychology and information processing: An introduction. Hillsdale, NJ: Erlbaum.

Licklider, J. C. R. (1965). Man-computer partnership. International Science and Technology, 41, 18-26.

Macdonald, N. H., Frase, L. T., Gingrich, P., & Keenan, S. A. (1982). The writer's workbench: Computer aids for text analysis. IEEE Transactions on Communication, 30, 105-110.

Mandler, J. M., & Goodman, M. S. (1982). On the psychological validity of story structure. Journal of Verbal Learning and Verbal Behavior, 21, 507-523.

Mandler, J. M., & Johnson, N. S. (1977). Remembrance of things parsed: Story structure and recall. Cognitive Psychology, 9, 111-151.

Meyer, B. J. F. (1975). The organization of prose and its effects on memory. Amsterdam: North-Holland.

Meyer, B. J. F. (1985). Prose analysis: Purposes, procedures, and problems. In B. K. Britton & J. B. Black (Eds.), Understanding expository text: A theoretical and practical handbook for analyzing explanatory text. Hillsdale, NJ: Erlbaum.

Murray, D. M. (1978). Internal revision: A process of discovery. In C. R. Cooper & L. Odell (Eds.), Research on composing (pp. 85-103). Urbana, IL: National Council of Teachers of English.

Newell, A., & Simon, H. (1972). Human problem solving. Englewood Cliffs, NJ: Prentice-Hall.

Nickerson, R. S. (1986). Using computers: The human factors of information systems. Cambridge, MA: The MIT Press.

Nold, E. W. (1981). Revising. In C. H. Frederiksen & J. F. Dominic (Eds.),
Writing: Process, development, and communication (Vol. 2, pp. 67-80).
Hillsdale, NJ: Erlbaum.

Norman, D. A. (1981). Twelve issues for cognitive science. In D. A. Norman
(Ed.), Perspectives on cognitive science (pp. 265-295). Hillsdale, NJ:
Lawrence Erlbaum.

Posner, M. I. (1978). Chronometric explorations of mind. Hillsdale, NJ:
Erlbaum.

Posner, M. I., & Boies, S. J. (1971). Components of attention. Psychological
Review, 78, 391-408.

Rader, M. H., & Wunsch, A. P. (1980). A survey of communication practices of
business school graduates by job category and undergraduate major.
Journal of Business Communication, 17, 33-41.

Rueckert, W. H. (1963). Kenneth Burke and the drama of human relations.
Minneapolis: University of Minnesota Press.

Scardamalia, M., & Bereiter, C. (1983). The development of evaluative,
diagnostic, and remedial capabilities in children's composing. In M.
Martlew (Ed.), The psychology of written language: A developmental
approach (pp 61-82). London: Wiley.

Solso, R. L., & Johnson, H. H. (1984). An introduction to experimental
design in psychology: A case approach. New York: Harper & Row.

Sommers, E. A. (1985). Integrating composing and computing. In J. L. Collins
& E. A Sommers (Eds.), Writing on-line (pp. 3-10). Upper Montclair, NJ:
Boyton/Cook.

Sommers, N. (1980). Revision strategies of student writers and experienced
writers. College Composition and Communication, 31, 378-387.

Sommers, N. I. (1979). The need for theory in composition research. College
Composition and Communication, 30, 46-49.

Stillings, N. A., Feinstein, M. H., Garfield, J. L., Rissland, E. L.,
Rosenbaum, D. A., Weisler, S. E., & Baker-Ward, L. (1987). Cognitive
science. Cambridge, MA: The MIT Press.

Stine, D., & Skarzenski, D. (1979). Priorities for the business communication
classroom: A survey of business and academe: Journal of Business
Communication, 16, 15-30.

Strassman, P. (1981, June). Information systems and literacy. Paper presented
at the Conference on Literacy in the 1980's, Ann Arbor, MI.

Strickland, J. (1985). Prewriting and computing. In J. L. Collins & E. A.
Sommers (Eds.), Writing on-line (pp. 67-74). Upper Montclair, NJ:
Boyton/Cook.

Weiss, E. H. (1985). How to write a usable user manual. Philadelphia: ISI
Press.

Wresch, W. (Ed.). (1984). The computer in composition instruction: A
writer's tool. Urbana, IL: National Council of Teachers of English.

AGING AND PERFORMANCE: A MENTAL WORKLOAD ANALYSIS

George Kellas

University of Kansas
Lawrence, Kansas

Greg Simpson

University of Nebraska-Omaha
Omaha, Nebraska

F. Richard Ferraro

University of Kansas
Lawrence, Kansas

It is estimated that by the year 2000, 31 million Americans will be 65 years of age or older (Ward, 1979). It is not surprising, therefore, that psychology has seen an increased interest in aging, in terms of basic psychological processes as well as the practical problems of dealing with an aging population. Of particular importance are the presumed effects of aging, both physical and cognitive, that may affect the elderly's role in society in general, and in the work force in particular. For example, questions of job advancement for older workers, and even mandatory retirement, are based on (possibly erroneous) assumptions about age-related declines in performance capacity.

Much of our thinking about the elderly begins with an assumption of the aging individual as one of steadily diminishing abilities, a view that the psychological literature has done little to dispel. Individual exceptions, elderly people of great energy and creativity, are, of course, easily found (e.g., Pablo Picasso, Georgia O'Keefe, Vladimir Horowitz, etc.). It may be, in fact, that such cases are less exceptional than they seem. A recent study by Horner, Rushton, and Vernon (1986) examined publication rates of psychological researchers between 35 and 64 years of age. They found that, although the rate of publication declines with age, there remains a substantial group of active older scholars that are more productive than many of their younger colleagues. Rybash, Hoyer, and Roodin (1986) have proposed a general model of adult changes in cognition (the encapsulation model) which holds that age-related changes may vary across different knowledge domains (i.e., interests and abilities). While information processing skills may show general decline with age, there may be little or no change within a domain in which an individual is "expert". The purpose of the present chapter is to explore changes that occur with age in psycholinguistic abilities and how such abilities are related to the allocation of attention, a basic psychological process. We will present the results of research showing that even as general and rudimentary a language process as the recognition of isolated words does not show a universal decline with age.

The research that we will discuss in this chapter concerns an examination of the attentional demands associated with the recognition of words by other adults. As adults grow older, they commonly show decreased performance on those tasks that place a demand on their attentional capacities. Although this phenomenon is well documented, its basis has been a matter of some controversy. Some researchers have proposed that there is a decrease with age in the amount of attentional capacity that one possesses (Craik & Simon, 1980), while others contend that performance differences reflect not diminished capacity, but rather a general age-related slowing of information processing abilities (Salthouse, 1982; Somberg & Salthouse, 1982). Neither of these accounts is very satisfying, in our opinion. Regarding the decreased capacity view, in the absence of any idea of how much attention any person has, or even of what the stuff of attention consists, it does not seem appropriate to propose that one group possesses less of it than another. The age-related slowing view, on the other hand, in positing that a speed loss is responsible for performance differences, essentially proposes the passage of time as a causal factor. Despite their differences, however, these views appear to share an assumption, the challenge of which will be a major focus of this chapter. Each approach has appeared to treat the elderly as a homogeneous group, universally showing decreased capacity or reduced speed. The possibility, indeed the likelihood, that there are large individual differences in the performance of attention-demanding tasks among older adults has implications that extend beyond the laboratory and into the workplace.

We have chosen the medium of word recognition for our studies of the attentional abilities of older adults. It is recognized widely that there are important changes in psycholinguistic abilities as adults grow older (Kausler, 1982; Kynette & Kemper, 1987). The language of older adults shows more sentence fragments and simpler syntactic constructions than does that of younger individuals. Such findings have important implications for America's aging workforce, in their suggestion that the ability to communicate may be affected by subtle age-related changes in language comprehension and production processes. Our research examines the possibility that it is age differences in attentional processes that underlie these changing psycholinguistic abilities. We believe that word recognition is an appropriate starting point for our exploration of the relationship between language comprehension and attention in aging, for two reasons. First, during comprehension, the initial identification of words is necessary before syntactic and semantic analyses can proceed. That is, word recognition can be seen as the foundation of spoken and written language comprehension. Second, recent work in cognitive psychology (including some of our own) provides a yardstick against which to measure age-related changes in these fundamental language processes. Therefore, we compared younger and older adults for differences in their patterns of attention allocation during the early stages of word recognition and the initial retrieval of word meaning. A dual-task procedure was employed, in which subjects performed a word recognition task and simultaneously responded to auditory tone probes. The logic of this task, along with a review of our current knowledge of attention and word recognition processes, is presented below.

ATTENTION AND WORD RECOGNITION

The role of attention in word recognition has generally been minimized, with many theorists assuming that the processes leading up to the identification of a word occur automatically (see Humphreys, 1985, for a review). Few researchers have examined explicitly the attentional demands associated with early stages of word recognition. Becker (1976) was the first to use a dual-task procedure to demonstrate that the operations involved in word recognition require attention. In Becker's research, college students decided whether visually presented letter strings were words (the lexical decision task) and, at the same time, responded to auditory probes. It is assumed that these two tasks draw upon the same limited-capacity resource pool and that performance on one task may be used to gauge the resource demands of the other. That is, as performance on one (primary) task becomes more demanding of a subject's attention, the less attention remains for performing a second task. Relatively poor performance on the second task, therefore, leads to the conclusion that the primary task is very demanding. Becker found that latencies to respond to the probe were longer when they were presented in conjunction with the lexical decision task than when the probe task was performed by itself. In addition, probe responses were slower when the letter string was a low-frequency word than when it was a more common word. These results showed that word recognition is resource demanding, and that the amount of resources that are required varies as a function of the frequency with which the words occur in printed English.

Recently, we conducted a similar experiment, also with college students as subjects (Kellas, Ferraro, & Simpson, under review). Rather than word frequency; however, we were interested in the attention demands associated with the early operations relevant to the retrieval of word meaning. Toward this end, we compared response latencies to probes presented in conjunction with multiple-meaning (ambiguous) and single-meaning (unambiguous) words.

The study of recognition of words with more than one meaning (lexical ambiguity) has received much attention from cognitive psychologists in recent years. The topic is of interest not only because of the frequency of ambiguity in the language but also because it presents particular problems that serve to shed light on word recognition in general (Simpson, 1984; Simpson & Burgess, in press). For example, data suggesting that multiple meanings of an ambiguous word are activated when such a word is encountered, regardless of context, have served as the primary evidence for the idea that word recognition in general is an autonomous process, unaffected by contextual constraints (e.g., Seidenberg, Tanenhaus, Leiman, & Bienkowski, 1982; Swinney, 1979). The study of ambiguous word recognition in isolation (i.e., without context) has been used to determine whether word recognition is best characterized as a serial search process through an internal lexicon (Forster & Bednall, 1976; Rubenstein, Garfield, & Millikan, 1970) or as a signal detection process in which one or more "logogens" (hypothetical word-detection devices) become activated beyond some threshold level (Jastrzembski, 1981). A complete explication of these issues is far beyond the scope of the present chapter, and not critical to its main arguments (see Simpson, 1984, for a more comprehensive review of the lexical ambiguity literature). The point to be made here is that multiple-meaning words provide an excellent special case of word recognition that allows us to explore the role that meaning plays in the early stages of word recognition.

In our research with college students, we asked them to perform lexical decisions while simultaneously responding to auditory probes. The lexical decision stimulus could be either a word or a pronounceable nonword (pseudoword). Word stimuli had been rated by another group of students as having either one or more than one meaning (unambiguous and ambiguous words, respectively). One of these stimulus types would be presented visually to the subject, who would then decide whether that stimulus was a word or nonword by pressing the appropriate response key. The subjects were also instructed to press a third key with the other hand when they heard a tone. The tone followed the onset of the letter string by 90, 180, or 270 milliseconds. This variable is referred to as the stimulus onset asynchrony, or SOA. The reaction time (RT) to the probe serves as an index of the amount of attention that has been allocated to word recognition: longer probe RTs suggest greater attention paid to the lexical decision. The SOA factor allowed us to chart changes in attentional allocation across the timecourse of the word recognition process. We found that ambiguous words showed faster lexical decisions than both unambiguous words and pseudowords, and also resulted in the fastest probe RTs. Similarly, unambiguous words showed faster responses on both tasks than did pseudowords. Further, all three stimulus types resulted in declining probe RTs across SOA. In summary, our principal conclusions from this research were that word recognition is a capacity-demanding process, and that processes associated with the early extraction of word meaning are implicated in these attentional operations. The latter conclusion emerged from the finding that, even at the earliest point of our measurement (90 milliseconds) the amount of attention required for word recognition was inversely related to the number of word meanings. Finally, we concluded that the demands of word recognition decrease across its timecourse, at a constant rate for all stimuli.

THE KANSAS PROJECT ON AGING AND COGNITION

The research to be reported was part of a larger program of collaborative research on cognitive aging that is being conducted at the University of Kansas. In addition to our work, the Project includes research on adult age changes in learning and memory strategies, complex linguistic (syntactic) abilities, the cognitive representation of interpersonal relations, and television viewing. In addition to a description of our preliminary results, we also will discuss briefly their relations to some of these projects.

In order to understand the role that attentional processes play in the language abilities of the elderly, we applied the procedures described above to a comparison between college students and a group of subjects averaging 70 years of age. By comparing the performance of elderly subjects on the dual-task procedure with that of college students, we have been able to assess adult developmental changes in the relationship between word recognition and attention allocation.

METHOD AND PROCEDURE

The subjects for this dual-task experiment were 26 undergraduate students and 34 elderly participants. The elderly adults were selected from a pool of retired faculty from the University of Kansas. Eight of the elderly subjects and 13 of the college students performed the probe task alone to provide a baseline measure for each age against which the resource allocation requirements of word recognition could be assessed. Our stimuli comprised a set of 60 ambiguous words, 60 unambiguous words, and 120 pronounceable nonwords. The ambiguity of the words was determined by a group of college student raters, who evaluated all of the stimuli according to their number of meanings. Ambiguous and unambiguous words were equated on frequency of occurrence in printed English (Kucera & Francis, 1967) and subject-rated experiential familiarity (Gernsbacher, 1984). Nonwords and both word types were also equated on length (number of letters) and bigram frequency (the summed frequency of occurrence in English of each successive letter pair).

The letter strings were presented to the subjects on the viewing screen of a tachistoscope. At the beginning of each trial, a warning signal (a plus sign) was presented for 500 milliseconds. The screen remained blank for one second following the offset of the warning. The letter string was then presented for 500 milliseconds. Onset of the letter string also started a millisecond clock, which was stopped when the subject made the lexical decision response by pressing one of two keys, marked "WORD" and "NONWORD," with the middle and index fingers of one hand. Either 90, 180, or 270 milliseconds after the onset of the letter string, a 70 dB 4kHz tone was presented binaurally to the subject through headphones. Presentation of the tone started a second millisecond clock, which stopped when the subject pressed a third key with the other hand. Subjects were instructed to render both the lexical decision and the probe response as rapidly and as accurately as possible.

RESULTS AND DISCUSSION

Our initial analyses of these older subjects' performance suggested a pattern very much like that seen in our college student subjects. Like the younger subjects, the elderly took less time to recognize ambiguous than unambiguous words and, in turn, responded to unambiguous words faster than to pseudowords. Overall, however, their lexical decision latencies were much longer than those of the college students. Similarly, the older subjects' probe reaction times were slower than those of the young, but followed the same pattern. Ambiguous words required fewer resources for their recognition than did unambiguous words, which required fewer than pseudowords. Probe RT, for all stimulus types, showed a constant decrease across SOA. Thus, one could conclude that the elderly processed these words, and allocated attention to them, in the same manner as college students did, but simply did so more slowly. Such a conclusion would be perfectly compatible with the prevailing hypothesis that aging is characterized by a generalized slowing of information processing abilities (Cerella, 1985; Salthouse, 1982). A closer inspection of our data, however, suggested to us that this could not be the entire story.

A more thorough comparison of the older subjects' data with those of the college students showed that, in addition to their slower mean probe RTs, the elderly displayed greater variability in their responding. The probe RT distributions for the elderly showed greater positive skew than did those of the younger subjects, and it appeared that this variability within individual subjects (i.e., intrasubject variability) was contributing disproportionately to the mean performance of the elderly in comparison to that of college students. This observation was confirmed by computing Pearson product=moment correlations between individuals' measures of central tendency and standard deviations. These correlations indicated that mean performance and variability were relatively independent for the college students (r = 0.35), but were strongly related for the older subjects (r = 0.83). In other words, the average performance of the elderly was highly influenced by the variability of responding that individual subjects showed from trial to trial.

This relative lack of consistent responding among some of the elderly has important implications for the hypothesis of a general age-related

Table 1. Mean Lexical Decision Reaction Times and Standard Deviations (in msec) for Lo-C Elderly, Hi-C Elderly, and Young Subjects as a Function of Stimulus Type

	Stimulus		
Group	Ambiguous	Unambiguous	Pseudoword
Lo-C	1573 (360)	1710 (465)	1983 (588)
Hi-C	984 (232)	994 (227)	1080 (255)
Young	773 (77)	802 (91)	896 (120)

Note: Standard Deviations are in parenthesis.

slowing of information processing. The high correlation among the elderly between average performance and variability suggests that the slower average performance may arise from extremely slow responses on some, but not all, trials. In short, what appears (from inspection of the group means) to be a general slowing in the elderly may arise instead from extremely slow responses by some subjects on some trials.

To explore this possibility further, we divided the older subjects' data into two groups based on a median split of the individual subjects' probe RT standard deviations. The subjects below the median standard deviation we refer to as the High-Consistency (Hi-C) group, and those above the median as the Low-Consistency (Lo-C) group. There were 13 elderly subjects in each of these groups, and we compared these to an equal sized group of college students.

Table 1 shows the three groups' mean lexical decision latencies, along with their standard deviations. All three groups showed the familiar pattern of fastest responses to ambiguous words, followed by ambiguous words, and finally pseudowords. Quantitatively, however, the groups are markedly different. The Lo-C elderly were 112% slower than young adults, whereas the Hi-C older subjects were only 24% slower than college students. The standard deviations indicate that Hi-C elderly were also less variable in their word recognition performance than were the Lo-C subjects. Note that the initial split of the elderly was based on variability in probe RT, not lexical decision. Nevertheless, the Hi-C group proved to be more consistent on both tasks than the Lo-C group, and more consistent even than college students in probe reaction time.

The data reflecting attentional allocation revealed several interesting results. The Lo-C probe responses were much slower than those of either the Hi-C elderly or the younger subjects. Like the college students, the Lo-C older subjects showed faster probe RTs to ambiguous than to unambiguous words, which in turn led to faster responses than did pseudowords. The performance of the Hi-C elderly, however, was quite different. First, their mean probe RTs were actually <u>faster</u> than those of the college students. In addition, stimulus type had no effect on this group's probe responses. That is, probe RTs were equivalent for ambiguous and unambiguous words and pseudowords. This pattern of probe RTs, in conjunction with the group differences seen in lexical decision performance, indicated that the Lo-C elderly committed <u>more</u> attentional resources to performance on the lexical decision task than did young adults. The Hi-C elderly, on the other hand, allocated <u>fewer</u> resources to the lexical decision task than did college students, but showed a comparatively small decrement in word recognition performance.

To confirm this account of differences in resource allocation among the groups, we computed a direct measure of attention, displayed in Figure 1, for the two elderly groups (right panel) and the college students (left panel). The attention scores shown in this figure represent differences in probe RT between the dual-task conditions (i.e., each stimulus type and SOA) and baseline performance of age-matched control groups who performed the probe task in isolation (i.e., unaccompanied by the lexical decision task). The data presented in Figure 1 confirm that more attention was allocated to word recognition by Lo-C elderly than by the young and that the Hi-C group showed the lowest degree of resource allocation. Also confirmed was the observation that, for the Hi-C older subjects, resource allocation was independent of word meaning. Finally, the figure suggests that the slope of the function related attention allocation and SOA, which indicates the withdrawal of resources over the timecourse of word recognition, is somewhat less for Hi-C elderly than for either of the other two groups.

This pattern of results leads us to conclude that the Hi-C elderly represent a group of "expert" word processors who are able to recognize words much more rapidly than their less consistent age-mates, and actually expend less attentional resources when doing so. In fact, the word recognition processes of these Hi-C older subjects appear to be automatic relative to the performance of college students. This conclusion is supported not only by the fact that their attention scores are lower than those of the younger group, but also by the lack of an effect of the number of word meanings and by the relative flatness of the SOA function for the Hi-C elderly. The absence of an effect for the type of the lexical decision stimulus indicates that these experts (the Hi-C group) required only minimal attention to recognize even unambiguous words and pseudowords, items which were relatively demanding for the college students as well as for the Lo-C elderly. If little attention is required by the Hi-C group for the early stages of the word recognition process, then the attention withdrawal across the course of a trial should be less dramatic, as confirmed by the decreased SOA slope for these subjects. Of course, if word recognition of the Hi-C group were fully automatic, the attention scores would be zero, which clearly is not the case. We would argue simply that the initial extraction of meaning from the printed stimulus is more highly routinized for these subjects than for college students or Lo-C elderly.

What conclusions about word recognition and attention in the elderly can be draw from these data? First, a model of a general age-related loss of information processing speed does not account well for these results. The overall data for older subjects did show generally slower responding on both tasks, in comparison to the results for college students, suggesting a speed-loss conclusion. The division of the elderly into responders of high and low consistency, however, indicates that this is a highly misleading characterization of older subjects' word recognition abilities. The lexical decision times of the Hi-C group were slower than those of the college students; but if a simple speed loss were responsible for this difference, we would not have expected the probe reaction time to be faster for the Hi-C group than for the younger subjects. Even the Lo-C group is not characterized best as merely responding more slowly. The high variability in their probe RTs suggests that, rather than showing a general slowing or less processing capacity, this group was simply less able to allocate and maintain attention across trials than was the Hi-C group. We examined this hypothesis by inspecting the standard deviations of the attention scores shown in Figure 1. These standard deviations, shown in Table 2, represent within-subject variability across trials, and thus can be interpreted as an index of the trial-to-trial consistency of attention allocation. These data show dramatically that the Lo-C elderly, in comparison to the other two groups, show a very high degree of fluctuation of attention across trials.

We would conclude, therefore, that older subjects do not necessarily show less attention than younger, but that they are less able to maintain attention and remain vigilant to the task at hand over an extended period of time. Even this conclusion does not hold for all older subjects, however, as our procedure has allowed us to identify a subset of expert elderly, who show word recognition processes that are somewhat slower, but apparently more routinized and less demanding, than are those of college students.

What do these data suggest more generally for statements about aging and cognition? First, we would argue that it is not appropriate to characterize the elderly as being generally slower or possessed of less information processing capacity than are the young. Not only did some of our elderly subjects contradict these characterizations altogether, but even the group that did show poorer performance cannot be described as universally slower than younger adults. Rather, their tendency toward slower average performance arises from an apparent difficulty in allocating and maintaining attention consistently across time.

Optimal Performance Analysis

If the difference between the Lo-C elderly and the other two groups is traceable to differences in the consistency of attentional allocation across

Table 2. Standard Deviations (in msec) of Absolute Difference Scores for Lo-C Elderly, Hi-C Elderly, and Young Subjects as a Function of Stimuli Type and Stimulus Onset Asynchrony (SOA)

		Stimuli		
Group	SOA	Ambiguous	Unambiguous	Pseudoword
Lo-C	90	280	322	469
	180	242	282	484
	270	320	269	430
Hi-C	90	163	191	169
	180	191	147	156
	270	123	137	162
Young	90	97	106	114
	180	93	97	123
	270	87	115	115

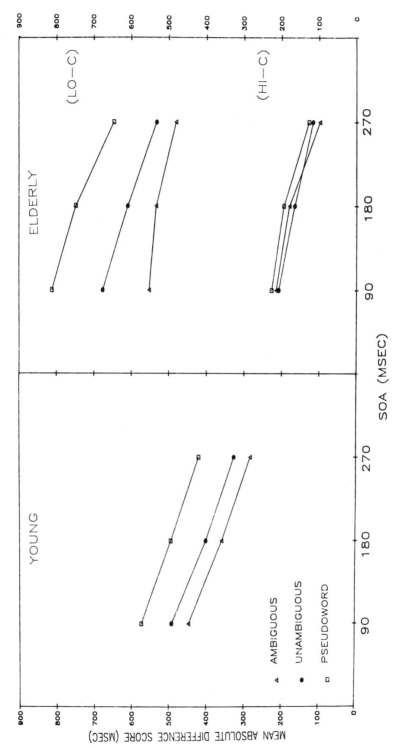

Fig. 1. Mean difference scores (in msec) for Lo-C Elderly, Hi-C Elderly, and Young subjects as a function of stimuli (ambiguous, unambiguous, pseudoword) and stimulus onset asynchrony (SOA; 90, 180, 270 msec).

43

Table 3. Mean Probe Reaction Times and Standard Deviations (in msec) for Three Fastest Probe Responses for Lo-C Elderly and Average Performance for Young Subjects as a Function of Stimulus Type and Stimulus Onset Asychrony (SOA)

| | | Stimulus | | | | | |
| | | Ambiguous | | Unambiguous | | Pseudoword | |
Group	SOA	M	SD	M	SD	M	SD
Lo-C	90	628	271	719	319	728	371
	180	599	264	631	287	654	367
	270	527	279	573	261	593	334
Young	90	623	128	658	155	747	143
	180	553	130	558	131	651	150
	270	464	140	477	127	592	145

Note: M = Mean, SD = Standard Deviation.

trials, then even these subjects should occasionally perform in a manner more like that of young adults. This, of course, is a natural conclusion to draw from the high within-subject variability of the Lo-C subjects. In order to assess the degree to which the best performance of the Lo-C group approximates that of college students, we re-examined the Lo-C elderly data, this time restricting our analysis to the three fastest probe responses in each condition (i.e., each combination of lexical decision stimulus type and SOA). Our principal criterion for so limiting the data was that these restricted "optimal performance" data should maintain the relationship seen in the full data set. That is, even when limited to the three fastest responses in each condition, the data still showed the typical differences among stimulus types and the decline of probe RT across SOA. The results of this optimal performance analysis are presented in Table 3, which shows the optimal performance in probe RT of the Lo-C elderly in comparison to the average performance of the college students.

The dramatic reduction in the age difference in probe RT is apparent in this table. Even these subjects, whose average performance is much poorer than the young adults', are equivalent to the average performance of college students when performing optimally. We take these data as strong confirmation of our hypothesis that the apparent slowing with age, rather than being universal, is instead a consequence of a disproportionate contribution of intrasubject variability to average performance. These results also contradict any hypothesis of an age-related structural change that would lead to a constant slowing with age. If such changes were responsible for the differences in average performance seen here (and in most cognitive aging research), we would expect that difference to be constant across trials. That is, such hypotheses (e.g., Salthouse 1985) leave no room for elderly performance to be sometimes as good as that of young adults.

Our hypothesis that it is difficulty in the consistent allocation of attention that underlies the apparent processing speed deficit in the elderly makes a further strong prediction: If we could make it difficult for college students to allocate attention, their word recognition performance should begin to resemble that of the elderly. That is, it should be possible to "age" younger adults artificially by affecting the facility with which they normally are able to allocate attention. In fact, we have completed an experiment with college students in which their word recognition performance was made to resemble that of our elderly subjects. In this experiment, college students performed the lexical decision task as described previously, either alone or in conjunction with another task. In this case, however, the second task involved maintaining a list of digits in memory. Prior to the onset of each lexical decision stimulus, the experimenter read to the subject a random string of seven digits. After the subject completed the lexical decision response, he or she then reported the digits that had been presented on that trial. If the speed of word recognition is sensitive to a person's ability to allocate resources, then diverting some of these resources to a memory task should result in slowed word recognition, even for young adults. Table 4 shows the lexical decision latencies for college students subjected to this memory load procedure, compared to a group that performed the lexical decision procedure alone. It is very clear from these data that performance on word recognition is both slower and more variable under the memory load conditions. In fact, like the data from the elderly subjects, the subjects in the memory load condition showed a stronger relationship between average performance and variability (r = 0.66 vs. 0.35 with no memory load). Consequently, when we make it difficult for young adults to allocate attention, by requiring them to perform a second capacity-demanding task, their word recognition performance begins to approximate that seen in the elderly. We are comfortable, therefore, in concluding that allocation and maintenance of attention are important factors in determining cognitive performance, and may represent major forces underlying adult age differences in cognitive performance.

Table 4. Mean Lexical Decision Times and Standard Deviations (In msec) as a Function of Condition and Stimuli

	Ambiguous		Stimuli Unambiguous		Pseudoword	
Condition	M	SD	M	SD	M	SD
Load	853	93	904	96	1038	140
No Load	736	73	770	77	848	76

Note: M = Mean, SD = Standard Deviation.

CONCLUSIONS AND IMPLICATIONS

Although our research has concentrated on a highly constrained cognitive domain, we do not believe that our conclusions are restricted to the recognition of isolated words. We believe, rather, that our division of the elderly into high- and low-consistency responders, and our identification of attentional fluctuation as an important factor underlying differences in performance, can serve as a model for the differences across domains in the cognitive abilities of the elderly. That is, just as "expert" word recognizers show very rapid and relatively automatic word recognition processes, experts in other domains may also be characterized by an ability to carry out the processes relevant to that domain in an efficient, routinized way. Further, we believe that the relative automaticity of a very basic process, such as word recognition, is reflected in all of the more sophisticated skills of which it is a part. Our finding of the consistency of attention allocation as a driving force in word recognition would be trivial if we did not believe that such consistency had implications for larger issues in language and communication. In fact, we do have some information regarding the generality of our attention measures beyond the word level.

As part of the larger Kansas Project on Aging and Cognition, we have examined the relationship between our attention allocation measure and the results of the research of other project investigators. The ability to allocate attention at the word level has been shown to be predictive of the percentage of sentence fragments produced by the elderly in a structured interview, and also the percentage of left-branching sentences used (these are sentences which begin with a subordinate clause and place a substantial demand on processing resources). Subjects who required less attention for word recognition also tended to show fewer sentence fragments and a greater percentage of left-branching constructions. Thus, the sophistication that these subjects showed in the recognition of single words was shown as well in their abilities in discourse production. In addition, a relationship was discovered between attention allocation and the amount of time that the elderly spend watching television programs of a sophisticated cultural content (e.g., documentaries, arts programs, etc.). If one assumes that such content is demanding of attention, it is not surprising that those showing more attentional facility during word recognition would show it as well in another domain. Indeed, we could even speculate that a greater ability to process the more sophisticated linguistic content that typically accompanies such programming is partly responsible for viewing choice. We realize that such a conjecture is going beyond our present data; but, if true, it points to the pervasive effects that a fundamental process, such as attention allocation, may have at all levels of communication abilities.

In conclusion, we would argue that our research has important implications for considerations of older individuals in the workplace. First, it suggests that a view of the elderly as showing a general decrement in functioning is inaccurate. Our work also provides some indirect support for the hypothesis that the elderly will show considerable variability of skills across domains, to the point of being very highly competent within one or more domains of expertise (Rybash et al., 1986), and suggests that abilities to perform tasks relatively effortlessly will be correlated with this domain-specific competence. Finally, we believe that communicative competence plays an important role in the work place (e.g., in the giving and understanding of instruction) and is undoubtedly strongly related to worker success. Our research has very direct implications for the older worker, therefore, in showing the role that a basic cognitive process, the allocation of processing resource, plays at every level of language processing.

SUMMARY

In this chapter, we have attempted to address the problem of adult age changes in performance through an examination of the relationship between attention and· psycholinguistic abilities. Research was presented which described younger and older adults' allocation of attention during word recognition. Although older adults were generally slower than the young, they showed much greater individual variation. From this age-related increase in intrasubject variability, we were able to identify a group of expert elderly whose word recognition and attention allocation was similar to that of college students. An analysis of the optimal performance of the highly variable elderly showed that even those subjects performed similarly to young adults on some trials. These results argue against any model of adult cognitive change that posits a universal slowing of information processing or a loss of processing capacity. Instead, it appears that the average slowing seen with age is traceable to a lack of consistency of attention allocation for some elderly across a series of trials. Finally, we discussed these results in terms of their implications for expert performance in a variety of domains. Indeed, our word recognition results were shown to be related to language production and to patterns of television viewing. Our research suggests that a consideration of individual differences is especially critical for any statement about changes in performance during adulthood, because of the high degree of intrasubject variability seen with many older individuals.

ACKNOWLEDGEMENTS

This research was supported by Graduate Research Fund grant 3247-X0-20-0038 and Biomedical Sciences Support grant 4382-20-0711-0 from the University of Kansas Graduate School (awarded to the first author), and in part by a United States Department of Education grant G008630072 to the Kansas Bureau of Child Research and the Learning Disabilities Center of the University of Kansas. The second author is currently a Postdoctoral Trainee in the Child Language Program of the University of Kansas. Address all correspondence to George Kellas, Department of Psychology, 426 Fraser Hall, University of Kansas, Lawrence, Kansas 66045.

REFERENCES

Becker, C. A. (1976). Allocation of attention during visual word recognition. Journal of Experimental Psychology: Human Perception & Performance, 2, 556-566.

Cerella, J. (1985). Information processing rates in the elderly. Psychological Bulletin, 98, 67-83.

Craik, F. I. M., & Simon, E. (1980). Age differences in memory: The role of attention and depth of processing. In L. W. Poon, J. L. Fozard, L. S. Cermak, D. Arensberg, & L. W. Thompson (Eds.), New directions in memory & aging: Proceedings of the George Talland Memorial Conference. NJ: Erlbaum.

Forster, K. I., & Bednall, E. S. (1976). Terminating and exhaustive search in lexical access. Memory and Cognition, 4, 53-61.

Gernsbacher, M. A. (1984). Resolving 20 years of inconsistent interactions between lexical familiarity and orthography, concreteness, and polysemy. Journal of Experimental Psychology: General, 113, 256-281.

Horner, K. L., Rushston, J. P., & Vernon, P. A. (1986). Relation between aging and research productivity of academic psychologists. Psychology & Aging, 1, 319-324.

Humphreys, G. W. (1985). Attention, automaticity, and autonomy in visual word processing. In D. Besner, T. Waller, & G. MacKinnon (Eds.), Reading research: Advances in theory and practice (Vol. 5). NY: Academic Press.

Jastrzembski, J. E. (1981). Multiple meanings, number of related meanings, frequency of occurrence, and the lexicon. Cognitive Psychology, 13, 278-305.

Kausler, D. H. (1982). Experimental psychology & human aging. NY: Wiley.

Kellas, G., Ferraro, F. R., & Simpson, G. B. (under review). Lexical ambiguity and the timecourse of attentional allocation in word recognition. Journal of Experimental Psychology: Human Perception & Performance.

Kucera, H., & Francis, W. (1967). Computational analysis of present-day American English. Providence, RI: Brown University Press.

Kynette, D., & Kemper, S. (1987). Aging and loss of grammatical forms: A cross-sectional study of language performance. Language & Communication, 6, 43-59.

Rubenstein, H., Garfield, L., & Millikan, J. A. (1970). Homographic entries in the mental lexicon. Journal of Verbal Learning and Verbal Behavior, 9, 487-494.

Rybash, J. M., Hoyer, W. J., & Roodin, P. A. (1986). Adult cognition and aging. NY: Pergamon.

Salthouse, T. A. (1982). Adult cognition: An experimental psychology of human aging. NY: Springer-Verlag.

Salthouse, T. A. (1985). A theory of cognitive aging. Amsterdam: North Holland.

Seidenberg, M. S., Tanenhaus, M. K., Leiman, J. L., & Bienkowski, M. (1982). Automatic access of the meaning of ambiguous words in context: Some limitations of knowledge-based processing. Cognitive Psychology, 14, 489-537.

Simpson, G. B. (1984). Lexical ambiguity and its role on models of word recognition. Psychological Bulletin, 96, 316-340.

Simpson, G. B., & Burgess, C. (in press). Implications of lexical ambiguity resolution for word recognition and comprehension. In S. L. Small, G. W. Cottrell, & M. K. Tanenhaus (Eds.), Lexical ambiguity resolution in the comprehension of human language. Palo Alto, CA: Morgan Kaufman Publishers.

Somberg, B. L., & Salthouse, T. A. (1982). Divided attention in young and old adults. Journal of Experimental Psychology: Human Perception & Performance, 8, 651-663.

Swinney, D. A. (1979). Lexical access during sentence comprehension: (Re) consideration of context effects. Journal of Verbal Learning & Verbal Behavior, 1, 645-660.

Ward, R. A. (1979). The aging experience. NY: Lippincott.

ARTIFICIAL INTELLIGENCE, EXPERT SYSTEMS, AND PRODUCTIVITY

Sally Yeates Sedelow and Walter A. Sedelow, Jr.

University of Arkansas at Little Rock and University of Arkansas Graduate Institute of Technology

This chapter discusses the terms Artificial Intelligence and Expert Systems before turning to a more general consideration of types of knowledge and their representation. Technology is leading us toward making knowledge algorithmic (procedural and ruleful). The implications of this development for productivity, especially as affected by resulting workforce attitudes, are likely to be monumental. Notably responsive will be not only blue-collar workers but also white-collar workers, whose stock-in-trade is symbolic manipulation. As technology becomes ever more facilitative of machine-based symbolic analysis and communication, traditional workforce roles, which hitherto were not threatened, inevitably will be affected. Nonetheless, in the near term, symbol systems (W. Sedelow & S. Sedelow, 1979, 1983) and the knowledge they represent pose formidable research and development challenges to technology-based productivity. Verbal symbol systems, with their ambiguities and vaguenesses, are especially difficult to manage in a multidomain-specific way; but there are promising approaches to these problems. Attention needs to be paid not only to such problem resolution but to the interfitting of Expert Systems, and Artificial Intelligence more generally, with Robotics.

Our association with Artificial Intelligence (AI) began almost exactly a quarter century ago when we joined what had been a division of The RAND Corporation: The System Development Corporation in Santa Monica, California. At that time, the field of AI had been founded not many years earlier and, to that date, had been heavily focused on such activities as building software for playing games against human opponents. There was no tight definition of AI and the commonplace way of characterizing it was to say: if the behavior of a computer-based system is what would be called intelligent behavior in a human, then we will call that computer-based system an example of AI.

There is, not at all surprisingly, a common phenomenon in the history of technological inventions such that some time is required before distinctive or even unique properties and powers in a new invention or system are discovered. That being the case, it is not surprising that, when first invented, systems tend to be used needlessly to ape some predecessor technology. In the instance of AI the effort was not, then, to find or create unique properties in any computer-based AI system and, more especially, unique properties which were complementary to human behavior but, rather, to make such a system "prove itself" by doing something that people did, such as playing a game as well or better. Just as Stephen Jay Gould recently has pointed out in The New York Review of Books that human beings often seem unable to categorize animal behavior except in anthropomorphic terms, so it often has seemed that computers invited "personalizing." It would not seem appropriate to develop a more abstract definition of intelligence--or better yet, of cognition--which could be applied differentially to humans and to certain sophisticated computer-based systems. In addition to thus encouraging attention to the ways in which computers can be made usefully to differ from human behavior in the performance of complex and productive tasks, such an intellectual move would have the effect of obviating problems with some of the numerous current disputes as to the cultural and class biases that have been built into existing definitions of intelligence--which, of course, is now also strongly urged upon us as a nonunitary phenomenon anyway.

As to the other computer-related term in the title, Expert Systems, we may say that with expert systems we have a heightening of the intelligence of AI, so that the system may be consulted--and consulted conversationally--as one would consult an expert or, better yet, the consensus wisdom of a specialized group of experts. Like AI more generally, expert systems represent a new and rather "ultimate" phase of that process of externalization whereby varied human capabilities are constructed so as to fulfill a human function without a person (e.g., the thread-spinning machines invented during the Industrial Revolution). In the case at the limit, this externalization process with reference to brain functions eventuates in what we have recently called Cognitive Robotics. With expert systems we may expect to see most significant knowledge, and a great deal which is only slightly consequential, reassembled outside of human brains and "embodied" in computer-based systems. That will not be a process of providing some operationalization to serve as a surrogate for knowledge but, rather, a realization in externalized form of the expert knowledge itself. And it probably should be stressed that one of the interesting and significant features of expert knowledge is that, perhaps somewhat paradoxically on the surface, knowledge is expert in proportion as it is not thoroughly worked out (formalized: W. Sedelow & S. Sedelow, 1979, 1983, in press) as knowledge. That is to say, insofar as knowledge is of a form which can be widely shared there does not need to be, nor can there be, an expert. Rather, we have experts in proportion as the knowledge is insecure, that is, insofar as there is a significant measure of noetic uncertainty. To develop symbol systems apt for representing such precarious knowledge, various specialized modes of knowledge representation (e.g., for statistical, probabilistic, and stochastic processes) have been invented. Other modes of knowledge representation are in process of being widely adopted (Fuzzy Sets and Possibility Theory), while still newer symbolic inventions attuned to the requirements of other forms of knowledge uncertainty (Rough Sets) are in process of emergence. Rough Sets, initiated by Pawlak in Poland (1981a, b) and continued in this country by Grzymala-Busse of the University of Kansas, is a form of expert knowledge representation research with which we ourselves are also associated.

In order to be presented to a computer in usable form, scientific and technical knowledge--in fact what we might call all "real" knowledge--will be decomposed, in a mathematical sense, and rendered algorithmic (often, in the implementation, employing recursive functions). Doing so of course will create enormous opportunities and interest in knowledge representation theory--the study of how to choose or invent (W. Sedelow, 1968) the symbol systems appropriate to the representation of particular types of knowledge. As the exposition in algorithmic form of knowledge becomes a widespread process, we offer the observation that the university which directly concentrates on creating and fostering a department of algorithmic science (i.e., the science of algorithms and science/knowledge as algorithms) will position itself to exert wide and significant influence, as in enhancing productivity (W. Sedelow, 1968). As has already happened with economics and psychology, for two examples, the exciting process of recapitulating the substantive content of science or technology in order to put that knowledge into a form usable by computers leads to the discovery of unwarranted assumptions and of logic holes, and also leads to the extension of that knowledge. Without doubt one of the intellectually pleasing prospects of the early 21st century will be to discover how "the second time around," so to speak, any given academic subspecialty will look different in its formal reconstitution--and "why." Careers doubtless will be made out of comparisons, and putative explanations of those comparisons, between the original human form of the science/technology and its newer, machinable form.

One of the major sources of enhanced productivity of use for scientific and technical knowledge will derive from a self-conscious effort at optimization as to the various "languages" within which that knowledge is represented. That process is already underway vis-a-vis medical expert systems. Efforts are being made to provide optimizations that relate to the processing of the knowledge on the machine, including the employment of that knowledge in the control of robotic devices. And, optimization against other criteria also will no doubt be implied ergonomically; that is to say, efforts also will be made to optimize some of the knowledge representation relative to the comfort of the user, whether the user is someone (a "packaging engineer") initially stowing the knowledge aboard the computer or someone in the role of intellectual longshoreman who is taking the knowledge off the machine. Again, in medical applications of expert systems, for example, such efforts are already underway.

Without question, one of the immediately evident implications for enhanced productivity in the reconstitution of knowledge in such formats as are machinable will be the utilization of the resultant expert systems in a pedagogical modality (such as in the Harvard Medical School's "New Pathways" learning option). And in addition to the other evident benefits of having so much knowledge available in machine form and hence, incidentally, in not necessarily institutionally controlled formats (thus available for "lifelong" and not school-dependent use), we observe that owing to the necessary completeness of the formulation of such knowledge it will be usable even by such students as are not effectively enculturated into the subcultures out of which the science emerged in the first instance. Among other implications, that suggests the greater accessability to knowledge for members of various minority constituencies and hence the possibility of a markedly heightened productivity for education both at home and abroad. Since "every step of the way" has to be taken explicitly in computerizing knowledge, there are no confusing, culture-dependent gaps in the knowledge. Hence it is much more widely understandable; there are no longer "dumb" questions since everything has to be made wholly explicit; and the learning from such systems can be comfortably self-paced as well.

But as we contemplate the implications of the rapid growth of expert systems, we do need to bear in mind that there can be very serious declines in human productivity if the implementation of expert systems is done in such ways as to bring about a kind of demoralization of the traditional (i.e., human) work force. It is probably a fair supposition that there will be--already may be--some short-term losses in productivity brought about either consciously or not in those who feel threatened by the possibility of even a partial, if substantial, replacement of their roles by computer-based systems. And it is of course worthy of notice that there is going to be comparatively little opportunity for groups of traditional white-collar experts to shelter themselves ("protectionism") from the impact of expert systems, especially when combined with a rich panoply of robotic devices. It is already the case that in some instances roboticized Japanese factories are able to retain their work forces until "attrited," and at the same time economically outperform their competitors despite the additional capital costs of having introduced fully robotic systems. We have there an indication of just how dramatic the productivity gains of further stages of computerization may come to be and of how, then, it easily may come to pass that the dislocations produced by the Industrial Revolution could be minor by contrast with the displacements--globally--in both the blue-collar and the white-collar workforces owing to computerization, automation, robotics, and, especially, cognitive robotics.

Twenty-five years ago, a question that we found intriguing was the extent to which computers were being used in order to facilitate the programming of computers. The answer to that question was, in brief, not much. But over these past two and one-half decades, we have seen the virtual disappearance of the coder as a professional and the decline in the role of the programmer in proportion as various devices for using computers to produce code and program increased. The notable emergence two decades ago of compiler compilers was but one big step taken along that path. And today, as is so widely known, it is also possible to obtain computer software which will markedly enhance the adequacy and productivity of decision making with reference to not only the design of computers themselves but also the configuring of available equipment and software for any given application. In the present context, the point, of course, is that we are going to have and in some measure are already beginning to have expert systems to help in expert system building and thus to, at least partially, replace the knowledge engineer whose workforce role was so designated only a few years ago by Feingenbaum (1983). Expert systems to build expert systems are emerging in tandem with robotic factories to build robots. Thereby productivity can be markedly enhanced. But, during the phase-in, we may expect to see, and very understandably, varied manifestations of antiproductive neo-Ludditeism. And when cognitive robotics is employed to build cognitive robots, the neo-Ludditeism may become the more subtle for emanating from white-collar workers in the professions.

It seems very evident that among the "determinants" that will affect whether over the next decade we see gains in productivity approaching technologically possible levels is the attitude of members of the work force toward the introduction of such advanced computing as we find in AI and, more specifically, in expert systems. The relationship of psychological factors, such as those attitudes, to economic process has been a source of interest to some social scientists for decades. An example was the work of Katona at the University of Michigan. We do not, however, even yet have an understanding at the level of brain sciences knowledge of such interactions between the perceptual and the behavioral. Such an effort as the new book by Winograd and Flores (1987) represents the merest beginnings towards achieving significant scientificity in that domain (W. Sedelow & S. Sedelow, 1978, 1979).

Although ideological and pragmatic factors in the United States have tended to forestall the development of such arrangements (guaranteed employment) as are more commonplace in some sectors of large-scale Japanese industry, and which facilitate the introduction of high productivity expert systems and AI, including robotics, there are examples of the same sort of approach here. A notable instance is the willingness of the longshoremen on the West Coast to, relatively unprotestingly, allow the introduction of robotic equipment. Owing to a type of "sweetheart" contract, the terms of which provide for protection of the economic interests of those who are currently longshoremen (even though, of course, the size of that component in the workforce will be inevitably reduced as the newer technologies are ever more widely employed), there has been comparatively little resistance to high-tech innovations on those docks. The immediate point at issue is that through the utilization of such an arrangement we do see one technique by means of which the introduction of machine-based high productivity can be facilitated in a "psycho-economic" way.

Some years ago, W. Sedelow (1978) spoke about the emergence of a mythology in the Occident which may be counterfunctional with reference to a criterion of effective introduction of expert systems and the like. Nervousness brought on by the implications of this culture"s own definitions and hypotheses concerning the nature of machines is seen in that paper to be the heart of the problem. In the West, historically, the differential definitions of human, in conjunction with the definitions of other categories both organic and inanimate, have compounded the situation in which powerful machines generate anxiety. By contrast, recently there have been those who have argued that the absence in Buddhism of such categorical separation of the human from the rest of the universe may be another factor giving the Japanese some edge in the more productive utilization of advanced computing.

Similarly, recently there has been considerable interest by historians in the implications of The Great Chain of Being (A. O. Lovejoy) as a mentalite factor in not only inadvertently encouraging ecological desolation but also, perhaps, through the threat latent in the idea of dominion, encouraging a sense of the possibility of machines in some way getting out of control, as was fantasized in the last century by Samuel Butler (Erewhon). Interestingly enough, the genius John von Neumann, through his contributions to automata theory and, especially, to the notion of the cellular automaton and the idea of the self-reproducing machine, in effect picked up mathematically on such possible conceptualizations and showed how they could be given attractive mathematical and theoretical significance.

If we seek to peer beyond our current horizons to determine the further implications of the development of AI, expert systems, and cognitive robotics, what do we perceive? A useful telescopic lens for that process is to be found in the work of Miller (1977) which, in its book format, is called Living Systems. As the result of a monumental effort stretched over decades at a variety of universities including notably the University of Michigan, Miller produced a synthesis of research material concerning the general nature of living systems, irrespective of scale. Coherently employing the same taxonomy and set of system relationships, Miller has set forth the nature of a living system from the scale of a cell up through the global ecosystem. In his enumeration of the necessary conditions for the functioning of such systems, we may find what, beyond current horizons, are fresh sets of challenges in the devising of advanced systems combining cognitive robotics with the robotization of afferent and efferent functions. Bionics and genetic engineering doubtless also will give us such devices in in/animate hybrid formats.

In a very different way, Holland (1975), of the University of Michigan, has offered us a rigorous mathematical generalization and extension to Darwinian notions of survival. In doing so, Holland has provided for us what we may use as a model in attempting to comprehend in advance what system characteristics are likely to lead to the survival, and also the demise, of such complex cognitive robotic systems as may be conceived and perhaps realized.

To date, it is probably the case that analogues to the afferent nervous system functions, centering on sensors and related capabilities, are the most fully developed of the components in the roboticization of the eye-brain-hand cycle. Consequently, it is not surprising that in the nearer term the greatest contributions to improvement in productivity through the building of smart robots will come through improvement in their effectors, the efferent nervous system analogues, and, especially, the building of hand-like equipment. The more effective simulation of brain functions is so much more complex a task than improving grippers and the like that the immediate payoff, in enhanced productivity, probably will emerge from the replication and extension of effector devices. Even so we would not want to minimize the complexity of the tasks implied, because it is true that realizing the versatility of the 20-jointed human hand has proved to be, of course, no easy matter.

As we reflect on what it takes and will take to produce computer-based brain functions of capability at least comparable in scale and quality to the human brain, though of course not duplicative of it, it is probably helpful to bear in mind that the very origin of the robot concept comes from the Czech language wherein cognates of robot signify serfs or statute laborers. The point here is that from the start--now nearly 65 years back for the specific word, robot--the idea was the achieving of an analogue to the capacities of the human being, rather than, simply, selected human mechanical skills. If we seek for the origins of that more modest goal of selected digital skills, we can recur all the way back to a dream of Aristotle's in which he presented the notion of weaving equipment (a loom) tending itself.

Although among the great pioneers in the conceptualization of modern computing, which is to say 20th century and especially (post-) World War II computing, each had his or her own perceptual sharpness in foreseeing implications of the computer. It is von Neumann among, let us say Juno Zuse, Alan Turing, and Norbert Wiener, who perhaps most clearly saw the "entelechy" of the computer. Even in the 17th century, Leibniz had an intimation of the great prospective logical power of a computing device with certain properties. And while Turing was the most powerfully reductive mathematically of the 20th-century pioneers, while Zuse in a remarkable way grasped intuitively (i.e., without the mathematics) the significance of a binary basis for hardware, and while Wiener foresaw some social implications of servomechanisms in general, it is to von Neumann that the credit must go for sensing that ultimately the greatest impact of the computer might be as instrumentation for understanding the functioning of the human brain, itself. And that reflexivity may well come to pass. In the process of doing so, it no doubt at least as dramatically will change the world around us as the major technological developments of the past century have changed the "world" of advanced industrial societies.

But what, especially in the remainder of this century, may we expect to see take place in the general powers of cognitive robotics and their implications in altered modalities of production?

Perhaps the most important proposition to advance is that, at least with reference to productivity implications and possibly more generally, expert systems and AI more comprehensively are likely to be tied to the interfitting of such computer-based systems with robots. That point needs to be emphasized inasmuch as a great deal of AI work to this date and almost all expert systems work has been done without reference to how it may come to be fitted into a more advanced kind of robotic system, wherein the intelligent functions implied will be taken care of by a type of cognitive robotics.

Somewhat ironic perhaps, given the general historical tendency of efforts to turn science to practical account resulting in a truncation of basic research with the resultant loss of the very levels of advantage being sought through "practicality," in the case of computer science vis-a-vis productivity we can quite clearly see that it is in no small measure a matter of the expansion of its theoretical base, which is to say automata theory, that is likely to give us the most potent forms of expanded productive capacity. Just as Zuse saw that it was advantageous (in part through the resultant conceptual/architectonic simplification) to build comprehensively binary machines, so one of the major reasons for making the theoretical component of computer science more central if we wish to achieve gains in productivity is that only through automata theory are we likely to be able to operate within one coherent symbolic system schema in understanding the computer functions, the software functions, the communication functions, and for that matter the ergonomic aspects of complex computer-based systems (W. Sedelow, 1976). Such unification and simplification of theoretical structures is a persistent theme in the history of scientific progress, and particularly where new paradigms are brought into play (Kuhn, 1970).

As indicated earlier, the development of nondeterministic, noncategorical symbolic systems for coping with knowledge under conditions of less than analytical certainty poses another major challenge to the building of expert systems which may contribute to enhanced computer effectiveness (W. Sedelow and S. Sedelow, in press). This is not the place to attempt a systematic investigation of the various symbol systems currently available for coping with informational uncertainty. But we may say here that, just as a decade or two ago it was an accomplishment to get graduate students to examine critically the repertory of possible programming languages to choose from when doing a particular piece of work so that there was not an "automatic" choosing of the language best known to the user, now we see, and even more foresee, that the underlying, critical choice of more fundamental knowledge representation/symbolism will come to be of increased urgency. Earlier on, we alluded to one example, Rough Sets, of a comparatively new development in the knowledge representation theory arena; here we simply note that such symbol systems will have to compete against ever more explicit and rigorous criteria as to whether they are to be the symbolic systems of choice in coping with any particular style of professional symbolization ("mentation"), such as diagnostician's. The dramatic gains implied by the recent efforts of Barnett and others at the Massachusetts General Hospital with DXplain are indicative of just how basic and comprehensive computer-based diagnostic systems are on their way to becoming. And although this Massachusetts General Hospital system product, supported in its development by the American Medical Association, is only in its first phases, we may well suppose that it will radically alter the work roles of the members of a medical clinic staff. More particularly, physicians may become more productive in part as a function of being able to assist nurses and other adjunctive personnel in being themselves more productive through the utilization of such expert systems as DXplain to provide preliminary screening of possible diagnoses and even patient management schemes in advance of the physician's meeting the patient. It is already possible in the area of clinical psychology and psychiatry, for example, to do much working up of information on clients through the use of computer-based systems, in advance of the clinician's (first) interview. And Weed, when on the University of Vermont Medical School faculty, sought to use computer-based information systems as a means to achieving team (e.g., nurses, pharmacist, et al., as well as physician) patient-management.

As an instance of how in the health-care domain we may see smart robotics changing procedures, it is apropos to note efforts in Japan to build systems which would fulfill some of the current functions of nursing staff, such as turning a patient in bed when desirable.

To date, without significant exception (although, especially in later version, DXplain may prove the rule), expert systems have been built to cope with only very narrow and restricted domains of knowledge. At the moment, though, we are seeing a return to more general and vastly more ambitious efforts to build systems with intelligence--which, as foreseen by Ashby (1952) in his Design for a Brain more than three decades ago, is, whatever else we may say, very much a matter of learning and hence adaptability. The emergence of a renewed interest in Rosenblatt's basic work at the Cornell Aeronautical Laboratory on The Perceptron, the growth of interest in parallel distributed processing (PDP) and in connectionist machines more generally, with their strong reminiscence of the models of Hebb and as encompassed in such recent literature as Minsky's Society of Mind, all point to the use of new types of supercomputer, post-Cray machine hardware, in conjunction with the development of intelligent systems and cognitive robotry. So, too, for our own research on the knowledge representational basis for domain-transcendent expert systems.

Knowledge representation research iteslf is taking new turns, following new paths toward these same goals of greater generality and power. By and large, it seems to use that, like efforts to define AI research, the task of knowledge representation has been taken to imply a search for useful analogues to inputs to the human central nervous system and analogues to (some of) central nervous system processing.

As an example of an analogue for processing, early on the AI field was preoccupied with the notion of a search space, as defined, for example, by the kind of means-end analysis typified by the so-called General Problem Solver developed at Carnegie-Mellon University. As the terms suggest, means-ends analysis entails re-presenting a problem (or knowledge about the problem) in terms of goals (ends) and the means to reach those goals. The approach was in a sense top-down, first specifying a general goal (e.g., travelling from Boston to California) (Winston, 1984), then specifying the means of reaching that goal (e.g., flying) which, in turn, usually entailed subgoals (e.g., getting to the airport) and the means of achieving those goals (e.g., driving to the airport). The kind of means-ends analysis used for the General Problem Solver can be characterized, or represented, as a search tree which grows in a depth-first manner.

Depth-first search trees might be thought of as a representation of a kind of impulsive, optimistic approach to problem-solving--that is, one assumes that the path taken is a good one and one keeps plunging ahead until either the goal is reached or one finds oneself in a dead end, at which point, one turns to depth-first search with backup. Very quickly these tree-like representations of search space took root and sprouted in AI texts (as well as in other computer-science literature). Now these representations are set forth, in AI texts as well as in introductory C.S. texts, as cookbook guides to program-writing rather than as representations, or outlines, of problem presentation (tree nodes) and problem solving (moving from node to node, as the nodes are generated). Here is an example of a type of narrowing of focus in science to rote solutions (reification) which in a near-term may well contribute to some types of productivity but also may rob us of the exploratory mind-set necessary for other types of problem solving (such as innovations for far more markedly enhanced productivity).

So far as the representation of inputs is concerned, visual input has received by far the most emphasis, with lesser attention to auditory input, followed by tactility. Characteristically, and inaccurately for written language, vision systems are separated in AI texts from natural language systems. As optical-character readers become ever better, the separation of vision and written natural language systems may seem less attractive. Perhaps a better division will be between (a) the visual signal, auditory signal, etc., as in some sense primary input modes which then interact with (b) other processes--such as a syntactic analyzer--to cope with verbal representations, pictorial representations, musical representations, etc. At present, AI and its restricted subcomponent, expert systems, muddle together into ad hoc structures, including robotic realizations, whatever representations of data input and problem-solving activity are needed to solve some very domain-restricted problem. There is neither in use nor in prospective use a coherent model which might, for example, make the introductory AI text a straightforward survey of visual and auditory signal processing which then interacts with other processes (e.g., the syntactic analyzer) in order to solve problems. Clearly, the attainment of such a model would suggest some sort of new plateau of scientific understanding as to intelligent functioning.

The work of Marr (1982) on vision provides an excellent example of the relationship between knowledge representation and potential productivity. Marr, an English mathematician and neuroscientist in the AI Lab at MIT, had noted that the approach of many computer scientists to the problem of visual perception implied that seeing required enormous stores of information. Early work on robotic vision emphasized matching shapes that are input to the robot (either as wave signals or in terms of position on various imagined axes) with shapes prestored in the computer's memory. As Rosenfield (1984) pointed out in an excellent review of Marr's (1982) book, using this approach computer scientists found that a

> seeing robot would need an enormous memory stuffed with photos, drawings, and three-dimensional reproductions of grandmas, teddy bears, bugs, and whatever else the robot might encounter in its preassigned tasks. They tried to simplify the problem by restricting visual scenes to minute worlds of toy blocks and office desks; and they concentrated on writing programs that could effectively and rapidly search computer memories for images that matched those in the robot's eye. Some of these programs worked very well (p. 53).

In what Rosenfield (1984) describes as a "theory of perception that integrated work in neurophysiology, psychology, and aritifical intelligence," Marr shifted away from such an approach apropos knowledge representation to an approach emphasizing stages common to all visual input before highly individualized objects must be dealt with. For example, Marr began with a retinal image consisting of various gray-levels from which, he argued, human beings compute a two-dimensional sketch, which he called the primal sketch. This sketch is based on the fact that changes in the illumination (gray-levels) of a scene occur just at the point where the edges and changes in surface contours of objects are located. Marr then went on to argue that the brain automatically transposes the contours implied by the primal sketch onto axes of symmetry which provide three-dimensional images. As Rosenfield (1984) said,

> (t)he problem of searching for catalogued information that had so preoccupied the artificial intelligence community when it first tried to build seeing machines occurs only at this final stage of visual processing. Nobody had imagined that so much information about shapes could be extracted from the retinal images before a search of catalogued information would be necessary. There is, consequently, a greater precision and simplicity to the search procedures we use in

identifying objects than has been previously assumed. What had been one of the central issues in vision research, what many thought might have "explained" vision, we now know is important only after the visual system has analyzed shaped in the physical environment (pp. 55).

Clearly, the possibility of lower-level processing basic to at least all nonverbal visual processing has enormous implications, long-term, for increasing the productivity of computer-based systems, as well as the productivity of those who create the computer-based systems.

In the verbal realm, one of the knowledge representation difficulties derives from the too-frequent assumption that the language we hear and speak and the language we see and write are, for any given specific language such as English or French, the same. Computer-based parsers of syntax—a representation that focuses on recognizable/acceptable sequences of parts of speech such as adjective-noun-verb—have shown that we rarely speak in the "correct" sequences we expect to see in written work. Although semantics, or meaning, might seem to be more consistent, whether in the spoken or written mode, in fact our experience suggests that at least there is often a greater diffuseness or vagueness in the spoken mode than in the written mode. In part that is due to the looser structure, including interjected a's, if you wills, you knows, etc. In part, it is due to the expectation of feedback from the auditor, which serves to force greater precision and, in part, it is due to the possibility of supplementing with other languages, such as gesture, pictorial representations, graphs, and so on.

Insofar as the effort to program computers to deal with natural language has sought after Marr-like low-level processes, the early focus for spoken input was upon the auditory signal and, for written input, upon syntax; as to written input, one could say that the work on optical scanners paralleled the work on the auditory signal. Optical scanners are designed to translate the visual signal into letters of the alphabet and auditory signal processors sometimes look for syllables and sometimes for individual phonemes which, when combined, make up syllables and words. Given the presumed recognition of some string of sounds or of alphabetic symbols, the next level is usually identified as the sequences in which these occur—the morphology and the syntax.

A morpheme is ordinarily defined as the smallest meaningful unit in a language. For example, in English the s at the end of desserts is a morpheme with the meaning of more than one; or the fit in fitted is a morpheme, just as is the ed, meaning past tense. Bear in mind that a morphologist generally feels free to assign meaning to such forms as s or ed but avoids trying to cope with fit, which would be regarded as within the province of semantics. Morphologists isolate affixes, including suffixes (endings such as ed) and prefixes (initial strings such as in in inconsiderable) and the stems (roots) to which those affixes can be attached.

Knowledge represented as morphemes can be used in natural language computing to convey information about the syntactic structure of, e.g., clauses; for example, suffixes such as ly generally signal the presence of an adverb, just as suffixes such as ed signal the presence of a verb. Prefixes, the other major type of affix, depart from the level of syntax; rather, as do stems and roots, prefixes tend to carry semantic information (note how the initial in changes the meaning of the considerable to which it is attached in the word inconsiderable).

Morphologists can work with both spoken and written language, as can syntacticians. But as we have already pointed out, in the large the syntax

60

of spoken language can be said either to fail to follow the syntactic rules of written language or to obey rules (possibly Rough) of its own. Current computer-based work uses the former assumption, so that now there is a good deal of research on "ill-formed input" and on so-called relaxation techniques for computer systems to use when dealing with such input. Using the other assumption—that spoken language obeys (perhaps noncategorical) rules of its own—is of course an open option that might well be pursued. Earlier we observed that spoken language often relies upon supplementation from gestures, pictures, and so on. Some computer-based tutorials, expert systems, and AI research programs use such supplementation to good effect, but always, to the best of our knowledge, in a studied, textbook way. As we gradually move toward computation with both spoken input and spoken output, we should perhaps begin to think of more "spontaneous" supplementation to cope with the problems of "ill-formedness" at whatever level they occur.

The difficulty with the processing "levels" as outlined so far is that the translation of the basic light or sound signal into an essentially arbitrary representation, such as an alphabetic character or a spoken "syllable," occurs at such an early stage in the process. Then researchers have piled on top further arbitrary representations for appropriate arrangements of morphemes and parts of speech, so that we are a long way from the primary signal at which one might hope for the kind of processing Marr hypothesized for vision. Further, as specialists in language research, with or without computers, are happy to say, correct syntax by no means guarantees meaningful sentences, as Chomsky's famous sentence "Colorless green ideas sleep furiously" was intended to demonstrate.

The (DARPA) speech understanding project of almost a decade ago concluded that, although various levels of language representation and processing might be usefully identified, the ambiguity problem made cooperation among the levels desirable at all stages of processing. Ambiguity sometimes arises from poor or loose sentence construction—or from the specific (quasi-) rules which apply to the spoken language. An example of such ambiguity-inducing construction, spotted recently on a local signboard, is: "This is a good time for cutting hair according to the stars." Is the time right because the Zodiac so indicates, or is hair to be cut in shapes based on constellations such as Ursa Major?

Or there is ambiguity of reference: for example, "Behind the table was a large table, and it needed to be moved so that we could reach it." To which table does each "it" refer?

Word sense ambiguity enriches the language but certainly complicates language understanding by computer-based systems. When a small child says to another, "We'll come in the wagon," will the child and sibling be rolling along in a wagon pulled by a parent, or bowling along in a station wagon driven by a parent and powered by metaphorical horses?

In all of these situations, as well of course as in others which could be cited, additional contextual knowledge ordinarily will resolve the ambiguity. AI researchers, as well as builders of expert systems, are using various approaches to the representation of linguistic knowledge to try to cope with the types of ambiguity illustrated through these examples. Case frames, which structure a sentence in terms of, for example, an agent doing something (the main verb) to something else (the patient) with something (the instrument), are very popular; and they can be incorporated into very domain-specific expert systems. So far, though, the elaborateness of the case frame needed for each sentence is very reminiscent of the pre-David Marr erroneous assumption that workers in vision made about the necessity of storing an extensive description of every object to be recognized—and the resultant preprocessing labor is enormous. Other models also are being used, but all entail much preprocessing. Our own approach (W. Sedelow & S. Sedelow, in press), in research now funded by NSF and based at the University of Arkansas at Little Rock and the University of Arkansas Graduate Institute of Technology, has been to try at least to avoid such additional levels or superstructures by focusing on the way words are associated with other words.

For a period extending over 20 years, but with gaps during that time, we (and many students and some faculty associates) have been working with Roget's International Thesaurus (3rd edition, 1962), with a view to finding a workable resource for the "real world knowledge" (representations) mentioned earlier when discussing information necessary for the resolution of ambiguity. In our view, the Thesaurus has an advantage in being a large culturally validated compendium of the English language. Including the index, it comprises about 210,000 entries. Further, it has the advantage over a dictionary of grouping words together on the basis of semantic association. An example entry is shown below:

    Class Six: Intellect
      I. Intellectual Faculties and Processes
        L. Conformity to Fact
          515. Truth
            Nouns
            515.3
              accuracy, correctness, rightness;

At the top level of its explicit structure, the groupings are so large and general as to be essentially useless. However at the category level (e.g., 515. Truth), the groupings are considerably more useful (e.g., we have successfully used this level to scan abstracts of SCAMC Proceedings so as to come up with a characterization of the conceptual content of the abstracts). There are 1,042 such categories in the Thesaurus. We have concentrated most attention at the lowest, semicolon group level (e.g., accuracy, correctness, rightness;) and at the entry level (correctness).

Our interest in the lower levels has been based on the assumption that the implicit, cross-hierarchical structure of the Thesaurus is at least as informative as the explicit structure. Using a mathematical model developed by a student of ours, Bryan (1973) of the San Francisco State University computer science faculty, we have been able to explore this implicit structure by using the multiple occurrences of individual words to "chain" through, in our preferred approach, semicolon groups in the Thesaurus. That is, if the word "correctness" appears in a semicolon group other than that listed above, there would be a link between the two semicolon groups. If both "accuracy" and "correctness" appeared together in the two semicolon groups, there would be a strong link between the two semicolon groups. Intuitively it is perhaps obvious that such links would begin to provide the context necessary to resolve various kinds of ambiguity. That is, using the number of links traversed as a measure of semantic distance, one can take several words from a textural context and trace their patterns of intersection so as to decide, for example, whether a de' sert was the topic under discussion or whether the concept of de sert' was the more likely.

Of course, in order to use the Thesaurus in this way, one must have a certain confidence in the way it's put together. Frankly, we were initially skeptical; but we have now tested the Thesaurus empirically in such a variety of ways and on such a variety of texts that we are persuaded of its general validity (we would not claim it is "perfect") as a representation of the real-world knowledge encoded in the English language (S. Sedelow, 1969,

1985; S. Sedelow & W. Sedelow, 1969, 1986a, 1986b). As you will infer, so far as knowledge representation of English verbalizations is concerned, we have opted for a structure which is certainly at a more basic level than the metastructures implied by case frames, schema, and other formats much in use in AI today. Since the Thesaurus is both descriptive and prescriptive as to the way words are conceptually associated in English, it provides a semantic structuring which does seem to cope with at least some ambiguities, and it also enables us to finesse some (not all) requirements for examination of syntax. Unlike a dictionary, it is simply a collection of words linked together through usage; it does not consist of words with individual definitions which, in turn must be analyzed in order to understand the word being defined. Thus, it eliminates much of the processing baggage implied by other structurings of the semantics of English and, in turn, has implications for productivity as we begin to anticipate an era in which not only data analysis but computer input and output will be heavily verbal (e.g., in expert systems)--and in human languages rather than in programming languages and with conversational computing probably the rule rather than the exception.

Little more than a century ago--in fact in the year 1884--Arnold Toynbee gave us the phrase "Industrial Revolution" in the title to a series of lectures. Toynbee thus initiated the use of a rubric which has come to provide the "great divide" in the history of productivity. But we may well suppose that well before 2084 a new rubric will be in place, and the great divide in the history of productivity will be seen to be the development of the computer, and especially its more advanced use in cognitive robotry.

To advance such a notion presupposes, and it is a dangerous assumption, that present trends continue. More especially, it assumes that the development of atomic weaponry has not led to catastrophic consequences and that the productivity history of the human species hasn't been otherwise radically changed, even by so horrendous a development as a wild growth in global population currently in process. Although as recently as 1933, in the first supplemental volume to the Oxford English Dictionary, the Industrial Revolution was defined as "the rapid development of industry owing to the employment of machinery." In retrospect it does appear to many scholars today that the utilization of machinery to substitute for muscle, through the development of water and steam technologies for the mills, and to substitute for digital skills in spinning, weaving, and the like, was less consequential than the organization of people to work in groups under the mill roof. Now for many specialists, that human factor (ergonomics) constitutes the most salient dimension of the process of modern industrialization. Interestingly enough, in the "prehistory" of modern computing, we see dispersed efforts, ranging from Henry Wallace at Ames, Iowa, to a member of the Hapsburg family in Vienna, attempting to organize people in groups to more efficiently perform computations. But in those cases, too, without the new technology (in that instance, of the computer) manipulating the human factor was grossly insufficient.

One could easily imagine that 100 years from now the provision of goods and services, including many of the services now performed by members of the professions, would be available through the use of computer-based systems. The theoretical limit on what can be done is a matter of what can be computed, a matter of what is computable; and, as we have noted, the development of new modes of knowledge representation continues to expand the scope of the computationally possible. Additionally, it should be noted that traditional as well as computer-based research has been plagued by inappropriate (and at least partially tacit) assumptions as to categoriality and lawfulness (W. Sedelow & S. Sedelow, in press) where "roughness" and/or "fuzziness" knowledge representations would obviate, or at least solve, some of the problems.

Interestingly enough, the most dramatic effects of the computer may come about through the application of cognitive robotics to the generation of knowledge itself. Were that process to emerge, as preliminary developments make it seem likely will happen, then we may suppose that, indeed, the sky is the limit. In papers published at the end of the last decade, we developed a typology for levels of scientificness, or scientificity (W. Sedelow & S. Sedelow, 1978, 1979). The highest such level goes beyond empirical description and taxonomy, beyond predictive adequacy, beyond the synthesis of the realities understood, to science itself as a subject of scientific knowledge, wherein through understanding the symbolic trajectories that constitute the public record of science, we are able to generate new science. Should that process come into use in a widespread and powerful fashion, as there is good reason to suppose will happen, then we will see one of the meanings latent in von Neumann's formulation that the most important use of the computer would be as instrumentation for understanding the human brain. Increasingly, a good route toward that goal appears to be by way of the understanding of combinatoric algebras as applied to processes of symbol string formation (W. Sedelow, 1985).

Inasmuch as for the foreseeable future, we may make the case that all major scientific developments are likely to be in some respects contingent upon the utilization of computing, and increasingly of advanced computing at that, there would seem to be the best of reasons for expecting that the productivity of science is likely to be enhanced by orders of magnitude beyond our present ability to comprehend--by means of cognitive robotics.

In summary, this chapter has focused upon:

1. the implications for productivity of rendering knowledge algorithmic;

2. the importance of AI in general, and Expert Systems in particular, for gains in productivity within a broad population, including industrial and business employees, members of the professions, and members of minority groups;

3. the threat to productivity posed by these same components of technology if careless implementation demoralizes the workforce;

4. the prospect of interfitting Expert Systems and AI with robots; although such interfitting is done on only a modest scale at present, long-term, great productivity gains are highly likely as the scale enlarges;

5. the potential of Automata Theory for unifying and simplifying conceptualizations ranging from Cognitive Robotics to limited effectors;

6. the still-underestimated importance of the choice of Knowledge Representation/Symbolism for any given task or set of tasks;

7. the specific issue of generalizable low-level representation of a great range of inputs (cf. Marr's decompositional work on vision) in contrast to highly restricted representation of (nondecomposed) individual objects or items; and

8. an extended discussion of the issue cited in 7 above, as applied to the authors' own work on English semantics and, in turn, the relevance of this work for productivity.

Significant segments of the early research on thesauri were supported by ONR Project NR348-005. Current research is supported by NSF Grant GA410.

REFERENCES

Ashby, W. R. (1952). Design for a brain. New York: Chapman & Hall.

Bryan, R. M. (1973). Abstract thesauri and graph theory applications to
    thesaurus research. In S. Y. Sedelow (Ed.), Automated language
    analysis (pp. 1972–1973). Lawrence: University of Kanses, Departments
    of Computer Science and Linguistics; also Defense Documentation Center,
    #AD 774-692.

Feigenbaum, E. A. (1983). Knowledge engineering. The applied side. In J.
    E. Hayes & D. Michie (Eds.), Intelligent systems: The unprecedented
    opportunity. New York: Halstead Press.

Holland, J. H. (1975). Adaptation in natural and artificial systems.
    Ann Arbor: University of Michigan.

Kuhn, T. S. (1970). The structure of scientific revolutions (2nd ed.,
    rev.). Chicago: University of Chicago.

Marr, D. (1982). Vision. San Francisco: W. H. Freeman.

Miller, J. G. (1977). Living systems. New York: McGraw-Hill.

Pawlak, Z. (1981a). Classification of objects by means of attributes
    (Institute of Computer Science #429). Warsaw: Polish Academy of
    Sciences.

Pawlak, Z. (1981b). Technical report #435, Institute of Computer Science
    #435. Warsaw: Polish Academy of Sciences.

Roget's International Thesaurus (3rd ed.). (1962). New York: Thomas Y.
    Crowell.

Rosenfield, I. (1984). Seeing through the brain. New York Review of Books
    (year, October 11), pp. 53–56.

Sedelow, S. Y. (1969). Prefix. In S. Y. Sedelow (Ed.), Automated language
    analysis, 1968–1969. Chapel Hill: University of North Carolina,
    Departments of English and Computer & Information Science; also DDC #AD
    691-451.

Sedelow, S. Y. (1985). Computational literary thematic analysis: The
    possibility of a general solution. In C. Parkhurst (Ed.), Proceedings
    of the 48th ASIS annual meeting 22 (pp. 359–362).

Sedelow, S. Y., & Sedelow, W. A., Jr. (1969). Categories and procedures
    for content analysis in the humanities. In G. Gerbner et al. (Eds.),
    The analysis of communication content (pp. 487–499). New York: John
    Wiley & Sons, Inc.

Sedelow, S. Y., & Sedelow, W. A., Jr. (1986a). The lexicon in the
    background. Computers and Translation, 1(2), 73–81.

Sedelow, S. Y., & Sedelow, W. A., Jr. (1986b). Thesaural knowledge
    representation. Proceedings of the Second Annual Conference of the UW
    (Canada) Centre for the New Oxford English Dictionary, Advances in
    Lexicology (pp. 29–43.

Sedelow, W. A., Jr. (1968). History as language. Computer Studies in the Humanities and Verbal Behavior, 1(4), 183-190.

Sedelow, W. A., Jr. (1976). From faceted to integrated human/computer systems theory. 8th Southeastern Symposium on System Theory Proceedings (pp. 283-288). New York: IEEE, Inc.

Sedelow, W. A., Jr. (1978). The mechanomorphic man and the anthropomorphic machine. Abstracts for 1st International Conference on Creatures of Legendry. Omaha: University of Nebraska.

Sedelow, W. A., Jr. (1980). Algorithm and empire: The new imperialism as an abstract machine theory instantiation. Omaha: University of Nebraska, European Studies Conference.

Sedelow, W. A., Jr. (1985). Semantics for humanities applications: Context and significance of semantic "Stores." In C. Parkhurst (Ed.), Proceedings of the 48th ASIS Annual Meeting (pp. 363-366), 22.

Sedelow, W. A., Jr., & Sedelow, S. Y. (1978). Formalized historiography, the structure of scientific and literary texts: Part I. Some issues posed by computational methodology. Journal of the History of the Behavioral Sciences, 14, 247-263.

Sedelow, W. A., Jr., & Sedelow, S. Y. (1979). The history of science as discourse. Journal of the History of the Behavioral Sciences, 15, 63-72.

Sedelow, W. A., Jr., & Sedelow, S. Y. (eds.). (1983). Formalization in literary and discourse analysis.... The Hague: Mouton. and (1979). Formal methods in language research. The Hague: Mouton.

Sedelow, W. A., Jr., & Sedelow, S. Y. (in press). Semantic space. Computers and Translation, 2, 235-246.

Winograd, T., & Flores, F. (1987). Understanding computers and cognition. Ablex. For extensive discussion of this book, see (1987) Artificial Intelligence, 31(2), pp. 213-262.

Winston, P. (1984). Artificial intelligence (2nd ed.). Reading, MA: Addison-Wesley.

SELECTION, TRAINING, AND PERFORMANCE

IMPACT OF SELECTION AND TRAINING RESEARCH ON

PRODUCTIVITY, QUALITY OF WORK LIFE, AND PROFITS

Wayne F. Cascio

Graduate School of Business
University of Colorado
Denver, Colorado

This chapter is not a comprehensive review of the research literature relevant to personnel selection and training research. Rather it attempts to place the subjects of selection and training in perspective--that is, in terms of their partial contribution to employee productivity, quality of work life, and profits. Then we will present examples of the contribution of four types of behavioral science interventions: an absenteeism control program, an employee assistance program, a goal setting and feedback program, and an assessment center selection program. Let us begin by defining our terms.

Productivity
_____

Productivity is generally considered to be a measure of the output of goods and services relative to the input of labor, material, and equipment. The more productive an industry, the better its competitive position because its unit costs are lower. Improving productivity simply means getting more out of what is put in. It does not mean increasing production through the addition of resources such as time, money, materials, or people. It is doing better with what you have. Improving productivity is not working harder; it is working smarter. Today's world demands that we do more with less--fewer people, less money, less time, less space, and fewer resources in general.

American workers are increasing their productivity, but not as fast as their Japanese and West German counterparts. Of 12 leading non-Communist industrial countries, West Germany has had the fastest record, with an increase in the average factory worker's production of 5.6% per hour, followed by Japan (5%), Belgium (4.6%), the United States (4.4%), Britain (3.4%), and France (3.3%). Sluggish U.S. productivity has been blamed for many of America's economic ills ("America Makes Gains," 1987).

What are some of the causes advanced by economists to explain the slow growth rate in U.S. productivity? One, the supply of labor that can be directed from inefficient productive activities, such as outdated steel mills, to more productive endeavors, such as electronics or health care, has shrunk. Lacking necessary job skills and trained only as steelworkers, these people are "structurally unemployed."

Two, complying with environmental and safety laws, among other government regulations, adds costs to production but does not increase it. Three, increasing dishonesty and crime generate costs that are reflected in increased production costs but do not increase productivity. Four, lower spending for research and development leads ultimately, and inexorably, to slower productivity growth over time.

These are not the only causes of slow U.S. growth in productivity. Indeed, economists admit that they cannot explain all of the reasons for the decline in terms of common economic measures (Dennis, 1979). Consider three other causes: (1) lazy workers and indifferent management; (2) government-induced inflation through practices such as cost-plus contracts, automatic cost-of-living increases in government spending, and big deficits to fight recessions; and (3) paper entrepreneurs, those who capitalize on legal and financial opportunities for profit rather than on improved methods of production. For example, consider that of every 10,000 citizens in the U.S. and Japan, the following ratios are found, respectively: Lawyers, 20 (US):1 (Japan); accountants, 40 (US):3 (Japan); engineers, 70 (US):400 (Japan) (Cascio, 1986). The net result of the trend toward paper entrepreneurship in the U.S. is that there is a serious "brain drain" away from genuine innovation in production, marketing, and sales.

Psychology cannot expect to have much impact on capital investment, spending for research and development, or compliance by organizations with government regulations. However, through behavioral-science-based interventions in personnel selection and training, it can have a major impact on structural unemployment, "lazy" workers, and indifferent management. In terms of the components of total productivity, psychology can reasonably expect to affect the contribution of labor, not the contributions of capital, materials, or energy resources. Improvements in the labor component therefore represent "partial measures of productivity" (Packer, 1983).

Quality of Work Life

There are two ways to look at what we mean by "quality of work life" (QWL) (Lawler, 1982). One way equates QWL with a set of objective organizational conditions and practices (e.g., job enrichment, democratic supervision, employee involvement, and safe working conditions). The other way equates QWL with employees' perceptions that they are safe, relatively well-satisfied, and are able to grow and develop as human beings. This way relates QWL to the degree to which the full range of human needs is met. Because the second view allows for differences among people--that not all people find the same set of objective conditions (e.g., democratic supervision) to be an important component of a good QWL--we will define QWL in terms of employees' perceptions of their physical and mental well-being at work.

Joint labor-management participation is the very essence of QWL; it is the common denominator that runs through almost all efforts to improve QWL in U.S. firms. Participation is used to identify problems and opportunities in the work environment, to make decisions, and to implement changes. Some of the most common forms of worker participation include the following:

1. Quality circles and other types of problem-solving groups.
2. Union-management cooperative projects.
3. Participative work design and new design plants.
4. Gain-sharing, profit-sharing, and Scanlon plans.
5. Worker ownership or employee stock ownership.

While the overall effect of worker participation depends on a number of factors (e.g., the extent to which the organization changes in a manner consistent with the democratic values and behaviors of the participation program), one of the most important of these factors is the extent of training and learning necessary to support worker involvement. Such training and learning frequently is underestimated. Workers need exposure to problem-solving, group processes, and business concepts. Managers need training in the listening and feedback skills necessary to work with groups of workers who are taking responsibility for decision making. Both workers and managers need to learn the basic interpersonal skills necessary to treat others with dignity and respect (Argyris & Schon, 1978). Psychologists have the opportunity to play major roles in this process. Current interest by managers suggests that they will have ample opportunities to do so ("Helping Workers," 1987).

Evaluation

Now that we understand what productivity and QWL are, and psychology's potential contribution to improvements in them, let us examine the impact of selection and training activities on productivity, QWL, and profits. Doing so requires that we consider the issue of evaluation--an area in which psychologists have special skills.

At the most basic level, the task of evaluation is counting--counting clients, counting interactions, counting dollars, counting hours, and so forth. The most difficult tasks of evaluation are deciding what things should be counted and developing routine methods for counting them. Managers should count the things that will provide the most useful feedback.

In the context of evaluating organizational interventions such as selection and training, there are at least four metrics that decision makers might find useful: (1) dollars; (2) the percentage improvement in job performance (output); (3) reductions in the number of workers required to produce a given amount of output, together with the linkage of this figure to human resource forecasts; and (4) reductions in payroll costs. Let us discuss each of these.

Dollars

Ever since the late 1940s, psychologists have known that the outcomes of human resource management programs could be evaluated in terms of dollars (Brogden, 1949). Indeed, Cronbach and Gleser (1965) presented a fully developed exposition of these ideas. Building on the principles of linear regression, they showed that the total dollar payoff to an organization resulting from, say, a selection program, relative to random selection of employees, is a function of the number of individuals selected, their average tenure on the job in question, the validity of the selection procedure, the standard deviation (SD_y) of job performance expressed in terms of dollars, the average predictor score of those hired, and the cost of the program. This general utility model can be expressed, in simplest terms, as:

$$\Delta U = N * T * r_{xy} * SD_y * \overline{Z}_x - N * C$$

where

ΔU = total gain in dollars over random selection; N = number of new hires selected under the new program; T = average tenure of new hires in the job in question; r_{xy} = validity of the new selection procedure; SD_y = standard deviation of job performance, expressed in dollars; $\overline{Z}_x$ = mean score on the predictor of those hired; and C = cost of the program per new hire.

Thus, if N = 10, T = 5 years, validity = .50, SD_y = \$15,000, $\bar{Z}_x$ = .33, and C = \$500,

$$\Delta U = 10 * 5 * .50 * \$15,000 * .33 - 10 * \$500$$
$$\Delta U = \$118,750$$

For illustrative purposes, we have expressed the gain resulting from the use of a selection program. A similar analysis also could be presented for a training program, or other type of organizational intervention. The only difference is that instead of the product $r_{xy} * Z_x$, we substitute d_t, the effect size. The effect size, d_t is just the difference between the means of two groups (e.g., experimental and control groups) expressed in standard score units. If the null hypothesis at the outset of a training program is that there is no post training difference between the performance of the trained and the untrained groups, d_t expresses the magnitude of that difference. When the standardized difference is corrected for unreliability in the performance measure, an estimate of the true difference in performance between the trained and untrained groups can be derived. Thus the term d_t.

Unfortunately, utility analysis was not widely used to evaluate behavioral science programs until the early 1980s, principally because of the difficulty associated with estimating SD_y. Traditionally it was thought that expensive cost accounting methods were necessary in order to estimate this parameter, but recent evidence (Greer & Cascio, 1987) has shown that such estimates are not more accurate than behavioral methods, and the behavioral methods are cheaper and quicker to accomplish.

At least six different behaviorally-based methods for estimating SD_y are available now. Each of these has been reviewed critically by Cascio (1987). Five of the six focus on direct estimation of SD_y for a **group** of employees. For example, the simplest approach is to estimate SD as 40% of the average salary paid to the employees in a job class (Schmidt & Hunter, 1983). This figure represents the lower bound of the 95% confidence interval, based on the cumulative results of studies that actually measured the dollar value of job performance of individual employees. Another method, CREPID (Cascio & Ramos, 1986), provides an estimate of the dollar value to the organization of the job performance of _individual_ employees. The advantage of both the group-based and individually-based methods for estimating SD_y is that they allow researchers to compute the mean gain in dollars per recruit per year.

Percentage Improvement in Job Performance

Instead of expressing the gain in job performance resulting from the use of a more valid selection program in terms of dollars, suppose we choose to express the gain in terms of the percentage increase in output per selectee. This can be done by changing the metric of SD_y. Instead of expressing it in terms of dollars, we need to express the standard deviation of output (SD_p) as a percentage of mean output. Given that wages and salaries average 57% of the total value of goods and services in the U.S. economy, 40% of salary corresponds to (.40) (.57) = 22.8% of mean output. In examining earlier empirical work, Schmidt and Hunter (1983) found that SD_y as a percentage of salary has ranged from 42% to 60%. As a rule of thumb they recommended that the lower-bound figure of 40% of salary be used when time or resources do not permit actual estimation of SD_y. If SD_y is expressed as a percentage of mean output, the corresponding upper and lower bound estimates are 22.8% and 34.2% (.60 * .57). Their 1983 study compared these upper and lower bound predictions to empirical figures for SD that were extracted from the cumulative research literature. The empirical data yielded value of 20%.

Thus, if we substitute 20 for SD_y in the general utility equation, utility may be expressed in terms of percentage increases in output. For example, to estimate the mean gain in output per year, let validity = .50, SD_p = 20, and $\bar{Z}$ = .75. The mean gain in output (ΔU) = 7.5. Hence output among new recruits can be expected to be about 7.5% higher as a result of using the selection procedure in question. If the average score on the predictor of new hires was a full standard deviation above the mean ($\bar{Z}$ = 1.0), then the gain in output would be 10%.

Reduced Labor Requirements and Payroll Costs

If, on average, new hires have 7.5% greater output, then the number selected can be reduced by about 7% with no decline in output (.075/(1+.075) = 0.0698). In this case, which might fit public sector employers quite nicely, managers might decide to take the productivity gains from improved selection in terms of reduced hiring--that is, in terms of a smaller labor force and reduced payroll costs. Thus if a particular organization projected 100 new hires over the next year, only 93 would be needed under the new selection system in order to provide the same level of output. If each new hire was paid $25,000 per year, the payroll savings would be expected to be $175,000 per year, excluding overhead.

In summary, we now have the ability to express the gains associated with the use of valid selection or training programs in terms of four different types of metrics: dollars, percentage increases in output, reductions in the size of the labor force needed to accomplish work, and the dollar savings in payroll costs associated with the reduced labor force. Certainly the special circumstances associated with any particular organization might render one or more of these metrics more or less useful (e.g., public sector versus private sector versus private sector firms). The important point is to communicate to decision makers the benefits of improved selection or training by choosing the metric that best "fits" the situation.

EXAMPLES OF SELECTION AND TRAINING EVALUATIONS

In the following sections we will examine four different examples of evaluations of selection and training efforts. These include an absenteeism control program, an employee assistance program, a goal setting and feedback program, and a selection program. Each illustrates the contribution of psychologically-based intervention programs to the improvement of workforce productivity.

An Absence Control Program Based on Positive Incentives

This program was evaluated over a 5-year period: 1 year before and 1 year after a 3-year incentive program (Schlotzhauer & Rosse, 1985). A 3,000-employee, non profit hospital provided the setting for the study. There were 164 employees in the experimental group and 136 in the control group.

According to the terms of the hospital's sick-leave program, employees could take up to 96 hours--12 days per year--with pay. Under the positive incentive program, employees could convert up to 24 hours of unused sick leave into additional pay or vacation. To determine the amount of the incentive, the number of hours absent was subtracted from 24. Four example, 24 minus 8 hours absent equals 16 hours of additional pay or vacation. The hospital informed eligible employees both verbally and in writing.

During the year prior to the installation of the incentive program, absence levels for the experimental and control groups did not differ significantly. During the 3 years in which the program was run, the experimental group consistently was absent less frequently, and this difference persisted during the year following the termination of the incentives.

The following variables were <u>not</u> related to absence: age, marital status, education, job grade, tenure, or number of hours absent 2 or 3 years previously. Two variables <u>were</u> related to absence, although not as strongly as the incentive program itself: gender (women were absent more than men) and number of hours absent during the previous year.

If the incentive program had been expanded to include all 3,000 hospital employees, net savings were estimated to have been $42,000 per year. However, this is an underestimate, for it does not consider such indirect costs as overtime pay, increased supervisory time for managing absenteeism problems, the costs of temporary labor, and intentional overstaffing to compensate for anticipated absences. Two other cautions are in order. One, the program may have no effect on employees who view sick leave as an earned "right" that should be used whether one is sick or not. Two, encouraging attendance when one has a legitimate reason for being absent—for example, hospital employees with contagious illnesses—may be dysfunctional.

Despite these limitations, the study warranted the following conclusions:

1. Absenteeism declined an average of 11.5 hours per employee (32 percent) during the incentive period.

2. Net dollar values to the organization (direct costs only) are based upon wage and benefit costs of $11.67 per hour.

3. Savings were $22,010 per year (11.5 hours * average hourly wage of $11.67 * 164 employees).

4. Direct costs to the hospital included 2,194 bonus hours at an average hourly wage (excluding benefits) of $8.98 per hour = $19,702.

5. Net savings were therefore $2,308 per year, for an 11.7% return on investment ($2,308/$19,702).

An Employee Assistance Program (EAP)

This study was conducted at the American Telephone & Telegraph Company by following each of 110 employees for 22 months before and 22 months after their involvement with the company's EAP program (Gaeta, Lynn, & Grey, 1982). The study yielded eight key findings:

1. The age, sex, ethnicity, and years of service of employees in the study reflected the actual characteristics of employees in the corporation. There was not a "typical" profile of an EAP client.

2. The corporation had a major investment in many of the employees who used the services of the EAP. In the group studied, 50% had over 11 years of service, and 77% were over the age of 30.

3. The location of the EAP in the medical department, combined with the supervisors' use of reduced job performance as a criterion for

referrals, was effective. Troubled employees were identified in all diagnostic categories: alcohol or drug abuse, emotional problems, family or marital problems, and work-related difficulties.

4. Alcohol and drug abuse accounted for the highest percentage (42%) of employee problems. Emotional problems were the second largest diagnostic category (39%), with family and work making up the remaining 19%. In terms of the source of referrals, 46 percent came from the medical department, 22% came from supervisors, 16% were self-referrals, and the remainder were referred by spouses or fellow employees.

5. The rate of rehabilitation or improvement for all cases was 86%. In the case of alcoholism, for example, rehabilitation was defined as 18 months of sustained sobriety. Improvement was defined as tangible efforts to overcome one's problem and participation in a rehabilitation program.

6. There was a significant decrease in accidents on and off the job, absenteeism, and visits to the medical department following EAP improvement. Among study group members, there were 26 accidents, resulting in 164 lost work days before participation in the EAP, but only 5, resulting in 19 lost days after participation in the EAP.

7. Among employees referred by their supervisors for poor performance, over 85% were no longer poor performers following EAP involvement. Prior to EAP involvement, these employees were in serious jeopardy of losing their jobs. Further, of this group, 41% were actually promoted during the post-investigation period.

8. Five variables for which objective dollar figures could be determined yielded a savings of $48,000 as a result of EAP activities. These variables were: on-the-job accidents, incidental absences, disability absences, visits to medical, and anticipated losses (that is, savings or costs not incurred as a result of the rehabilitation of employees who potentially would have been lost). However, the cost savings in these five areas are conservative since they do not include such hidden factors as the dollar value of improved productivity, employee morale, and the more effective use of supervisory time. Since the effects of this EAP program were studied over a period of $3\frac{1}{2}$ years, the results are likely to be quite reliable.

A Goal Setting and Feedback Program

Training is big business in the United States. According to a recent report (American Society for Training & Development, 1986), firms spend $30 billion on formal training activities and an additional $180 billion on informal or on-the-job training. Given expenditures of this magnitude, an obvious question from decision makers is, "What are we getting in return?" Can expenditures for training be justified economically? The answer in many cases is yes, returns in terms of improved job performance are far greater than the cost of the training itself. Unfortunately, cost is the factor that receives major attention in many instances. Yet the technology is available now to allow training results to be expressed in terms of dollars, or as we saw earlier, in terms of the percentage increase in improved job performance (output).

As an example, let us consider a goal setting and feedback program. Let us assume that benefits from the program continue to accrue over a 4-year period, and that the program is run only once, at a cost of $50,000

(50 employees trained at a cost of $1,000 each). Let us assume further that the average salary per trainee is $35,000, and therefore the standard deviation of job performance (SD_y) can be estimated conservatively at 40% of this amount, or $14,000.

In order to estimate the dollar returns from a training program or other type of organizational intervention, a measure of effect size, or the degree of departure from the null hypothesis, is required. In the evaluation of any training activity, the null hypothesis is that the job performance (or any other dependent variable considered useful and important) of trainees is no different from that of untrained individuals. To the extent that this null hypothesis is not true, there will be a difference between the scores of the trained and untrained groups. True experimental or quasi-experimental designs (cf., Cook & Campbell, 1979) can and should be used to assess the magnitude of this difference or effect. Common statistical indexes such as r, t, or F can be transformed into an index of effect size, d, which represents the difference between the means of the experimental and control groups in standard (z) score units. See Hunter, Schmidt, and Jackson (1982) for details. If the resulting effect size index, d, is corrected for unreliability in the criterion measure, then an index of the true difference in performance between the trained and untrained groups can be derived. This index of effect size, d , is substituted for the product of $r * \overline{Z}_x$ in the general utility equation, and the utility analysis proceeds as before.

Meta-analyses of the effects of behavioral science interventions on workforce productivity have been conducted by Guzzo, Jette, and Katzell (1985). According to Guzzo et al., the expected effect size from a goal setting and feedback program is 0.75, with a lower bound of the 95% confidence interval of 0.57. This represents an expected improvement in job performance of almost 20% (one SD = 34%; .34 * .57 = .194).

Substituting this value into the general utility equation, along with the values specified earlier, allows us to compute an estimated pay off from the training program:

$$\Delta U = 4 * 50 * .57 * \$14,000 - (50 * \$1,000)$$

$$\Delta U = \$1,546,000$$

This is what we may call the "unadjusted" payoff, for we haven't taken into account three important economic factors that affect payoffs. These are: discounting (to account for the fact that a dollar received 1, 2, 3, or 4 years out is not worth the same as a dollar received today); variable costs (to account for the fact that some costs to the organization, such as bonuses and commissions, will rise along with improvements in productivity as a result of the training program); and corporate taxes (assuming that a nonpublic, for-profit organization is involved). Exact procedures for taking these economic factors into account have been derived by Boudreau (1983). The modified utility formula that results is as follows:

$$\Delta U = N * \{\sum_{t=1}^{N} [1/(1+i)] * SD_y * (1+V) (1-TAX) * d_t\} - C(1-TAX)$$

where

ΔU = the total dollar payoff in terms of improved productivity for one cohort of trainees over the 4-year period; N = number trained; i = the discount rate; t = the number of time periods; SD = the dollar-valued standard deviation of job performance; V = variable costs expressed as a percentage; TAX = the corporate tax rate; d = the true difference in job performance between the trained and untrained groups, expressed in terms of standard (z) score units; C = the overall cost of the program.

In the context of our goal setting and feedback program, let us assume that the discount rate is 10% over four years, that variable costs comprise -5%, and that the corporate tax rate is 46%. Substituting these values into the adjusted utility equation, along with the values specified earlier, yields:

$$\Delta U = 50 * [3.17] * \$14,000 * (.95) (.54) * .57 - \$50,000 * (.54)$$

$$\Delta U = \$621,858$$

This value is only 40% as large as the unadjusted payoff, but arguably it is more realistic. It represents a dollar-valued gain in performance of over \$3,100 per trainee per year in improved job performance. To the extent that the program is repeated with other cohorts of trainees, the total gains will be even greater.

A Selection Program

As our final example, let us consider the payoffs associated with one selection program, the assessment center, to management productivity. Assessment centers have been widely used in the selection of managers both in the U.S. and abroad. Although they are tailored to fit the requirements of any given managerial job and job level (e.g., first-line supervisors, technical services supervisors, bank officers), they all share three common characteristics. One, they use multiple assessment procedures, such as written tests, interviews, and group- and individually-based behavioral simulations of job-relevant situations; two, they use standardized methods for interpreting the results of the assessment procedures; and three, each candidate's final rating is the result of the pooled judgment of the assessors who have evaluated him or her. For more information on the assessment center method, see Thornton and Byham (1982).

Hundreds of individual validity studies of assessment centers have been conducted, but quantitative cumulations of these results in studies by Hunter and Hunter (1984) and Schmitt, Gooding, Noe, and Kirsch (1984) reported similar results. Both meta-analyses found an average validity of about .43 for assessment centers when performance ratings or measures of productivity are used as criteria.

In computing the payoffs associated with an assessment center, the same adjusted utility equation is used as was used to compute the payoffs associated with training programs. The only difference is that instead of d_t, we substitute the product of the validity coefficient times the average score on the predictor of new hires, that is, $r * \overline{Z}_x$.

Let us assume that the assessment center in question is applied to candidates for first-level management jobs. Let us assume further that 100 persons are assessed at a cost of \$1,000 per person; their average tenure in first-level management jobs is 5 years; the validity of the assessment center is 0.43; SD_y = \$15,000; the average standardized predictor score of each person promoted is 1.4; the discount rate is 10%; variable costs comprise -5%; and the tax rate is 46%. Substituting these values into the adjusted utility equation yields:

$$\Delta U = 100 * (3.79) * \$15,000 * (.95) (.54) * (.43) (1.4) - 100 *$$

$$(\$1,000)/(.20) (.54)$$

$$\Delta U = \$1,755,676 - \$270,000 \text{ or } \$1,485,676$$

This is the total gain over random selection over 5 years. The gain per newly promoted manager over 5 years is $14,857 or about $2,970 per new hire per year. To determine the net gain over the procedure that currently is used, the dollar payoffs from that procedure must be subtracted from $1,485,676.

SUMMARY

Psychologists have made great contributions to improving workforce productivity, quality of work life, and profits. These contributions have been realized at the level of the individual firm as well as the national level (Schmidt, Hunter, Outerbridge, & Trattner, 1986). Unfortunately, psychologists have not been as adept as those in other disciplines in communicating these contributions in terms that decision makers can relate to easily. In this chapter we considered examples of four types of interventions where psychologists have developed and applied new technology and experimental methods that allow results to be expressed in the language of business--that of dollars. It's not that behavioral or statistical results are not meaningful; it's just that business decision makers relate more comfortably to financial concepts than they do to statistical ones.

The first intervention we examined was a 5-year absence control program based on positive incentives. A total of $19,702 was invested in the program, and a net savings of $2,308 resulted, for a return on investment of 11.7%.

The second program we examined was an employee assistance program at American Telephone & Telegraph Co. Each of 110 employees was followed for 22 months before and 22 months after the EAP. Five variables for which objective dollar figures could be determined yielded a savings of $448,000 as a result of the program.

The third intervention was a goal setting and feedback program. Using data from meta-analysis and utility analysis, we demonstrated how such a program could yield savings of $3,100 per trainee per year in improved job performance.

The final program we considered was a selection program--the assessment center. Using data on validity, and the standard deviation of job performance expressed in dollars, we showed the payoff from a valid selection procedure to be $14,857 per person over 5 years for first-level managers.

In short, the technology is available now for psychologists to demonstrate the dollar value of improved productivity and quality of work life interventions. Experimental design, data analysis, and evaluation traditionally have been the special strengths of psychologists. We need not trade in those tools for expertise in finance, economics, and accounting. It's just a matter of changing metrics, and it's time we got on with the job.

REFERENCES

America makes gains in productivity. (1987, January 9). Business Times, p. 5.

American Psychological Association, Society for Industrial and Organizational Psychology. (1987). Principles for the validation and use of personnel selection procedures (3rd ed.). College Park, MD: Author.

American Society for Training and Development. (1986). Serving the new corporation. Alexandria, VA: Author.

Argyris, C., & Schon, D. A. (1978). Organizational learning: A theory of action perspective. Reading, MA: Addison-Wesley.

Boudreau, J. W. (1983). Economic considerations in estimating the utility of human resource productivity improvement programs. Personnel Psychology, 36, 551-576.

Brogden, H. E. (1949). When testing pays off. Personnel Psychology, 2, 171-185.

Cascio, W. F. (1986). Managing human resources. New York: McGraw-Hill.

Cascio, W. F. (1987). Costing human resources: The financial impact of behavior in organizations (2nd ed.). Boston: Kent.

Cascio, W. F., & Ramos, R. A. (1986). Development and application of a new method for assessing job performance in behavioral/economic terms. Journal of Applied Psychology, 71, 20-28.

Cook, T. D., & Campbell, D. T. (1979). Quasi-experimentation: Design and analysis issues for field settings. Chicago: Rand-McNally.

Cronbach, L. J., & Gleser, G. C. (1965). Psychological tests and personnel decisions (2nd ed.). Urbana, IL: University of Illinois Press.

Dennis, E. F. (1979). Accounting for slower economic growth--The United States in the 1970s. Washington, D.C.: The Brookings Institution.

Eaton, N. K., Wing, H., & Mitchell, K. J. (1985). Alternate methods of estimating the dollar value of performance. Personnel Psychology, 38, 27-40.

Gaeta, E., Lynn, R., & Grey, L. (1982, May-June). AT&T looks at program evaluation. EAP Digest, pp. 22-31.

Greer, D. L., & Cascio, W. F. (1987). Is cost accounting the answer? A comparison of two behaviorally-based methods for estimating the standard deviation of job performance with a cost accounting approach. Journal of Applied Psychology, 72, 588-595.

Guzzo, R. A., Jette, R. D., & Katzell, R. A. (1985). The effects of psychologically-based intervention programs on worker productivity: A meta-analysis. Personnel Psychology, 38, 275-291.

Helping workers to work smarter. (1987, June 8). Fortune, pp. 86-88.

Hunter, J. E., & Hunter, R. F. (1984). Validity and utility of alternative predictors of job performance. Psychological Bulletin, 96, 72-98.

Hunter, J. E., Schmidt, F. L., & Jackson, G. B. (1982). Meta-analysis: Cumulating Research finding across studies. Beverly Hills, CA: Sage.

Lawler, E. E. III. (1982). Strategies for improving the quality of work
    life. American Psychologist, 37, 486–493.

Packer, M. B. (1983, February–March). Measuring the intangible in
    productivity. Technology Review, 86, 48–87.

Schlotzhauer, D. L., & Rosse, J. G. (1985). A five-year study of a positive
    incentive absence control program. Personnel Psychology, 38, 575–585.

Schmidt, F. L., & Hunter, J. E. (1983). Individual differences in
    productivity: An empirical test of estimates derived from studies of
    selection procedure utility. Journal of Applied Psychology, 68,
    407–414.

Schmidt, F. L., Hunter, J. E., McKenzie, R. C., & Muldrow, T. W. (1979).
    Impact of valid selection procedures on work force productivity.
    Journal of Applied Psychology, 64, 609–626.

Schmidt, F. L., Hunter, J. E., Outerbridge, A. N., & Trattner, M. H. (1986).
    The economic impact of job selection methods on size, productivity, and
    payroll costs of the federal work force: An empirically-based
    demonstration. Personnel Psychology, 39, 1–29.

Schmitt, N., Gooding, R. Z., Noe, R. D., & Kirsch, M. (1984). Meta-analyses
    of validity studies published between 1964 and 1982 and the
    investigation of study characteristics. Personnel Psychology, 37,
    407–422.

Thornton, G. C. III, & Byham, W. C. (1982). Assessment centers and
    managerial performance. New York: Academic Press.

FINANCIAL INCENTIVES AND THEIR

VARYING EFFECTS ON PRODUCTIVITY

Richard A. Guzzo

New York University
New York, NY

The premise for this paper is simple: The impact of financial incentives on productivity is quite variable. In some instances financial incentives are powerful stimulants to increased productivity by individuals, work groups, and entire organizations. In other instances, financial incentives have little or no impact on productivity at work. And, on occasion, the introduction of financial incentives precipitates a decline in productivity.

This chapter examines the varying effects of financial incentives on productivity. The chapter has three main goals. The first is to present evidence supporting the assertion that financial incentives do not have stable, consistent effects on productivity. The second is to probe reasons why the productivity effect of financial incentives varies. And the third goal is to present constructive propositions regarding both the future use of financial incentives and research on their effects. To accomplish these goals, the chapter first makes clear what is meant by the terms financial incentives and productivity.

FORMS OF FINANCIAL INCENTIVES

Money is used as an inducement for increased productivity in a seemingly endless variety of ways. Financial incentive plans differ greatly in the rules determining who gets a reward, the magnitude of the reward, and so on. However, it is possible to speak of three broad types, or categories, of financial incentive pay plans: individual, group, and organization-wide (Lawler, 1971).

Individual Incentive Plans

Of the three types of incentive pay plans, individual incentive plans are the most familiar. They include piece-rate pay plans, through which earnings are at least partly determined by an individual's output. Output might be assessed in terms of the number of things produced within a fixed period of time, the quality of production (e.g., as assessed by wasted materials or number of defects), or the speed with which work is done (e.g., the average time a bank teller spends per customer). Sales workers whose pay is based on commissions also work under an individual incentive plan.

Individual incentive plans are most frequently used with employees at lower levels in the organizational hierarchy, partly because these employees tend to have well circumscribed jobs with measurable outputs in defined periods of time. However, individual incentive plans also can be used with employees farther up the organizational hierarchy, whose jobs are less circumscribed, less time-bounded, and whose outputs are more difficult to measure. We call these employees managers. The individual incentive plans for managers are usually referred to as merit pay plans.

Merit pay can be based on quantifiable indicators such as profitability, cost reductions, and frequency of customer complaints. However, managerial merit is more often determined by the judgments of others, especially superiors. Annual performance appraisals are mechanisms for systematically collecting evaluations of the performance of managers during a past year. The resulting assessments are then translated into financial rewards. These rewards usually take the form of salary increments but could also come as a bonus or other tangible benefit.

Some chief executive officers (CEO) of firms also are subject to individual incentive pay plans. A CEO sits at the pinnacle of an organization's hierarchy with organization-wide responsibilities. Therefore, the indicators of CEO performance used to determine individual financial rewards are usually indicators of overall organizational performance, such as growth in market share or profitability.

Skill Based Pay. A recent variant in financial reward systems to reward individual accomplishments is skill based pay. Here, pay is linked to the number of discrete competencies mastered by individuals. Thus, the greater number of jobs a person is qualified to perform, the higher is his or her pay. Skill based pay rewards the enhanced capacity to perform work. It does not directly reward the actual productive accomplishments of an individual within a specified time frame, as individual incentive plans are meant to do. Skill based pay, then, will not be considered an individual incentive plan comparable to piece-rate, commission, and merit schemes.

Group Incentive Plans

Group incentive plans distribute financial rewards on the basis of a unit's (work group's, team's, small department's) performance, not on the basis of individual accomplishments. An example of a group incentive plan comes from a major department store chain. Rather than paying certain sales employees through individual commissions, the firm provides financial rewards on the basis of the sales performance of teams of employees in stores. Teams are defined along product lines (e.g., housewares, sporting goods), and the monthly sales volume of the team determines how much incentive money is earned. More specifically, the team qualifies for bonus pay if the dollar sales volume of the most recent month exceeds that of the same month in the prior year. The greater the gain, the larger the bonus, up to a limit. Each team member's share of the bonus is determined by the number of hours worked during the month.

Some other examples of group incentive pay plans include teams of brokers and their support staffs who are paid periodic bonuses based on team revenues. Production teams, too, gain financial rewards through group incentive plans. Production teams in the famous Hawthorne studies of the '20s and '30s were paid, in part, through a team bonus plan (Roethlisberger & Dickson, 1939).

Financial rewards paid on the basis of team performance can be allocated to team members in various ways. In the above retail store example, members' shares of the team bonus were based on time spent at work. The financial rewards earned through team accomplishments can be shared equally among team members, for example, or can be allocated on the basis of seniority. The allocation of group bonuses paid to members in the Hawthorne studies was based on seniority. Also, group financial rewards can be allocated on the basis of individual performance. That is, although a financial reward is made available to a team only if collective performance surpasses some criterion, each member's share in that reward can be determined by the magnitude of his or her contribution to the team's performance.

Organization-Wide Incentive Plans

In organization-wide incentive plans, employees earn monetary rewards based on the performance of the organization as a whole. For this type of incentive plan, "organization" can be defined as a business unit, a distinct facility (e.g., a manufacturing plant), or as the total enterprise. Rewards could be paid monthly, quarterly, annually, or on some other cycle. As with group incentive plans, the financial rewards are usually in the form of bonuses rather than increments to base pay.

One form of organization-wide incentive pay plans is the Scanlon Plan (e.g., Lawler, 1971). Scanlon plans have two essential qualities. One is the provision of monetary gains. The other is the extensive participation of employees in the design and monitoring of the plan. That is, Scanlon plans call for employees (typically through representatives) and management to decide jointly the substantive issues governing the operation of the plan. These include establishing a standard (e.g., a production goal) of organizational performance which, if exceeded, provides a basis for determining how much money gets distributed as reward. Such standards usually exist for monthly performance, though other periods may be adopted. When the standard is exceeded, the company realizes some value, and decisions must be made about how much of that value is to be retained by the company versus distributed to employees. A common split is 50-50: half for the firm, half for the employees. Decisions must also be reached concerning how much of the money allocated to workers in any period, actually gets distributed. In some plans moneys are held in reserve to be distributed during periods when no bonus is attained. In this way cycles of "feast or famine" in take-home pay are avoided. Rules of eligibility to participate in the plan must also be established. For example, employees may be required to work one year before sharing in bonuses and higher levels of management may be excluded from payouts. Rules for allocating bonus money to eligible recipients must also be established. Should everyone get an equal share? Should bonus shares reflect base wages? Agreements must also be reached regarding monitoring the plan and revising its rules. In short, numerous decisions must be made to implement a Scanlon plan. And to help ensure its acceptability and success, extensive collaboration between workers and management is suggested. Other forms of organization-wide incentive plans do not have the extensive participation in decision making characteristic of the Scanlon Plan.

Summary

The three types of financial incentive plans of interest in this chapter are individual, group, and organization-wide plans. An organization may seek to use any or all of these plans to stimulate increased productivity in a work force. The inconsistent success of these plans in raising productivity is the focus of this chapter. Before turning to evidence of the inconsistent effects of financial incentives, it is useful to clarify the meaning of the term productivity as it is presently used.

THE MEANING OF PRODUCTIVITY

Productivity is a term with many meanings (e.g., see Guzzo, in press). However, at the core of most definitions of productivity is a ratio of outputs to inputs. The more favorable the ratio of outputs to the cost of inputs, the higher the productivity. Although productivity can be measured at many levels (e.g., national, industrial, organizational), this chapter concerns the productivity of individuals, work groups, and organizational units. Aspects of productive output include the quantity of things produced, their quality, the dollar value of sales revenue, and so on. Input costs principally reflect the costs of labor (in terms of wages) but also in terms of absenteeism, turnover, accidents, and other expenditures.

It is thus easy to see that productivity gains can be realized either by getting more output for the same amount of input or by decreasing the costs of input per unit of output. To what extent do financial incentives bring about productivity gains in individuals, groups, and organizations, either by stimulating output or minimizing input costs? This chapter argues that financial incentives can indeed bring about productivity gains, but that the effects of financial incentives on productivity are neither consistent nor reliable. Evidence of the varying effects of financial incentives on productivity appears in the next section.

EVIDENCE: FINANCIAL INCENTIVES AND PRODUCTIVITY

The concern of this section is with the effects of any of the three forms of financial incentives (individual, group, organization-wide) on productivity in any of its aspects (output quantity or quality, costs of absenteeism and turnover, etc.). Most of the existing research evidence concerns the effects of individual incentive plans, and most focus on the effects on quantity of output. Nonetheless, a sufficient amount of research data exists to permit some general conclusions.

One recent report contrasted the effects of financial incentives to the effects of other types of psychologically-based productivity programs (Guzzo, Jette & Katzell, 1985; Locke, Faren, McCaleb, Shaw, & Denny, 1980). Guzzo et al. (1985) examined studies conducted in employing organizations in the United States during an 11-year span. This report provided a meta-analysis of these studies' findings. Meta-analysis is a technique useful for estimating the strength of the effect of financial incentives on productivity. As 11 different intervention programs were studied, the strength of effect of financial incentives on productivity was compared to the strength of productivity impact of 10 other interventions. Locke et al. (1980) examined the relative impact of four programs for raising productivity and estimated the strength of effect in terms of average percentage increases in productivity attributable to the programs.

Both of these reviews reported a positive average effect of financial incentives on productivity. Guzzo et al. (1985) reported a mean effect size of .57 for financial incentives. If we assume that productivity is normally distributed, an effect size of .57 indicates that the productivity of workers exposed to financial incentives is greater than about 67% of the workers not working under financial incentives. Locke et al. (1980) reported average increases of 30% when piece-rate pay replaced hourly wages and average gains up to 39% for various types of incentive plans.

These are substantial gains. However, the data indicated that the effects of financial incentives are quite variable. That is, sometimes financial incentives can work quite favorably to raise productivity but at other times they may have little or even a negative effect on productivity. In fact, the effects of financial incentives on productivity were found to be more variable than the effects of any of the 11 other types of productivity programs examined by Guzzo et al. (1985). These other programs included such things as goal-setting programs, training, job enrichment, the use of flexible working hours, and realistic job previews. Guzzo et al. also reported that the effect of financial incentives on measures of output (quality and quantity) were generally more favorable than the effects of financial incentives on aspects of employee withdrawal from the work place. Locke et al.'s (1980) review also detected sizable variation in the productivity effects of financial incentives.

Jenkins (1986) looked very closely at the difference in effects of financial incentives on quality versus quantity of output. He reviewed evidence from field studies, as did Guzzo et al. (1985) and Locke et al. (1980). He also examined controlled laboratory studies and work simulations involving financial incentives. Jenkins reports that 50% of the laboratory and simulation studies reviewed found evidence that financial incentives raise output (quality or quantity) while the remaining 50% found no ameliorative effects of financial incentives. On the other hand, 75% of the field studies of financial incentives reported gains in output while 25% did not. Looking more closely at the effects of financial incentives on quality of output, Jenkins concluded that "financial incentives do not improve performance quality" (p. 172). However, he further concluded that financial incentives do tend to improve performance quantity, though there is little unanimity among research findings concerning the amount or nature of this effect.

Thierry (1987) reviewed a very large number of financial incentive reports published between 1945-1985. Thierry's review was not bound by methodological concerns, relative to the above reviews. Thus, virtually any report on the effects of financial incentives was eligible for review. Consequently, Thierry's review has the merit of being based on a far greater number of reports than any of the reviews cited thus far. On the other hand, the review may contain findings obtained by less-than-adequate research methods. Nonetheless, Thierry's findings are instructive. Thierry found that individual piece-rate incentive systems and organization-wide incentive plans (especially the Scanlon Plan) had the most frequent positive effects on performance. Individual bonus plans, however, had far more variable effects on productivity than did piece-rate pay. Merit pay systems, interestingly, were more frequently associated with unfavorable rather than favorable productivity outcomes. Group bonus plans, were also more frequently associated with adverse rather than propitious outcomes.

These recent reviews of research, then, indicate that, while financial incentives often have positive effects on productivity, their effects are neither systematic nor stable. Further, quantity of productive output seems to be more readily raised by the use of financial incentives than quality. Additionally, it is not at all certain that financial incentives can consistently enhance productivity by decreasing the costs of employee withdrawal.

These conclusions are consistent with other recent reviews. Kopelman (1986), for example, reported that individual incentive plans bring about increases in quantity of output (when contrasted with time-based pay) but offers no conclusions about financial incentives' effects on quality. Kopelman further concludes that group and organization-wide incentive plans can raise productivity, although their effects on productivity are more variable than those of individual incentive plans. This view generally is in accord with previous reviews of research on financial incentives (e.g., Davison, Florence, Gray, & Ross, 1958; Lawler, 1971; Marriott, 1968; Viteles, 1953).

Most often, financial incentive pay plans have been used to compensate nonmanagerial employees. More recent times have seen the use of financial incentives applied to managerial employees. Data concerning the effects of financial incentives on managerial performance are nonabundant, in part because measures of personal output quality or quantity are often difficult to obtain and performance spans a long time. The data that exist, however, are consistent in their inconsistency. That is, the existing research literature shows quite mixed results (Pearce, Stevenson & Perry, 1985). In some, but not nearly all, instances managerial performance has been positively affected by financial incentives. Pearce et al.'s own study showed that financial incentives for managers had no demonstrable effect on performance.

Do financial incentives raise productivity? A qualified yes is the answer. Financial incentives appear to most consistently raise productivity in terms of quantity of output, especially with non-managerial employees. However, financial incentives appear to have no reliable, positive impact on the quality of productive output for either managerial or nonmanagerial employees. As well, some evidence exists that financial incentives can be used to decrease the costs of employee withdrawal from work (in the form of absenteeism and turnover). The evidence for this is neither exceptionally clear nor are effects on withdrawal especially strong. Financial incentives work some of the time for some of the people to stimulate increases in some--but not all--aspects of productivity. Why this should be so is addressed in the next section, which is based on work by Guzzo and Katzell (1987).

SOURCES OF VARIABILITY IN THE EFFECTS OF FINANCIAL INCENTIVES

1. <u>The Value of Pay</u>. For financial incentives to be useful in stimulating increased productivity, the employees subject to a financial incentive plan must value money as a reward for work. For most people, pay indeed is a valued reward. However, studies of the relative ranking of the importance of work rewards show that pay ranks highly, though it is not usually the highest ranked work reward (Lawler, 1971). Further, there may be strong individual differences in the extent to which pay is valued. Financial incentives may be less powerful in some professions, perhaps because of the nature of the people working in them, than in other professions. Nurses, for example, may be "in it for the money" less than are stock brokers. Additionally, the amount of money offered through a financial incentive plan must be of sufficient magnitude to induce increased effort on the part of employees. Also, some jobs may provide many more rewards than just pay. These rewards might be recognition, status, learning, travel, and so on. Manipulations of the financial gains in such jobs may have weak effects because money is but one of several valued outcomes. Thus, how pay is valued by different people, the amount of potential earnings, and the availability of non- monetary rewards from a job may account for some of the variation in the effects of financial incentives on productivity.

2. <u>Pay Satisfaction</u>. The link between satisfaction and the quantity of performance has been much discussed. The prevailing view holds that pay is at best a weak determinant of output. Literature reviews such as that of Iaffaldano and Muchinsky (1985) consistently find modest empirical relationships between satisfaction and output measures of performance.

Pay satisfaction, however, is one component of overall job satisfaction. And, overall job satisfaction has been found to relate to the tendency to remain in an organization (e.g., Mowday, Porter & Steers, 1982). Thus, pay satisfaction may play at least an indirect role in determining productivity-related costs of employee turnover. To the extent that different financial incentive plans bring about differing degrees of satisfaction with pay, the effects of these plans may vary.

3. Performance Goals. There is strong evidence that specific, challenging goals enhance performance. In the presence of such goals at work, pay can provide the incentive to pursue them and then enhance the satisfaction experienced with their attainment. When pay is clearly linked to specific, difficult levels of performance, those levels of performance become objectives that can direct effort on the job. Variations in the clarity of the link between financial rewards and levels of performance, or variations in the difficulty of the performance level required to gain a financial reward, may be a reason why some financial incentive plans succeed in stimulating productivity increases while others fail to do so.

4. Social Context. The variable effects of financial incentives on productivity can be understood with reference to the social context of work. This is true in two senses: (1) incentive pay changes the social context of work and (2) the existing social context can influence the effects of financial incentives on productivity.

Financial incentives, depending on how they are implemented and administered, can make for radical changes in the existing social relations among employees. This is well illustrated in the case of a work group in a retail store subject to a new individual sales commission incentive plan (Babchuk & Goode, 1951). When the store changed to a new pay plan that compensated employees on the basis of the dollar value of goods they sold, the work group experienced considerable disharmony and conflict. In addition, many tasks were left incomplete, such as re-stocking display shelves and taking inventory. These are tasks which can be thought of as helping not only one's own efforts to sell but also one's co-workers and failing to perform these tasks was counterproductive for all concerned. In response to the new pay plan, the group "defeated" the new pay plan by establishing a system in which all group members received credit for equal amounts of merchandise sold. Thus, each group member received equal amounts of incentive pay. The strained interpersonal relations returned to a more satisfactory state and tasks that previously had been shirked were once again completed. Interestingly, productivity was high under both management's individual incentive plan and the group's modification of it. Other examples of how pay plans affected social relations—and employee responses to the plans—are given by Horsfall and Arensberg (1949), Viteles (1953), and Whyte (1955).

While pay plans can alter existing relationships, the prevailing social context also can shape the impact of a newly implemented financial incentive. For example, if a climate of mistrust exists between management and employees subject to an incentive pay plan, the plan may be resisted and ultimately have little or no impact on productivity. Whyte's (1955) classic investigation of pay and the social environment at work is filled with examples of incentive plans gone awry or succeeding because of socially determined reactions to pay plans.

Quite simply, the effects of financial incentives on productivity often depend on social factors such as employee group norms, shared attitudes, and trust of management. Studies of the impact of financial incentives on productivity of the sort reviewed by Guzzo et al. (1985) often ignore the influence of social factors. This is unfortunate, because the influence of social factors could be great.

6. Use of Resources. In some work settings resource sharing is required. That is, employees must share space, tools, information, and

other things essential to performing the job. A top management team, for example, may need to share information obtained from subordinates, publications, outsiders, and other sources. Sales clerks in a retail store may need to share display racks, phones, staplers, accounting forms, and other items necessary to sell merchandise and serve customers. Incentive pay plans, depending on their nature, can either foster or obstruct the effective sharing of resources.

Organization-wide and group incentive plans can be expected, generally speaking, to facilitate the sharing of resources within the rewarded unit. Individual incentive plans, however, may sometimes provide disincentives for resource sharing, particularly if the plan encourages competition among individuals vying for limited financial rewards. Very little research on the effects of financial incentives has examined the extent to which resource sharing is required among the employees subject to the pay plan. However, it is plausible that variation in the effects of financial incentives relates to the amount of required resource sharing. For example, individual incentive plans may show smaller positive effects or more numerous negative side effects when used in situations demanding resource sharing than when used in other situations. Further, organization-wide and group incentive plans may be most effective when resource sharing by employees is important.

7. <u>Contingency Between Reward and Performance</u>. According to several theories of work motivation, employees must perceive a link between efforts and reward in order to respond to the promise of an incentive. Expectancy theory (Vroom, 1964), for example, asserts that the stronger the belief that one's effort will result in valued outcomes (such as pay), the greater the motivation to work. Said another way, employees must see that a nontrivial opportunity exists to earn financial gains through work.

The perception of a contingency between performance and rewards can be strengthened in many ways. Repeated communication of the contingency to employees can help. Having employees participate in the design of the pay plan and its contingencies also promotes a clearer perception of a link between performance and reward. Also, paying out incentive earnings as soon as possible after the required level of performance is achieved strengthens the perceived connection between performance and rewards.

In general, individual incentive plans appear to provide more certain perceptions that one's efforts will result in financial gains compared to group and organization-wide incentive plans. In the latter two types of financial incentive plans, one's monetary gains are determined not only by one's own efforts but also by the efforts of others. Consequently, a reduced sense of opportunity to gain additional pay under group and organization-wide incentive plans may partially explain Kopelman's (1986) finding that these forms of financial incentives have less certain effects on productive output than do individual incentive plans.

8. <u>Equity</u>. Equity concerns a judgment of sufficiency of outcomes, such as pay. The judgment is generally thought to be reached via a social comparison. That is, individuals compare the outcomes they gain through work, relative to their efforts and contributions, to the outcomes gained by others (relative to other's inputs and contributions). These comparisons are highly subjective. When they indicate that things are in balance, equity exists. When not, feelings of inequity arise. Inequity can then motivate a variety of behaviors, some of which may be counter to an employing organization's interests.

Pay is a salient outcome of work. It is likely that most people are sensitive to differences in pay and make comparative judgments concerning the fairness of their own pay relative to what others earn. One of the real dangers of incentive pay plans is that they might set off perceptions of inequity. Any of the three major types of incentive pay plans--organization-wide, group, and individual--may initiate perceptions of inequity. Consider, for example, an organization-wide incentive plan in which each employee receives an equal financial reward because overall organizational performance was excellent. Employees who feel they contributed more to overall performance than did a co-worker may feel it unfair to receive the same amount of bonus money as that co-worker. One possible consequence is that employees experiencing this inequity may reduce their effort in the future as a way of psychologically redressing the perceived injustice. The same scenario could hold for group incentive plans. Individual incentive plans, too, can be a cause of perceived inequity because individuals may feel their performance was under-rewarded relative to others. Incentive pay plans also can be seen as equitable. One that replaces an existing, (perceived) inequitable pay plan could be a godsend for improving productivity.

Much of the apparent inconsistency in the effects of financial incentives on productivity may be due to differences in the extent to which incentive plans bring about feelings of inequity or equity.

9. _Adequate Criterion_. Perhaps more than anything else, a good financial incentive pay plan requires a good criterion for assessing performance. A good criterion or yardstick for distinguishing between high and low productivity goes a long way toward preventing perceptions of inequity and promoting clear perceptions of the link between performance and pay. A good criterion often is not easy to come by. Individual incentive plans for sales workers, for example, often are based on the dollar amount of sales made in a certain period of time. As a criterion on which to base distributions of incentive pay, sales is excellent if the observed differences in sales truly reflect differences in the effort or skill of the employee. However, if the observed differences are due to differences in advertising, or merely location of the sales agent, or seasonal variation in product demand, or a host or other confounding factors, the criterion loses its meaningfulness as a basis for differentially rewarding employees.

Perhaps it is most difficult to establish criteria of productivity for managerial rather than for nonmanagerial jobs. As pointed out earlier, the literature shows that the effects of financial incentives on managerial productivity are considerably less positive than their effects in nonmanagerial jobs, and the criterion problem may be one reason for this. Differences in the adequacy of criteria could account for other inconsistencies in findings concerning the effects of financial incentives on productivity.

CONCLUSION

Research evidence shows that the effects of financial incentives on productivity are neither consistent nor stable. Financial incentives often have a positive impact on productivity. But, quite often, no effect or a negative effect occurs. There are many possible reasons why the effects of financial incentives are variable. These include the nine factors just reviewed as well as other potential sources of variance in the effects of financial incentives. Clearly, financial incentives can be used to improve productivity. The success of their use, however, appears to depend on many factors related to the employees subject to an incentive pay plan, the nature of the plan, and features of the situation. In light of this state of affairs, the next section offers some considerations about what we should do in the future regarding research on the effects of financial incentives and the practice of using them to improve productivity.

Future Research

I have but two modest proposals for future research on the use of financial incentives to improve productivity. The first is that we need shotgun, not pinpoint, marksman-like research on the productivity effects of financial incentives.

By shotgun-style research I mean that we need to ask many questions in each research study and thus measure many variables. For example, we ought to look closely at the various aspects of productivity when examining the effects of financial incentives. These aspects refer not only to different attributes of output at work (quality, quantity, rate) but also of input costs (absenteeism, turnover, disruptions, accidents). Financial incentives appear to differentially affect the various aspects of productivity, and future research should investigate this more closely.

Shotgun-style research also means we ought to be measuring features of the situations in which incentive pay plans are implemented, both in terms of how the effects of such pay plans are shaped by situational forces as well as how financial incentives change the existing work situation. Many of the situational factors of interest are social in nature (e.g., relations among employees, employees and management, and so on). Other situational factors to be investigated could concern properties of the technical system or amount of resource sharing required in a work setting.

Additionally, when implementing financial incentive pay plans we ought to change more than just the way in which people are paid. That is, change in situational factors (goals, interpersonal relationships, work procedures, resources) in conjunction with the adoption of an incentive pay plan could help illuminate the conditions under which financial incentives are most powerful for improving productivity. From a scientific, cause-and-effect standpoint, changing several things at once and then observing the consequences complicates the chore of disentangling the findings to determine exactly which factor caused what consequence in any one study. However, such causal connections become more evident as many such studies are conducted and their results cumulate. In complex situations like work settings, complicated changes might be surprisingly informative.

In short, research on the effects of financial incentives must become more multivariate for us to advance our knowledge of why financial incentives sometimes work well but sometimes fail. Existing research reports are too often focused on single issues or single variables, typically missing contextual variables while closely examining attributes (e.g., timing of distribution of rewards) of a specific incentive pay plan. More needs to be attended to in future research on financial incentives than has been the case in past studies.

The second proposal is to forego research in simple settings. That is, future research on the effects of financial incentives ought either to be conducted in existing employment settings or in complex simulations of those settings. Simple settings of the sort to avoid are mainly laboratory experiments which are characterized by a highly controlled environment, primitive tasks, short time durations, undeveloped social relations among participants, and a negligible monetary import to participants.

The suggestion to avoid simple research settings is not predicated on the assumption that the results of laboratory studies often do not generalize to the field. Rather, the suggestion is consistent with the proposal that research on the effects of financial incentives explicitly be multivariate, especially concerning situational factors that shape the impact of financial incentives. The settings in which we do research must

allow for the interplay of multiple factors for
advance our understanding of financial incentives
way.

Future Practice

Four suggestions appear below regarding the us
at work. Some of the suggestions follow closely
analysis. Others are generally good ideas to kee¡
significant changes in managerial practices, such
financial incentive pay plan.

First, diagnose the situation before implemen   ─ınancial
incentive pay plan. That is, make a careful assessment of factors that can
influence the success of the plan. These factors include existing social
relationships (and how the incentive plan might change them), the need for
resource sharing, the availability of good criteria of performance that will
serve as the basis for distributing incentives, and so on. In short, it is
desirable to assess the likelihood with which any of the several sources of
variance in the effects of financial incentives will help or hinder the
particular incentive plan put into place in an organization.

Second, it will often be useful to try a financial incentive plan at
first in one part of an organization, with the idea of spreading it to other
parts of the organization if it succeeds. Giving an incentive plan a trial
run can help identify unanticipated problems and help fine-tune the plan.
However, a trial run also means that the effects of the plan must be
monitored. Not only must aspects of productivity be measured for changes in
response to the incentive plan; but also, changes in the context as a result
of the plan should be examined.

The third point is an extension of the second: Always monitor the
effects of the incentive plan when implemented, whether implemented for a
few or many employees. Further, it may be useful to keep a long time frame
in mind when studying the effects of financial incentives. Their effects
may not be immediate, for example, or may appear quickly but dwindle over
time. Conditions change, too, and an incentive plan that once worked well
may no longer be effective, as changes occur in the work force, technology,
and other factors.

The fourth point I wish to suggest is that organizations communicate
what they learn about the productivity effects of financial incentives. The
actual use of financial incentives far exceeds the number of good research
reports available on the effects of incentives on productivity.
Consequently, we have a rather imperfect understanding of financial
incentive plans. Seemingly, one of the best ways of forging a better
understanding of variability in the effects of financial incentives is to
compile a large number of single-organization, multivariate studies of
incentive plans. These findings can then be examined comparatively and
integrated into better theoretical and practical statements of the effects
of financial incentives on productivity.

REFERENCES

Babchuck, N., & Goode, W. J. (1951). Work incentives in a self-determined
    group. American Sociological Review, 16, 679-687.

Davison, J. P., Florence, P. S., Gray, B., & Ross, N. S. (1958).
    Productivity and economic incentives. London: George Allen & Unwin.

n press). Productivity research in review. In J. P.
& R. J. Campbell (Eds.), <u>Individual and Group Productivity in</u>
zations. San Francisco: Jossey-Bass.

R. A., Jette, R. D., & Katzell, R. A. (1985). The effects of psychologically based intervention programs on worker productivity: A
meta-analysis. <u>Personnel Psychology</u>, <u>38</u>, 275-291.

Guzzo, R. A., & Katzell, R. A. (1987). Effects of economic incentives on
productivity: A psychological view. In H. R. Nalbantian (Ed.),
<u>Incentives, cooperation, and risk-sharing</u>. Totowa, NJ: Rowman &
Littlefield.

Horsfall, A. B., & Arensberg, C. M. (1949). Teamwork and productivity in a
shoe factory. <u>Human Organization</u>, <u>8</u>, 13-25.

Iaffaldano, M. Y., & Muchinsky, P. M. (1985). Job satisfaction and job
performance: A meta-analysis. <u>Psychological Bulletin</u>, <u>97</u>, 251-273.

Jenkins, G. D. (1986). Financial incentives. In E. A. Locke (Ed.),
<u>Generalizing from laboratory to field settings</u>. Lexington, MA: D. C.
Heath.

Kopelman, R. E. (1986). <u>Managing productivity in organizations</u>. New York:
McGraw-Hill.

Lawler, E. E. (1971). <u>Pay and organizational effectiveness</u>. New York:
McGraw-Hill.

Locke, E. A., Faren, D. B., McCaleb, V. M., Shaw, K. N., & Denny, A. T.
(1980). The relative effectiveness of four methods of motivating
employee performance. In K. A. Duncan, M. M. Gruneberg, & D. Wallis
(Eds.), <u>Changes in working life</u> (pp. 363-388). New York: Wiley.

Marriott, R. (1968). <u>Incentive pay systems: A review of research and
opinion</u> (3rd ed.). London: Staples.

Mowday, R. T., Porter, L. W., & Steers, R. M. (1982). <u>Employee-
organization linkages</u>. New York: Academic Press.

Pearce, J. L., Stevenson, W. B., & Perry, J. L. (1985). Managerial
compensation based on organizational performance: A time series
analysis of the effects of pay. <u>Academy of Management Journal</u>, <u>28</u>,
261-278.

Roethlisberger, F. J., & Dickson, W. J. (1939). <u>Management and the worker</u>.
Cambridge, MA: Harvard University Press.

Thierry, H. (1987). Payment by results systems: A review of research
1945-1985. <u>Applied Psychology: An International Review</u>, <u>36</u>, 91-108.

Viteles, M. S. (1953). <u>Motivation and morale in industry</u>. New York: W. W.
Norton.

Vroom, V. H. (1964). <u>Work and motivation</u>. New York: Wiley.

Whyte, W. F. (1955). <u>Money and motivation</u>. New York: Harper & Brothers.

PERSONALITY, TEAM PERFORMANCE, AND ORGANIZATIONAL CONTEXT

Robert Hogan and Susan Raza

The University of Tulsa
Tulsa, Oklahoma

James E. Driskell

Eagle Technology

Most great human achievements are the products of coordinated group efforts: the moon shot, the exploration of the sunken Titanic, the original Mount Everest expedition, the Allied invasion of Europe in WWII. These undertakings all required the mobilization and orchestration of a group effort. Obviously some group efforts are more successful than others--there are victorious armies and failed Antarctic expeditions. As is the case with every human effort, some groups are more successful than others in achieving their goals.

Presently there is a good deal of discussion about such topics as the competitiveness of American industry and the combat readiness of the American military. At stake, many people believe, is little less than national survival. At some level and on some occasions, the concept of team effectiveness will come up in these discussions because, despite our faith in the myth of the technological fix, our technology must be operated, maintained, and repaired by teams. What does modern psychology have to say about team effectiveness? We are tempted to say that "It all depends on the situation and circumstances." A more serious answer is that the profession seemed to lose interest in this question in the early 1960s.

Team effectiveness has not been seriously studied since the 1960s. Why might this be? There are both philosophical and professional reasons. On the philosophical side, we Americans are largely committed to an indivi-dualistic perspective on human affairs, a perspective that derives from our capitalistic economic system and our puritan ancestry (Hogan, 1976). Our economy is based on individual entrepreneurship, our legal system is designed to protect individual rights, and we must seek religious salvation alone. Even our models of achievement in the popular culture honor the lonely author, scientist, or musician, working alone, late at night, seeking to prevail by determination and force of will. Our heroes are not coalition builders, movement organizers, or loyal upholders of tradition; they are brave, stubborn, singleminded people, fighting against the odds, ignored or misunderstood by others--Jesus alone in the desert, Freud alone with his neurosis, Lincoln alone with his conscience.

Some writers even doubt the meaningfulness of the concept of a group. It is interesting to note that it is usually the solitary researcher who questions the existence of groups. Those who work with groups in applied settings, however, usually understand the concept of team performance. In a recent preseason interview, a well known college football coach was asked about his team's prospects for the upcoming season. Was this going to be a great team? "Is this a great team--I don't know," he responded. "This is the best material we have ever had. But a great team? I just don't know." This response tells us two things. First, the coach almost surely had a good team. Football coaches normally play down their prospects in the preseason. This, of course, serves to lower the fans' and alumni's expectations and makes the coach a hero if he has a decent season. Second, this quotation tells us that real-world group managers--coaches, administrators, military leaders--often intuitively understand what makes a good team. They know that individual skill is only one determinant. Non-technical factors such as trainability, conscientiousness, and leadership determine whether a group will become a good team. In sum, those who work with groups on a day-to-day basis often appreciate effective team performance. They also understand that technical competency alone does not determine team effectiveness. However, we psychologists have not been able to provide real-world managers with an explanation of team effectiveness.

The professional reason for ignoring the problem of team effectiveness has to do with the fact that research on the topic failed to cumulate or replicate. In particular, earlier research on the relationship between personality and team performance produced varying results. There are two explanations for this lack of convergence. First, the research on personality and team performance lacked a common or agreed-upon definition of personality; each investigator defined it differently, and usually in terms of a "personality" measure of convenience (e.g. self-esteem, anxiety, locus of control, dogmatism). Because personality was defined differently across studies, convergence was hard to find. Second, Morris (1967) showed that the strongest single influence on the behavior of a team is the team's task. Earlier research did not adequately control for differences in team tasks, thereby further insuring a lack of convergence in research results.

Moreover, in this earlier work, researchers often confounded process with performance in that they used different "bottom line" measures of outcome. Consequently, the earlier body of research on personality and team performance failed to cohere, but the reasons for this incoherence are interpretable in retrospect.

An additional reason why people lost interest in the topic of team effectiveness has to do with the social climate of America in the 1960s. During that time many intellectuals seriously challenged the traditional values of American culture. Although these values may have been associated with the achievement of a reasonable national standard of living, they also supported institutionalized racism at home and right wing dictatorships abroad. Consequently, social scientists stopped inquiring about the determinants of team effectiveness and began studying team process and whether members found group membership growth enhancing and personally satisfying.

In the absence of systematic research guidelines, managers in the real world normally compose work teams on the basis of technical competency. In the case of a professional basketball team for example, the players generally have played organized sports for perhaps ten years and a good deal of self-selection has taken place. Consequently, players with the talent to perform at the professional level have also been prescreened for the appropriate personality style--aggressive, industrious, coachable, team players. But what about a group of astronauts? In this case combat fighter pilots are suddenly required to work as a team. What about the crew of a nuclear submarine? Other than some psychiatric screening, crews are chosen on the basis of service records and technical talents.

If an organization considers psychological variables in team composition, it usually adopts a defensive posture and asks "what are the characteristics we want to avoid?" NASA, for example, selects astronaut crew candidates by screening out undesirable characteristics. Although this screening eliminates the unqualified candidates, it tells little about the characteristics that typify effective or exceptional team performers. The most we can say about this is that it doesn't seem to be the best possible way to assemble a team.

This paper presents a perspective on the relationship between personality, team effectiveness, and organizational context. It is a reductionist perspective; we believe that effective teams are built one member at a time and that some teams are more effective than others. At the same time, we realize that contextual considerations can override the performance of the best teams.

Before we begin the main point of our analysis, we need to define our terms. The word "personality" has two very different meanings and serious confusion results when these meanings are not kept distinct. In its first sense, personality refers to a person's public reputation, to the manner in which he or she is described and evaluated by his or her friends, family, co-workers, and other associates. Personality in this sense is reflected in and captured by trait words (pleasant, honest, hardworking, etc.), and it is closely linked to a person's interpersonal style. Personality in the second sense refers to the processes inside people that cause them to behave the way they do. Personality in this second sense is described differently by the various theories of personality that we have inherited over the years. We tend to focus on the first meaning of personality because it can be studied relatively easily--people can quickly appraise any personality in this first sense by conferring among themselves and coming to a consensus about that person.

If you look at personality in this manner often enough, you will discover three interesting properties of personality as defined in this way. First, everyone can be described using the same relatively small number of trait words. For example, we may refer to others as smart, outgoing, or friendly. This fact has given rise to what some people call the "Big Five Theory." This refers to the fact that five broad trait categories seem to underlie personality descriptions. These trait categories can be labelled as follows:

1. Intelligence
2. Adjustment
3. Prudence
4. Sociability/ambition
5. Likeability

Second, people can be described with these categories in quantitative terms: e.g., "Jones ranks at the 90th percentile for Adjustment but at the 20th percentile for Prudence." More importantly, it is possible to estimate the reliability of these descriptions. And finally, individual differences in placement along these dimensions have demonstrable implications for a person's occupational or job performance. That is, people's reputations reflect their past performance; and, as we know, that is the best predictor of future performance. The most important point here is that we now have a generally agreed upon methodology or system for classifying personality in terms of individual social reputation. Moreover, this will prove helpful when we study the influence of personality on team performance.

As noted earlier, a second problem that plagued earlier research on team performance was how to classify team tasks. Our assumption is that different types of tasks require different behaviors. To specify the relationship between personality and team effectiveness requires that we specify task environments. In a recent review of this problem, Driskell, Hogan and Salas (1987) found some convergences of opinion regarding task classification. Driskell et al. examined the task classification systems of Hackman (1968), McGrath (1984), Holland (1966), Guilford, Christensen, Bond, and Sutton (1954), and others, and developed a six factor task taxonomy. These six task categories, which are most closely represented by the Holland (1966) and Guilford et al. (1954) models, are:

1. Mechanical/Technical
2. Intellectual/Analytic
3. Imaginative/Aesthetic
4. Social
5. Manipulative/Persuasive
6. Logical/Precision

Evidence suggests that tasks can be quickly and reliably classified within this taxonomy (Gottfredson, Holland, & Owaga, 1982). We crossed this taxonomy with Herold's (1978) simple/complex task schema. This complexity dimension is not an explicit part of the other task taxonomies.

We generated a list of about 150 team tasks. Then, we asked teams of raters to classify these tasks by distributing ten points across the task categories and rating the task for complexity. We found that raters can do this with good reliability, that some tasks are easier to classify than others, that adults can do it more reliably than college students, and that persons familiar with this model can use it to classify team tasks more reliably than persons who are unfamiliar with it.

At this point we felt we had the conceptual tools necessary to begin a systematic study of the effects of personality on team performance. If we developed a set of team tasks that are prototypical examples of each task category (controlling for complexity), then we could do a series of composed group experiments and determine empirically the optimum composition of a team for a particular task.

We defined a group task as one that an individual cannot do alone and in which the product is the result of the efforts of the members working together rather than merely the sum of the efforts of members working as individuals. This definition excludes serial tasks in which the performance is limited by the group's weakest member. This definition also considers the team as a group, rather than as a collection of separate individuals.

We developed two Mechanical/Technical team tasks designed to simulate shipboard work--the Navy sponsored the research. One was a "replenishment at sea" problem that involved coordination of efforts to move freight from one ship to another, using a crane and simulated highline transport system.

We also developed two Social team tasks dealing with informing and helping others. For one task, teams prepare a video explaining the techniques of persuasion to navy recruiters in training. The other task asks teams to provide image consultation to a video-taped individual sadly in need of such help.

We then encountered the performance measurement problem. A thorough review of the literature initially created more confusion than solution but did suggest that there may be a useful distinction between group processes and performance. Cohesion (personal liking) and types of communications (Bales' Interaction Process Analysis categories) are measures of group process, whereas number of pieces of freight moved, errors made, and adaptation of presentation content to the needs of the audience are measures of group performance. Borrowing heavily from earlier studies, we were able to put together a series of measures of group process that can be used for all types of group tasks. We found this impossible to do for performance measures. Therefore, our performance measures systematically vary as a function of the type of team task.

We then began testing male undergraduates with the Hogan Personality Inventory (HPI) in order to identify people who should do well or poorly on a mechanical/technical team task, as predicted by our theoretical perspective. At this point we encountered two serious practical problems. The first was that there is not a great deal of variety among the men who comprised our initial subject pool; those who (a) join fraternities or (b) play football. The second problem, as other experimental researchers are aware, was that it is very difficult to get three male undergraduates to show up simultaneously and participate in an experiment. Thus, our research was hampered by the lack of variety and dependability in the potential subject pool at a small, private university.

We videotaped each experimental session, coded team performance, and assigned scores based on performance. There are four conclusions from this initial work that we would like to pass on. The first two are "clinical" insights based on studying the video tapes; the third and fourth come from the data analysis. The videotapes are a marvelously rich data source, almost overwhelming in their complexity. Nonetheless, two fairly consistent phenomena can be discerned. On the one hand, structures of control or heirarchy emerge very quickly. The participants rapidly settle on a pattern of communication, with certain people initiating directions and certain people following them. One also senses that if the interaction were repeated over a longer period of time, this could become a problem--some participants seem to say, "I don't like this, but I will put up with it for 30 minutes and not cause a scene." In a nutshell, tension over status issues could easily disrupt task performance in a team composed of strangers--and this says something about the importance of status issues in social interaction.

On the other hand, there is a complex but distinctive interaction between personality and role in these very simple groups. For example, in the replenishment at sea task, there is a mismatch between the anticipated power associated with one of the three roles and its actual power. Thus, dominant people tend to avoid the role of supplier and take that of crane operator or unloader. Once they see that the supplier really controls the actions of the entire team, they attempt to take control by issuing orders. Depending upon the nature of the supplier, problems may develop very quickly. We were unable to control this complex personality by role interaction, and it undoubtedly makes our research less interpretable. It may, however, be ultimately simple and related to the first problem--status issues need to be resolved early; and one key to this is to pay close attention to role assignment, even in presumably leadership groups.

The third and fourth conclusions are that personality patterns are significantly associated with team performance and that these patterns differ as a function of the type of team task. Table 1 presents the quantitative results regarding personality and team performance on a

Mechanical/Technical task. What those results indicate is that teams with high average scores for Prudence, Ambition, and Likeability perform better than teams with low average scores for these personality variables. The size of this group is 36 people on 12 teams. We believe that Likeability is important because it contributes to cohension. People with high scores on Likeability are even tempered, tolerant, and congenial. Driskell (1987) argues that cohension is generally associated with team performance--provided that the team is committed to performance norms in the first place.

Table 1. Selected Correlations: Team Performance and Personality-Mechanical/Technical Tasks

| | | Team Performance | |
Primary Trait Homogenous Item Composite	Total Score	Positive Points	Negative Points
Prudence	.38	.22	−.59**
Good Attachment	.51*	.40	−.55*
Appearance	.61**	.50	−.61**
Mastery	.48	.35	−.57*
Impulse Control	.29	.11	−.59**
Not Thrill-Seeking	.25	.05	−.61**
Ambition			
Competitive	.46	.28	−.68**
Likeability			
Even-Tempered	.45	.31	−.57*
Trusting	.44	.29	−.62**

$\underline{N}$ = 12 teams, * $\underline{p}$ <.10, ** $\underline{p}$ <.05

Table 2 presents a schematic interpretation of the influence of Ambition and Prudence on Mechanical/Technical team performance. Ambition is associated with competitiveness and hard work at the high end, apathy and indolence at the low end. Prudence is associated with caution and role compliance at the high end, risk taking and nonconformity at the low end. Tables 1 and 2 suggest that the optimal mechanical/technical team will be cohesive, hardworking, and careful to maintain proper procedures. Other combinations are suboptimal. Earlier research concerning the characteristics of effective bomb disposal technicians corroborate and support these findings and speculations.

Table 3 presents the quantative results for our Social tasks. We defined Social task performance in terms of the quality of oral communication, the degree of adapting the presentation content to the needs of the audience, and informing and advising the audience rather than persuading. The results indicate that teams with high average scores for Prudence and low average scores for Intelligence, Ambition, Sociability, and Likeability perform better than teams with the opposite scores on these personality variables. Among the most interesting things about these results is the indication that groups who performed poorly on the Social tasks did so for

Table 2. Prudence, Ambition, and Team Performance

	PRUDENCE	
	Low	High
High	High output High errors	High output Low errors
Ambition		
Low	Low output High errors	Low output Low errors

Table 3. Selected Correlations: Team Performance and Personality-Social Tasks

Primary Trait Homogenus Item Composite	Team Performance		
	Oral Communication	Audience Adaptation	Informing Advising
Intelligence	.04	-.51*	-.23
Mathematics	.42	-.02	-.50*
Science	-.09	-.52*	.15
Curiosity	-.34	-.55*	.08
Prudence			
Good Attachment	.24	.52*	-.50*
Not Experience Seeking	.33	.60**	.16
Not Thrill Seeking	.60**	.36	-.18
Ambition			
Status	-.25	-.39	-.49*
Competitive	-.18	-.12	-.51*
Sociability			
Exhibitionistic	-.45	-.53*	-.31
Likes Parties	-.36	-.32	-.51*
Likeability	.09	-.36	-.52*
Even-tempered	.15	-.25	-.54*
Trusting	.31	-.26	-.62**
Not Autonomy	.40	-.21	-.59**

$\underline{N}$ = 13 Teams, * $\underline{p}$ <.10, ** $\underline{p}$ <.05

different reasons. Groups with high average scores for Intelligence performed poorly because they seemed to make presentations to satisfy their own curiosity and intellectual interests rather than to meet the needs of their audience. In contrast, teams with high average scores for Ambition, Sociability, and Likeability performed poorly primarily because they attempted to persuade or, occasionally, forcefully convince the audience to accept their point of view.

Organizational Context

We can now specify with modest confidence the relationship between personality and team performance on Mechanical/Technical tasks. Effective teams are cohesive, prudential, and ambitious. This is not a trivial finding. Most of the work teams in the military and in industry are concerned with Mechanical/Technical tasks—building, repairing, and maintaining the technology that is supposed to save us. Our findings for Social tasks are somewhat more tentative. However, it appears that effective Social teams are dependable, concrete-minded, conforming, unassuming, and reserved. This is an important point because such groups will tend to be the teams who train others to perform the Realistic tasks.

However, work teams don't exist in a vacuum; they exist in the context of larger organizations. And the effectiveness of a team is only partly a function of the team itself. The larger organization moderates and modifies the performance of its work teams in very powerful ways.

First, organizations are responsible for composing almost all non-voluntary work teams. The organization must ensure that adequate technical skills are available within the group for it to accomplish its tasks. Beyond this, however, nontechnical factors determine team effectiveness. Consequently, an organization should also try to ensure an optimal match between personality and task demands. For example, assigning four supersalespersons (who invariably are sociable and ambitious) to an Intellectual/Analytic task (which requires reasoning and pure intellectual effort) is not the most effective use of personnel.

Organizations should also attempt to match the role structure within work groups to the personality strengths of the members. We assume that certain types of individuals will excel on certain types of tasks, and have prescribed what seems to be the optimal traits for Mechanical/Technical team tasks. But the analysis is formal; consequently, there should be different optimal teams for different tasks. However, for any particular task, there are also positions within the group that must be filled, and that process also requires taking personality into account. Work teams often include the role of leader or task coordinator who is responsible for task completion, social coordinator who ensures smooth interpersonal relations, and salesman who presents the group product to the public. Teams will perform best by matching individuals to appropriate task roles. A good recipe for failure is to assign a high achiever to a peripheral or support role in a team, and assign a socially orientated interpersonal specialist as the technical leader. Good managers and team leaders intuitively match the person to the job. The problem for research is to make this intuitive process explicit so that poor managers can do the same thing.

A second way that organizations mediate the effectiveness of groups is through their choice of goals and strategies. Organizations can defeat the efforts of well-composed and well-trained work teams by adopting ill-advised goals and strategies and then sending the teams on fools' errands. Military history provides many, many examples of this—Custer's Corporations are understandably eager to avoid discussing blunders in managerial strategy. Suffice it to say, no matter how competent the work teams might have been, nothing could have saved the Edsel.

In other instances, goals may be well-advised but poorly communicated. A well performing team will get somewhere; but without a clear prior statement of purposes or goals, that "somewhere" may not be where the organization wants to go. In other cases, goals may be ambiguous or mixed, providing incongruent or inconsistent task information. We have all spent time in pointless meetings with murky agendas, wherein the group accomplished little more than frustrating itself. A work team that understands what it has to accomplish and how that relates to organizational goals has clear task direction and less potential for interpersonal tension. Latham and Baldes (1975) provide an example of the effect of clear goals on performance. When truck drivers transporting logs were given broad goals, to "do their best," they carried about 60% of the legal load limit. When they were given clear goals, to transport 95% of the limit, they even made minor modifications to their trucks to meet this goal. Clear goals give direction and provide a standard of performance.

In most cases, providing a sense of direction is the responsibility of the organization. Moreover, achievement-oriented people are not only oriented toward individual achievement but will also achieve for their organization if their energy can be harnessed. The organization can do this by ensuring that individuals are aware of organizational goals, can relate those goals to the work group's task, and perceive the organizational goals as their own.

Third, organizations must reward group performance. They must provide incentive that foster group cooperation and accomplishment. Most formal reward structure in organizations (e.g., pay) promote individual achievement and are implicitly based on competition. Consequently, it is critical for organizations also to provide rewards (recognition, etc.) that promote group cooperation. Blau (1954) provides an example of the effect of reward structure on group performance in an examination of an employment agency. Interviewers in an employment agency must share information on applicants and openings in order to achieve efficiently the organizational goal of high placements. They must work as a team. When this organization emphasized cooperation, interviewers worked together and productivity was high. When, in another group, the organization stressed competition, interviewers hoarded information and everyone's placement rate declined. Organizations that reward group performance will foster group productivity.

There is an exemption to this rule and that is when the group task is a coactive or additive rather than an interactive. Interactive tasks require that team members share resources and coordinate efforts to solve the task. Most of what we would term true team tasks are interactive. Coactive tasks simply require that someone sum the individual contributions of all team members. In this case, group members can simply work individually to accomplish the task. The singles competition of a U.S. Davis Cup team tennis match is a good example. Each member must perform individually for the team to excel. For this type of group task, when group members work independently of one another, a competitive reward structure can be effective.

Finally, in many cases, the organization must choose the work team supervisor or leader. There are a variety of methods for doing this, but we rarely meet organizations that choose first-line supervisors on the basis of managerial skill or competency. For example, how do universities choose departmental chairs? On a seemingly random basis. Most organizations do a bit better than that; they often choose team supervisors on the basis of technical competence--so, the best mechanic in the garage becomes the garage foreman. As a result, the company loses a good mechanic and gets a mediocre foreman. And this has very interesting consequences. In study after study beginning with Herzberg's research in the 1950s, regardless of the job or geographical location, about 70% of the work force reports that the worst single feature of their job is their immediate boss. This in turn leads to absenteeism, illness, burnout, and poor performance generally. Perhaps the worst offender in this area is the military, which appoints team supervisors primarily on the basis of seniority. In addition, however, the military has institutionalized an authoritarian model of leadership that is inconsistent with everything we know about effective management. Two predictable and highly undesirable consequences follow from this. On the one hand, this method of selecting first line supervisors tends to degrade team performance because the team members become alienated and angry. On the other hand, it exacerbates attrition from the various military technical specialties. This is a waste of the original training dollars and the lack of personnel contributes to the poor maintenance and low operational readiness of the increasingly sophisticated equipment on which the military relies.

Are there leadership traits that characterize effective leaders? Although decades of leadership research concludes that effective leadership depends on the task environment, we can offer a prescription in terms of our trait taxonomy. First, leaders must be well-adjusted. Poorly adjusted persons are moody and unpredictable and tend to disrupt team interaction. Leaders must not only coordinate team performance but also serve as a source of inspiration for the group. For any team task, poorly adjusted leaders will compromise team performance. Second, leaders must be ambitious and achievement-oriented. Leaders must promote the organizational goal of excellence as the team goal and pursue this outcome. Third, their achievement-orientation must be tempered with interpersonal qualities inherent in the likeability trait. Leaders do not have to be loved, but the effective leader must be concerned with individual well-being and must establish relatively congenial relations in the group. Thus, effective leaders must adequately understand human motivation and have the interpersonal skill necessary to promote smooth group relations. Groups led by tyrants are at a competitive disadvantage.

So we see that team effectiveness is a function of team composition, but it is a slave to corporate policy. For those persons who currently work for an incompetent boss, it should be comforting to know that the only solution may be to do such a good job for that person that he or she will get promoted and become someone else's problem. The bad news is that seven out of ten replacements for that person will also be incompetent, but probably in different ways. Consequently, you should take pride in the performance of your group and let that particular virtue be its own reward.

REFERENCES

Blau, P. (1954). Cooperation and competition in a bureaucracy. American Journal of Sociology, 59, 530-535.

Driskell, J. E. (1987). Effects of group cohesiveness and collective orientation on performance: A review and empirical study. Orlando, FL: Eagle Technology.

Driskell, J. E., Hogan, R., & Salas, E. (1987). Personal and group performance. In C. Hendrick (Ed.), Personality and social psychology review (pp. 91-112). California: Sage.

Gottfredson, G. D., Holland, J. L., & Ogawa, D. K. (1982). Dictionary of Holland occupational codes. Palo Alto: Consulting Psychologists Press.

Guilford, J. P., Christensen, P. R., Bond, N.A., & Sutton, M. A. (1954). A factor analysis study of human interests. Psychological Monographs, 68 (Whole No. 375).

Hackman, J. R. (1968). Effects of task characteristics on group products. Journal of Experimental Social Psychology, 4, 162-187.

Herold, D. M. (1978). Improving the performance effectiveness of groups through a task-contingent selection of intervention strategies. The Academy of Management Review, 3, 315-325.

Hogan, R. (1976). Egoism, altruism, and culture. American Psychologist, 31, 363-366.

Holland, J. L. (1966). A psychological classification scheme for vocations and major fields. Journal of Counseling Psychology, 13, 278-288.

Latham, G. P., & Balders, J. J. (1975). The "practical significance" of Locke's theory of goal setting. Journal of Applied Psychology, 60, 122-124.

McGrath, J. E. (1984). Groups: Interaction and performance. Englewood Cliffs, NJ: Prentice-Hall.

Morris, C. G. (1967). Task effects on group interaction. Journal of Personality and Social Psychology, 5, 545-554.

THE EMPLOYEE ASSISTANCE PROGRAM: RAISING

PRODUCTIVITY BY LIFTING CONSTRAINTS

Jeffery Scott Mio

Washington State University
Pullman, Washington

Craig K. Goishi

Institute for Motivational Development
Newport Beach, California

INTRODUCTION

The employee assistance program (EAP) movement has gained strength in recent decades. The goal of the EAP is to work hand in hand with management and labor to increase the productivity of troubled workers by addressing alcohol, drug abuse, or other types of mental health related problems.

In the present chapter, we give a broad overview of the history, description, implementation, and ethical concerns of EAPs. We present case material from supervisory sessions we have had with EAP counselors and coordinators. We then examine some of the recent research evaluating the effectiveness of such programs. Research has indicated that for the most part, EAPs have been unsuccessful in reaching white-collar workers. We offer reasons for this problem, and we suggest strategies for reaching this evasive population.

HISTORY

The historical roots of EAPs date back to the 19th Century. In the 1880s, a movement known as the social betterment movement began to take hold. According to Sonnenstuhl and Trice (1986) "these services included inexpensive housing, company-sponsored unions, sanitary working conditions, insurance, and pension plans, as well as facilities for banking, recreation, medical care, and education" (p. 3). This movement ended for at least three reasons: (1) disenchantment with corporate paternalism, (2) the Depression, which forced companies to be penurious, and (3) the Wagner Act of 1936, which outlawed company-sponsored unions.

Personnel counseling was the next historical movement, taking hold as the social betterment movement subsided in the 1920s and 1930s (Sonnenstuhl & Trice, 1986). Personnel counseling arose out of studies from Western Electric's Hawthorne plant, well known for the so-called Hawthorne Effect (Roethlisberger & Dickson, 1939). Supervisors and industrial consultants felt that there were pressures at work to interfere with maximum productivity. This was seen, correctly or incorrectly, as an irrational, noncooperative stance workers took against their employers. In order to counteract this stance, management trained some shop workers to be listeners--counselors, if you will--to wander the workplace and listen to workers' problems. This was management's demonstration of care for its workers, thus lifting pressures to resist management's requests to be optimally productive.

The final historical employee assistance movement cited by Sonnenstuhl and Trice was the occupational mental health movement. This arose as a response to a perceived need due to World War II. Many individuals who had never worked before were needed to aid the war effort. Thus, mental health workers were hired in order to respond to actual mental health crises in the workplace and to prevent other workers from becoming emotionally distressed. Because the objective of these programs was to help integrate new workers into the workforce, companies discontinued these programs after the war ended.

As the occupational mental health movement disbanded, a new movement began to rise. This was the Occupational Alcohol Movement of the 1940's. This is generally acknowledged as the direct predecessor of the EAP movement, both in content and form (e.g., Good, 1986; Jerrell & Rightmyer, 1982).[1] It was recognized that alcoholism was a serious impediment to productivity in the workplace. Drawing from the strength of the Alcoholics Anonymous programs, businesses sought to assist troubled workers whose problems prevented them from operating at maximum efficiency.

Concern over alcohol abuse in the workplace continues today. Alcoholism is an ever-increasing drain upon American society. Blum (1984) estimated that alcohol-related costs to society were upwards of $42.75 billion in 1977. This figure rose to $120 billion by 1983. Nearly half of the alcohol-related costs to society are directly traced to lost productivity in industry (Quayle, 1985). The pain and suffering alcoholism causes to the alcoholics and those around them are immeasurable. The original intent of the EAP movement was to help businesses avoid the loss of productivity they might otherwise have incurred. Apparently, there remains a desperate need for this service in industry, as measured by the rapid contracting for EAP services in recent years. In 1970, there were an estimated 350-400 programs throughout the country; by 1986, 5,000-10,000 such programs existed (Sonnenstuhl & Trice, 1986).

Although alcohol problems are still emphasized, there is a growing movement within the EAP field to include all types of problems that may interfere with worker productivity. These problems include drug abuse, emotional or behavioral problems of the offspring of employees, and financial or legal problems. This new orientation is called the "broad-brush approach" to employee assistance (Jerrell & Rightmeyer, 1962). This expanded emphasis has undoubtedly contributed to the sharp increase in the number of EAPs in recent years.

While expanding a company's EAP from a purely alcohol emphasis to a broad-brush approach is in many respects a more humanitarian move, it adds much more uncertainty to the policy's implementation. How does one define general mental health or factors preventing such help? Where does an EAP coordinator draw the line between intervention and nonintervention? Briar and Vinet (1985) give a hypothetical (but all too realistic) example of a company engaging in a major reorganization that necessitates massive employee lay-offs. Clearly, this is a prescription for mental health difficulties. Does an EAP coordinator intervene? It is important for EAPs to have a realistic and comprehensible mission that is able to anticipate as well as respond to a wide variety of situations. Successful EAPs have clear guidelines that are understood by all levels of management and employees. However, the act of confronting a worker with a problem is still a delicate matter.

Constructive Confrontation

Trice and Beyer (1984) reported that in the early 1960s, a strategy called "constructive confrontation" was developed to address problem workers. Trice was one of the forerunners in the development of this strategy (Trice, 1962). This strategy combined disciplinary actions presented in a positive manner along with rehabilitative measures. Firing was seen only as a last resort. The reasoning here was that if workers still had something to lose (i.e., their jobs), they would likely be more motivated to follow through on requests that they seek treatment. Also, in either a work or a rehabilitation setting, there would be external monitors of their behaviors. However, if workers were simply fired, no such external controls could be exerted, and there is a likelihood that if the workers were to secure other jobs, their cycle of unproductivity would continue.

Constructive confrontation involves a supervisor of an employee confronting the employee about his/her deteriorating job performance and pointing out that there is a company program (the EAP) designed to assist employees in trouble. The confrontation is done orally, so there is no formal, written document that goes into the company's file. The confrontational component gives the employee specific feedback on unacceptable job performance and also carries with it a warning that continued unacceptable job performance will lead to formal discipline or dismissal. Important aspects of this component are (1) it reiterates the group's internal values, i.e., acceptable levels of work performance are expected of all workers, (2) it points out that the worker is not conforming to these values, and (3) it establishes social distance between the individual and the group. The constructive component reminds the employee that the company provides assistance to employees with similar problems through their particular EAP. Important aspects of this component are (1) it expresses emotional support, (2) it points out that group membership can be maintained or reacquired if the worker's performance conforms to the group norms, and (3) it specifies a particular mode through which the worker can regain acceptable job performance.

An important difference between the alcohol and the broad-brush approaches to EAPs is the emphasis placed upon constructive confrontation. Programs emphasizing alcoholism are influenced by the Alcoholics Anonymous (AA) tradition and management theory. AA suggests that alcoholics are excellent at denying or avoiding their problems. Thus, the only way to get an alcoholic to take steps towards recovery is to confront him/her with the problem, breaking through the denial. The constructive confrontation strategy places primary emphasis upon the supervisor and the worker. The rise in the broad-brush approach came in the 1970s, when many trained therapists were employed by EAPs. Because of the therapists' training in theories of psychotherapy, their tendency was to place emphasis on counseling rather than constructive confrontation. Constructive confrontation was seen as coercive and antithetical to traditional therapy. Therefore, emphasis was placed upon the therapeutic relationship between the therapist and the worker. However, as Sonnenstuhl and Trice (1986) point out, all EAPs contain some form of constructive confrontation and counseling.

To examine the effectiveness of constructive confrontation, Trice and Beyer (1984) examined the managerial style of 474 managers in a major corporation. The corporation employeed over 120,000 workers over 50 locations throughout the United States. Of these companies, 19 were selected through a stratified random sampling procedure so that all areas of the corporation (e.g., manufacturing, service, etc.) and all geographic areas would be represented. From these sites, two samples of managers were selected. One sample consisted of 153 managers who had had to deal with an employee with a drinking problem within the previous three years. The other sample consisted of 321 managers who had had to deal with a problem employee during the same 3-year period whose problem did not involve drinking. Among the 474 managers, only four declined to participate in the study. The data consisted of one and a half hour structured interviews.

From their results, the authors concluded, "...it was the balanced use of both constructive and confrontational elements in oral discussion that produced positive outcomes among problem-drinking employees" (pp. 402-403). The authors found that while exclusive use of confrontation was related to workers agreeing to address their drinking problems and increasing their productivity subsequent to the confrontation, exclusive use of this strategy was also associated with employee intransigence and some quitting their jobs. Application of constructive confrontation to nonalcohol-related problems was also successful, but it was less consistently so. Note that the authors discussed the oral use of constructive confrontation. This is consistent with the feeling by many (e.g., Heyman, 1976, 1978; Sonnenstuhl & Trice, 1986) that informal initial contact is much more effective than a more formal, written memorandum in dealing with problem employees. Anecdotally, the company's EAP was considered to be a success, as the managers reported an 80% improvement for general conduct and a 74% improvement for work performance after EAP intervention.

Hoffman and Roman (1984) question the importance of supervisors using the constructive confrontation strategy. They feel that supervisors tend to be task-oriented or emotion-oriented in their styles of interaction. The constructive confrontation strategy asks supervisors to be facile in both skills, so it is an inherently difficult task. In their examination of 84 supervisors, Hoffman and Roman found that supervisors did not seem to need to be adept at both task and emotional orientation in order for the EAP to be successful. Instead, supervisors harboring generally positive views towards the EAP is a much better predictor of the success of the program. The authors recommend that organizations spend time "selling" their programs, thus giving supervisors a superordinate goal towards which they all can work. It is much easier to change attitudes toward a policy than it is to change fundamental supervisory styles.

We feel that although Hoffman and Roman (1984) raise an important issue, and their notion of "selling" a program is valid, they seem to miss the essence of the constructive confrontation strategy. This strategy does not require that individual supervisors possess both the task and the caring components. Instead, the strategy itself possesses both components. Supervisors need only to confront employees with their problems, primarily through the observance of job deterioration. The supervisors can do this through a matter of fact stance or through a caring stance. However, with this confrontation must come a reminder that there is a mechanism established in the company through which the employee can receive help.

Sonnelstuhl and Trice (1986) indentified what they considered to be seven essential elements of EAPs: (1) There must be a clear, written policy regarding assistance. (2) There needs to be management support for the programs. (3) An EAP coordinator needs to be present at the company. (4) Supervisors need to be trained to implement the company's policy. (5) Employees need to be educated about the policy. (6) There needs to be a counseling component in the program. (7) Union support and involvement is needed. Each of these elements will now be developed more fully. The reader must keep in mind that each element is a necessary component but not sufficient by itself.

Clear, Written Policy

Sonnenstuhl and Trice's first essential element for a successful EAP is that there must be a clear, written company policy regarding assistance. Good (1986) examined three different companies' EAP policies, all with varying degrees of balance between workers' privacy and company's needs. One company's policy was particularly clear and balanced. It stated that if an employee were to volunteer to seek help via the EAP staff, confidentiality would be maintained, including job promotion eligibility in the future. However, if the supervisory staff were to detect the abuse in what otherwise would have been clandestine behavior, the disciplinary action would be taken. The policy also addressed off-the-job behavior. On a case-by-case basis, the company and a union representative would assess whether or not off-the-job substance abuse adversely affected work performance. This company actively sought union cooperation on this policy, particularly with respect to off-the-job behavior as it related to on-the-job safety. In a year, this company went from six union-sponsored grievances involving substance abuse to none.

Management Support

Management needs to be supportive of EAPs from top to bottom. Noncooperation at any level of management can undermine the goals of even the most solidly constructed program. Of course, there are a number of possible motives behind management support of EAPs. Rinella (1986) indicated that companies are examining ways of cutting expenses of employee health benefit packages while still providing services. While mental health services account for a small percentage of benefit costs, they are among the first to be eliminated or reduced. Therefore, programs such as EAPs have seen a dramatic increase in recent years. While Rinella's assertion may be partially correct, EAP researchers have not found cost-cutting pressures to be foremost in the decision making process to include EAPs in worker's benefits. Instead, many have suggested that a company's sense of social responsibility is the primary reason for adoption of EAPs (e.g., Miller, 1986; Putnam & Stout, 1985; Sonnenstuhl & Trice, 1986). For example, Putnam and Stout (1985) contacted 377 organizations in Rhode Island, interviewing organizational officers in a questionnaire format. About one-third of these organizations had adopted EAPs. Based upon a step-wise multiple regression procedure, the authors concluded that organizations adopting EAPs tended to have reputations in the community of being progressive, especially in their concern for workers. Furthermore, these organizations tended to be large, autonomous, and highly unionized. Characteristics of nonadopting organizations tended to fear that a written policy on alcoholism would hurt the company's public image, and that outside influence (i.e., EAPs) would interfere with internal personnel procedures.

There needs to be an EAP coordinator within the company. Some believe that almost anyone with a caring attitude would be sufficient to fill this coordinator position (e.g., Wrich, 1980). Others (e.g., Manuso, 1983) contend that the coordinator should be a clinical psychologist, psychiatrist, or clinical social worker because of the diagnostic and clinical issues that arise in EAPs. According to its Information Director, the Association of Labor-Management Administrators and Consultants on Alcoholism (ALMACA) has recently developed a certification procedure for EAP consultants, including a certifying examination (R. Bickerton, May 1988). This is a four-hour examination covering the full range of EAP duties. Upon completion and passage, the candidate is awarded a Certified EAP Professional certificate. ALMACA has certified over 3,000 individuals throughout the country in the first 18 months of the certification procedure. This large number of awardees is in part a reflection of the number of individuals who have been functioning in the EAP field and who were "grandfathered in" as being certified professionals. It is anticipated that the procedures will be more restrictive in the future. Another anticipated change is that ALMACA will change its name to de-emphasize alcoholism and to reflect the broad brush trend in EAPs. According to Bickerton, only one state has pending legislation to require certification of all EAP consultants but the trend is for many more states to follow suit.

The EAP coordinator is the individual around which the entire system revolves. An ineffective coordinator will make the program unnecessarily costly, so selecting an efficient coordinator is important in the final cost-benefit analysis. Franz (1986) identified some important issues relevant to referral making and the selection of a coordinator. First is the organizational context. Is it an alcohol-specific program or a broad-brush one? What are the company's policies? Are there in-house or off-site services? How comfortable is the potential coordinator with these contextual factors? Next is the attitude of the coordinator. Are all problems referred out, or is referral seen as a last resort? If all problems are referred out, the program will be overly costly. If referral is seen as a last resort, this will implicitly discourage employees from using the services. Personal qualities of the coordinator are also important. Are there some types of clients about whom the coordinator has particularly negative feelings (e.g., child abusers, demanding clients)? If so, are these feelings held in check or are they allowed to interfere with the referral process? Are there important deficits in the coordinator's training? Finally, resource familiarity is an important coordinator quality. The coordinator must be aware of, or willing to learn about, all resources available, both within the company and within the surrounding community. In this way, more cost-effective referrals can be made.

Once established, the EAP coordinator needs to be aware of the process involved in referral making. Franz (1986) identified four steps involved in this process. Step I is the engagement phase. Here trust and rapport are built to maximize the probability that the employee will follow through on the referral. Step II is the identification and analysis of the problem. This is important in making the most appropriate referrals. Step III is the implementation phase where the actual referral is made and the employee follows through on the referral. A strategy that is often successful is to give the employee a range of appropriate referrals allowing the employee to choose the specific one with which s/he feels most comfortable. Step IV is the follow-up and evaluation phase. It is important to examine the effectiveness of the particular referral site and/or to have an on-going analysis of which types of problems seem most appropriate for which sites.

Training of Supervisors

While the EAP system revolves around the EAP coordinator, the system is not set in motion until supervisors make referrals to the coordinator. Thus, supervisors need to be trained in recognizing and acting upon problems that arise. Our previous discussion of the constructive confrontation strategy underscores the importance of this element in the success of the EAP. Moreover, as will be discussed later, it is often quite difficult to detect alcohol problems as they relate to job performance (Edwards, 1975; Schramm, Mandell, & Archer, 1978); broad-brush problems would be even more difficult to detect. One must also be aware of the fact that supervisors have other responsibilities that take precedence over EAP-related issues, thus making the detection of problems still more difficult. In an effort to help supervisors accept the added responsibilities of EAP-related issues, Sonnenstuhl and Trice (1984) suggest that training involve the following four components:

> (1) defining program policy, (2) emphasizing the degree of management support for it, (3) explaining the supervisors' role in implementing it, and (4) demonstrating how it can be integrated into supervisor's existing responsibilities for employee job performance (p. 16).

Employee Education

As discussed earlier, Hoffman and Roman (1984) recommend that organizations need to "sell" their EAPs. A major component of this is to educate employees about the benefits of the program.

The importance of this factor can been seen in Lesser and Cavaseno's (1986) report on promoting their hospital's EAP. The EAP had been functioning under the hospital's Employee Health Services (EHS) Department. However, the program was shifted over to the Department of Social Work Services (DSWS). The DSWS decided to make their EAP a model program to not only encourage utilization by hospital employees, but also to encourage Social Work Departments in other hospitals to take on such responsibilities. The authors felt that if social workers were to expand their roles from patient care to all hospital concerns, they will be more visible and more invaluable within a hospital setting. Thus, the authors' orientation was a politically motivated one, but one that provided the context for excellent dissemination of EAP policies and services. The DSWS informed all new employees about the EAP in hospital orientation meetings, sponsored seminars for supervisors designed to train the supervisors in identification and referral techniques, held seminars for employees that dealt with a range of topics, many of which dealint with mental health issues, developed and provided written materials on the subject, dispersing material throughout the hospital, and networking throughout the various departments to establish personal contacts to all who might be in the position of referring troubled employees.

In a little over one and a half years, 342 cases were seen through the social-work sponsored EAP. This marked a 160-case increase (88%) from the two-year period just previous to the DSWS program. Initially, most of the referrals came from EHS (72%), with supervisor referral (18%) and self-referral (10%) comprising the rest of the referrals. However, in the second year of the new program, there was a marked increase in supervisor referral (25%) and self-referral (18%). The 57% referral from the EHS in the second year under the DSWS may reflect some degree of friction between the two departments. The increase in employee utilization is somewhat indicative of the ineffectiveness of the EAP under the sponsorship of the EHS, and the authors reported some strained relations, between the two departments. However, this still does not detract from the importance of promoting the EAP and getting all concerned to see the value of such programs.

Counseling Component

Because of the increasing number of trained therapists serving as EAP coordinators, the counseling component has gained in importance. In-house services are often available in larger companies that can afford to pay therapists, whereas external services are the more common treatment overall, especially for small companies (Sonnenstuhl & Trice, 1986). External services may be preferable because of the higher probability of conflicts of interest for on-site therapists. The major drawback of external EAP services is that those agencies may have minimal experience with the work setting, so productivity of the worker is de-emphasized in favor of counseling and more expensive treatments. As an alternative to the internal vs. external strategies, there is what is termed the "community resource network." Here, the EAP coordinator is in charge of training supervisors and union officials regarding their role in the process. The coordinator also maintains close contact with the various community services that are available and are covered by the company's benefit package. The coordinator then provides employees with information about these community resources.

Union Support

As indicated in the Putnam and Stout (1985) study, besides a company's willingness to institute an EAP, union involvement is a necessary component to a successful program. Thus, businesses wishing to implement an EAP would be wise to consult with the relevant unions. This recommendation has been suggested by many in the field (e.g, Albert, Smythe, & Brook, 1985; Briar & Vinet, 1985; Good, 1986; Sonnenstuhl & Trice, 1986). A major part of the reason for this is the historical tension between labor and management (Briar & Vinet, 1985). In bringing the unions into the process at the inception stage of implementation, more trust and cooperation will ensue in support of the EAP. Still, a certain amount of tension will be felt by the EAP coordinator. Because the basic mission of an EAP is to assist a worker in need, the natural therapeutic stance would be to be an advocate for the worker. Thus, management will view the EAP with suspicion, especially regarding cost issues. There could be implicit or explicit threats for an EAP to side with management or else the contract will be awarded to another program. Unions, also, have been ambivalent about EAPs. On the one hand, unions are in favor of helping workers. On the other hand, they feel that in some instances, EAPs are the company's way of usurping union power (Sonnenstuhl & Trice, 1986).

THERAPEUTIC PROBLEMS

We turn now to some therapeutic problems unique to EAPs. These problems are largely due to the potential number of individuals involved in such programs. However, many problems may simply be due to the relative newness of EAPs, especially the more recent therapy component.

Dilemmas of Implementation

Once an EAP is in place, there are still difficulties that may arise.

Although EAP coordinators are expected to make professional referrals, carefully matching the employee's needs with the most appropriate community resource, this cannot always be achieved. For one thing, in a large metropolitan area, it is unlikely that an EAP coordinator will have been able to visit all of the community facilities available, much less all of the staff members associated with those facilities nor the countless number of individual therapists that may be of potential use. Moreover, in large corporations, the EAP coordinator quite often has only telephone contact with the troubled employee. Quite often, this contact is far too brief for adequate evaluation to take place.

As an illustration of the pragmatic difficulties facing EAP coordinators, the following vignette is offered.[2] Jim O., an EAP coordinator, presented to us his frustrations with telephone referrals. If the phones happen to be slow, he could spend more time with clients, carefully evaluating their respective conditions. However, on busy days, he would receive upwards of 25 calls. On these days, he found himself being on the curt side with clients. He expressed his personal anguish to us:

> I have 15 minutes, sometimes less, to make some very critical
> judgment about people's lives. Although I always try to give them
> options, I know my tone of voice is different if, on the one hand, I
> think the person is in a serious crisis or, on the other hand, just
> complaining about a passing problem or simply seeking attention.
> Clients will act on the implied recommendations that are given. I
> know highly skilled psychotherapists would only make these sorts of
> judgments after psychological tests or several in-person meetings.
> Often I would worry that I am in over my head...too many important
> decision hinge on a 15-minute phone call.

Part of the dilemma facing EAP coordinators and counselors is that there are a number of interrelating systems exerting influence upon the coordinator. Ford and Ford (1986) identified at least ten such systems:

1. all of the formal elements of the EAP
2. the upper level management of the company
3. the middle and supervisory managers charged with the responsibility of identifying problem employees
4. the staff employees
5. the employees' families
6. the labor union(s)
7. the community facilities and social services providing care
8. the insurers and payors of health care services, including both private and governmental bodies
9. the community of like employers (e.g., if one car company offers an EAP, the community of car companies becomes a relevant system)
10. the immediate public community, including residents, politicians, and the media

When making various decisions and referrals, EAP coordinators must recognize that they may be hearing directly from one or more of these systems. Coordinators must be mindful of the fact that quite often, interacting systems may have differing and even conflicting goals. Decisions must respect the goals of each system, finding a proper balance upon which all can agree. For example, employees want to get better, health care providers want to give the best possible treatment, and upper level management wants to be mindful of costs associated with the care. The following vignette illustrates the many influences from different directions exerting pressure upon EAP coordinators: An EAP coordinator expressed to us her frustration that much of her job involved diffusing crises rather than facilitating treatment. She would generally have one to three phone and/or office contacts with her clients prior to referring them for treatments. With one or two phone contacts, she often felt she did not know enough about the client to make treatment recommendations. On the other extreme, she would often find that after building rapport with clients over the phone and then seeing them for three sessions, clients would express their irritation at having to explain their situation all over to a new counselor after the referral has been made.

On the positive side, through careful monitoring, this same coordinator was able to facilitate the transfer of a client from a hospital to a residential care facility. Although hospital treatment was effective, the residential care was equally appropriate at a fraction of the cost. Neither the primary therapist nor the hospital would have been sufficiently motivated to make the transfer without the EAP coordinator's input. In this single case, the self-insured company saved over $100,000.

Another problem of implementation involves defining the scope and nature of the EAP duties. Alice H. was the on-call EAP staff counselor in the following case. She was called late one evening by a manager of the client company. Apparently, a visiting customer of the company was exhibiting bizarre behavior after a corporate sales presentation and dinner. He appeared to be drunk or otherwise impaired and was becoming anxious and hostile. The manager wanted an EAP counselor to go to the restaurant to calm down the customer. In order to avoid negative publicity, the manager did not want to involve the police nor a public mental health agency. Alice was concerned about the scope of her duties, including (1) whether the customer was in fact a covered client, and (2) whether a restaurant was an appropriate location for intervention. Alice was also concerned about being constrained from involving the police even if she deemed this to be a prudent course of action.

As one can see, therapeutic dilemmas of EAP coordinators and counselors are varied and at times frustrating. This is due in large part to the numerous interacting systems impinging upon the EAP representative. Traditional therapy allows for an educative process, where the client learns the boundaries of therapy over time, and inappropriate requests or expectations abate over time. This educative process is much more complex when multiple systems interact. Many involved in the system are not even known to the EAP representative, so more than a general educative program is difficult if not impossible to deliver.

Confidentiality

When seeing an individual in therapy, unless the client is gravely disabled or is a danger to him-/herself or others, therapists are sworn to confidentiality, not revealing anything about the client's case to anyone else. The exception to this standard is when the therapist is either being supervised on the case or if there is a formal consultation established between the therapist and a colleague. Violation of confidentiality is considered to be an ethical violation, and therapists are subject to disciplinary action, including loss of license. However, EAPs offer an interesting challenge to conventional notions of ethical considerations. There is not a clear therapist-client relationship, so issues of confidentiality become confused. For example, the organization employing the services of the EAP is the company instituting the program, the recipient of the services is the troubled worker, the service provider is the individual or facility to whom the worker is referred, and the payor of the services is the insurance company used by the employer of the troubled worker. An employer needs to have some sense of the progress the worker is making in treatment in order to make decisions on a temporary or permanent replacement for the worker. The EAP coordinator needs to have some sense of the effectiveness of the facilities to whom workers are being referred. A worker needs to have a sense that his/her treatment is confidential, or the treatment will be doomed to failure. The relevant union needs to feel confident that a given employee is being treated fairly by the company or else the union will withdraw support for the company's program.

Briar and Vinet (1985) take the position that the therapist-client relationship is still the primary one that needs to be protected. This means that confidentiality between the care provider and the troubled worker needs to be respected. The authors feel that all systems involved should take the stand that what is best for the worker is ultimately what is best for all concerned parties. Sonnenstuhl and Trice (1986) suggest that the proper balance is one where the needs of various systems are respected and a written consent form is signed by the client to those parties. However, only that specific information that is absolutely necessary is consented to be released. So, for statistical purposes, an EAP coordinator may need to know the mode of treatment used by the care giving facility, the duration of the treatment, and the facility's assessment if the worker's condition has improved, deteriorated, or remained the same. This specific information should appear on the consent form to be signed by the worker being treated, and no other information may be released to the EAP coordinator without another consent form to be drafted and signed.

Dual Relationship

Another ethical violation is that of dual relationship. A therapist cannot both be functioning as a therapist and, say, the troubled worker's co-worker on an assembly line. Should any sort of dual relationship exist, it is incumbent upon the therapist to refer the client to another therapist. However, quite often EAPs accept contracts that lead to gray areas of the dual relationship standard. The following case illustrates this point: Joan C. came to supervision extremely concerned upon learning that her EAP had accepted a contract with an airport. Part of the contract involved having EAP counselors supervise urine specimen collection for drug testing purposes. Her initial concern had to do with the fact that his was a new and unusual task. Counselors are almost never requested to supervise medically-related procedures. However, as we discussed the situation further, it became apparent that there were other problems as well. One was a potential dual relationship: participating in drug testing may interfere with the way in which the EAP was viewed by the employees. Was its primary duties counseling or policing? Moreover, Joan might have occasion to counsel one of the employees whose drug testing she had supervised. This dual role may also be seen as a dual relationship.

Conflict of Interest

The classic conflict of interest situation involves money. How motivated are care providers to terminate treatment if they are being paid for services without any specific time limit to treatment? In an environment that stresses monetary prudence, is it a conflict of interest if a particular facility offers a discount for a certain number of referrals? Rinella (1986) was particularly concerned about such issues: "Since their inception, EAPs have been fertile territory for a variety of ethical problems. The most obvious, largely undocumented, but an 'open secret' among providers and employers, is the frequency of exclusive 'sweet-heart' arrangements between EAPs and particular providers" (p. 129). These arrangements include kick-backs from referred-to facilities and discounts for exclusive referrals. Rinella also warned against opting for a less effective treatment merely for its cost-saving value. "One may assume, of course, that in the long run, employers will pay more for misdirected decisions.... However, the long view is generally given a back seat to next year's balanced budget" (p. 131).

RESEARCH ON EAP EFFECTIVENESS

There has been extensive research on the efficacy of EAPs, yet there continues to be disagreement on the meaning of the results (Sonnenstuhl & Trice, 1986). The major reason for the dispute focuses upon the inherent nature of the problem to be studied. How does one measure impaired job performance? How does one measure improved job performance? How are costs associated with impaired or lost job performance measured? How does one balance costs against humanitarian intentions to help a troubled worker? Because of these inherent problems, it has been suggested that many skilled program evaluators have chosen not to conduct EAP research (Sonnenstuhl & Trice, 1986). Still, research examining aspects of EAPs is an important endeavor. Only then can we refine our methods and improve the quality of service delivery. Such work may convince nonadopting organizations to finally adopt EAPs in the service of their employees.

The essential selling point of EAPs is that there is a cost-benefit element to them. As Jerrell and Rightmyer (1982) noted, "The scope of problems being addressed by EAPs has expanded considerably, but the primary emphasis remains on improving the work performance of the employee and minimizing the costs associated with these problems" (p. 256). However, as Shain, Suurvali, and Boutilier (1986) point out, there are four kinds of cost-benefit models: cost-recovery, purchase of service, benefits, and ecological. The cost-recovery model examines issues such as medical cost reduction, reduced absenteeism, and reduced training costs and compares these cost reductions with the costs associated with the installation and maintenance of the EAP. Does the EAP cost more than it is saving the company? The purchase of service model takes a different stand altogether. From this stand, the EAP is a given, akin to other services a business is likely to purchase. The relevant research question from this model asks if the costs associated with this particular EAP are reasonable when compared with similar services provided by other EAPs. Thus, issues of efficiency are important. The benefits model takes a slightly different stand from the purchase of service model. The research questions are similar, but the benefits model takes the position that the company is not purchasing a service for itself but it is providing a benefit for its workers. Thus, the EAP is seen as part of the overall benefits package workers receive. Finally, the ecological model is predicated on the view that work takes mental and physical resources away from workers, and it is both humane and necessary to replenish these resources. Thus, both cost and benefit are amorphous terms, and accepting the philosophical stance is justification enough to provide an EAP for one's workers.

As one can see, the four cost-benefit models are arranged from the most concrete (cost-recovery) to the most abstract (ecological). They are also arranged from the model emphasizing the most economic benefit to the company to the one emphasizing the most humane view of the worker. Shain et al. (1986) note that the cost-recovery model seems to be the most researched model. This is not surprising since there are clear numbers associated with the dependent variables, such as the number of days absent, the cost of hiring replacement workers, and hospital charges.

116

However, these measures may not be assessing the true costs of problem workers nor the true benefits of returning such workers to work. Thus, the proliferation of cost-recovery studies may be more a function of convenience of measurement rather than of ecological validity. Moreover, Shain et al. found that company executives view the benefits model as the most compelling justification for utilizing EAPs. The purchase of service and ecological models were the next most emphasized model, with the cost-recovery model having the lowest impact of argument. This is consistent with research we cited earlier on the characteristics of companies adopting to EAPs.

Difficulties in EAP Research

Groeneveld, Shain, Brayshaw, Keaney, and Laird (1985) note: "A consistently recurring theme in the EAP tradition is the cost-effectiveness notion.... Although the notion of cost effectiveness is very firmly ingrained in the field's cultural context, the evidence to support this postulate is still weak" (p. 75). Albert et al. (1985) agree, and they criticize many EAP practitioners for "their uncritical acceptance of findings from the EAP research literature" (p. 175). Many with a critical eye (e.g., Jerrell & Rightmyer, 1982; Sonnenstuhl & Trice, 1986), although recognizing the flaws in EAP research, conclude that EAPs are generally an effective way of dealing with alcoholism and other problems that might interfere with worker productivity. Jerrell and Rightmyer (1982) note that part of the overall difficulty in evaluating EAPs is that their roles are continually being expanded. Time series and nonequivalent control group designs are the appropriate techniques for handling the type of naturalistic situations of which EAPs are a part. These require somewhat stable baseline and follow-up measures. But if an EAP's role is changing as a study is being conducted--say, from an alcohol emphasis to a broad-brush approach, then expanding duties within the broad-brush approach--there is an inherent difficulty in the study.

Albert et al. (1985) offer some of the most serious challenges to EAP researchers. For one thing, "job deterioration" is not a very explicit or objectifiable criterion. It tends to be whatever a supervisor defines it to be. Also, differential status carries with it differential--and more difficult--performance assessment.

The performance of a vice-president of finance must be measured differently from the performance of an assembly line worker. It is a truism of organizational theory that the more complex and abstract the job, the more difficult it becomes to quantify performance using objective criteria like "attendance" or "productivity" (p. 176).

We will return to the difficulties regarding white-collar involvement in EAPs in our final section.

Another difficulty is that many alcoholics function adequately on the job, even in the middle to late stages of the disorder (Edwards, 1975; Schramm et al., 1978). Many have argued that if a company were to catch alcoholism early, loss of productivity would have been prevented. However, the above findings render "early detection" a useless concept. Albert et al. (1985) suggest that a more fruitful avenue to pursue may be to determine the point at which detection may be maximally beneficial. We feel that although in fact productivity may not be affected by alcoholism for a long period, this latter view loses sight of the humanitarian component to EAPs.

Many assume that self-referrals are more desirable and are evidence for a more effective program. For instance, the Lesser and Cavaseno

(1986) study reviewed earlier noted, among other things, that the percentage of self-referrals increased after their promotion campaign. Conversely, coercing employees into treatment by imminent job dismissal, for example, is seen as an ineffective procedure. However, Albert et al. (1985) challenge the voluntary vs. coerced distinction as valuable measures to be taken by EAP researchers. They point out that in some cases, high amounts of self-referrals may be a symptom of poorly trained supervisors. Also, coercing late stage alcoholics may be absolutely helpful and evidence that all of the interrelating systems are working in concordance, whereas coercing an early stage alcoholic may be counterproductive.

Finally, the notion of "successful outcome" lacks clarity and consistency across studies (Albert et al., 1985; Jerrell & Rightmyer, 1982). Some studies rely upon the caregiver to assess progress, others on supervisors, and still others on EAP coordinators. Others use "objective" measures, such as absenteeism, cost of medical care in ensuing years, or cost of insurance premiums. However, as Groeneveld et al. (1985) point out, many of these post-treatment measures reflect relapse costs because many programs do not provide for aftercare treatment. In examining the available research, Albert et al. (1985) conclude that it is premature for EAPs to argue for their effectiveness on the basis of cost-benefit analyses. The above methodological problems need to be addressed before one can even state if EAPs are even successful, much less cost efficient. Although we strongly agree with the Albert et al. conclusion, we would like to underscore that their orientation is from a cost-recovery model perspective. If we can take company executives' words at face value, the cost-recovery model is the least relevant one for choosing to adopt an EAP.

Penetration Rate

Because the cost-recovery model may not be the most appropriate model to examine, issues of effectiveness and efficiency of EAPs come to the fore. In many respects, efficiency is measured by value judgments. An EAP coordinator often needs to make decisions such as referring a worker to an excellent but expensive facility versus a less expensive facility that also provides aftercare. Aftercare can help prevent relapses, but the additional time away from work may result in a more costly commitment. Which program is more efficient? The coordinator's judgment of efficiency may be more a reflection of personal preference than of "objective" evidence. It is much easier to measure effectiveness than efficiency, for there is much more consensus about the criteria relevant to effectiveness. Shain and Groeneveld (1980) stated that effectiveness is judged by two common measures: penetration rates and success rates. As was indicated in the last section, measures of success are inconsistent across studies and are fraught with other methodological and definitional problems. Still, many respected researchers agree that EAPs deserve credit for producing positive results (e.g., Jerrell & Rightmyer, 1982; Sonnenstuhl & Trice, 1986). Thus, this section will concentrate on penetration rate.

Penetration rate is defined as the degree to which an EAP actually reached the total number of workers in need of assistance. Put in formula form, it is:

$$\frac{\text{\# workers utilizing EAP}}{\text{\# troubled workers}}$$

The problem with this statistical measure is that it is difficult to know to any degree of certainty how many troubled workers there actually are in any given company. This problem is more severe within the broad-brush approach. As Albert et al. (1985) pointed out, with a strictly alcohol emphasis, EAP researchers at least have some general guidelines they can follow to estimate the extent of the problem for a given company. Within the context of a broad-brush EAP approach, it is almost impossible to estimate the number of troubled employees with any precision.

Perhaps because of the difficulty in measuring penetration rates, it is a statistic rarely kept by EAPs. Korr and Ruez (1986) sent surveys to 25 EAPs randomly selected from a list of programs registered in Illinois. Nineteen of the 25 surveys were returned. Among the items in the survey was a question about penetration rates. Only five of the 19 programs kept this statistic, and only one of these programs conformed to the standard use of the term. Even this program inflated its figures by using the number of referrals in the numerator of the equation as opposed to the number of actual utilizers of the service.

Shain and Goeneveld (1980) reported that penetration rates are disappointingly low in practice, estimating the true range to be from .1 to 1.5%. Therefore, even if EAPs perform perfectly--if every single worker involved in the program becomes maximally productive once again--the companies are increasing their overall productivity by only a small amount. In order for EAPs to be considered truly effective in increasing companies' productivity levels and provide humanitarian assistance to those in need, EAPs need to find a way to more effectively penetrate the troubled worker population. No segment of this population has been less penetrated than the white-collar worker. It is this segment to which we now turn.

WHITE-COLLAR RESISTANCE TO EAPs

Unquestionably, white-collar workers[3] underutilize EAP services (Jerrell & Rightmyer, 1982; Schramm, Mandell, & Archer, 1978; Shain & Groeneveld, 1980; Shirley, 1985; Trice, 1962; Trice & Beyer, 1977; Virgil, 1986). Although many have discussed this problem, few have carried out empirical studies on the topic. Trice and his colleagues are notable exceptions (e.g., Trice, 1962; Trice & Beyer, 1977).

Trice and Beyer (1977) examined 71 Federal Civil Service installations employing over 50 individuals. All installations had a formal alcoholism program. They categorized workers into six different skill levels, which was equated with higher status levels within groups of employees. Consistent with their predictions, there was an inverse relation between job status and the probability of utilizing EAP services. The authors divided these findings into two broad classes of interpretations: (1) low-status drinkers tend to be more visible in the workplace, and (2) alcoholism policies tend to be more vigorously applied to lower-status employees.

Visibility

According to Trice and Beyer (1977), lower-status employees tend to be more open in their discussion of their drinking behaviors than higher-status workers. Lower-status problem drinkers tend to get drunk with their fellow employees, whereas higher-status problem drinkers tend to drink "normally" when around co-workers, getting drunk when alone, or at least away from their colleagues. The authors also note that many mental health studies suggest that lower socio-economic status (SES) individuals are more susceptible to mental health problems, so it may well be that lower-status workers do have a higher prevalence of alcoholism. We view this latter interpretation with caution, for lower SES individuals have a range of problems fundamentally different from those problems lower-status individuals might face. Still, it is a hypothesis worthy of further examination.

Vigorous Application

Alcoholism policies may be more vigorously applied to lower-status employees for two separate but interrelated reasons. The first is that it is easier for higher-status employees to cover up their alcoholism due to the nature of their positions. The second reason deals with social distance and relative power.

Cover-up. Trice and Beyer note that lower-status employees tend to be absent after drinking episodes. This spotlights their drinking behavior and also provides supervisors with objective evidence of job deterioration. On the other hand, higher-status employees tend to show up at work regardless of their condition after drinking episodes. This is known as "on-the-job absenteeism" and is possible because of the nebulous way in which many higher-status jobs are defined. On-the-job absenteeism is also a convenient way one can deny one's drinking problem. "Failure to appear would spotlight the executive, whereas physical presence acts to deny deviant behavior and thus slows down its detection" (p. 60). Besides latitude of performance for executives, their jobs tend to be more cyclical in nature. What this does is allow the executive to cover up past mistakes during the next cycle. In contrast, lower-level jobs tend to require alertness that can be impaired by hang-overs and on-the-job drinking. This is immediately detectable, especially if some form of accident occurs as a result. Because on-the-job accidents are almost nonexistent for executives, this cannot be a measure for detection. Also, higher-status drinkers are able to cover up on-the-job drinking or on-the-job absenteeism because they have more privacy. Not only do higher-status employees tend to have their own offices, but they are quite often able to set their own work schedule and have other similar freedoms.

Another form of cover-up comes from the immediate subordinates of higher-status drinkers. This is done either for benign reasons, such as the sense that "loyalty" means that one should make one's boss "look good," or the cover-up could be for manipulative reasons, such as gaining power for oneself. The flip side of this argument is that the higher-status drinkers "traded off a large measure of their power and authority for the protection they received from their trusted lieutenants" (Trice & Beyer, 1977, p. 61). Regardless of the motivations of the subordinates assisting in the cover-up of the problem, they may be considered to be codependents of the problem (Cermak, 1986). Codependency is a term gaining wider usage in the substance abuse literature. It is applied mainly to family members who help the substance abusers to maintain their disorder. However, the term is gaining expanding usage (Gierymski & Williams, 1986) and is being applied to close friends and associates who are also helping substance abusers maintain their disorder.

Social Distance. Trice and Beyer (1977) suggest that it is difficult to confront higher-status drinkers because of the loss of social distance. In the work setting, the major difference in status is between labor and management. Thus, it is easier for management to confront labor with drinking problems due to the inherent distance between the two levels. However, even if an individual is supervising a manager and is clearly higher in status, there is psychologically less social distance between these two individuals, so there are impediments to confrontation. Also, if a supervisor or manager is confronted by a higher-status individual, there are more avenues for him/her to equalize the power relationship by bringing in an advocate of equal or higher power as the confronter. Supervisors of higher status employees tended to harbor attitudes of resolving problems informally and among themselves rather than to use company policies. Part of the reason for this is due to the perceived low pay-offs for the policy. As Trice and Beyer indicated, these supervisors saw EAP policies as unwanted irritants. There were few organizational rewards and many potential problems. In comparison, supervisors of lower-status workers expressed none of the concerns of their higher-status counterparts. In fact, they seemed to have a readiness to observe misconduct among their supervisees. Rather than seeing few organizational rewards, they saw many rewards. These rewards included proving themselves to their superiors and furthering their organizational advancement.

A View from the Other Side

Clearly, it is more difficult to detect and to confront white-collar alcoholism and, by extension, other mental health related problems. However, there are indications that those with problems would welcome a helping hand. Shirley (1985) individually interviewed 25 top executives who had undergone treatment for alcohol while holding their executive positions (vice president or above). All subjects in the study had been recovered for at least one year at the time of the interview. All had been in the late stages of alcoholism when they entered recovery (e.g., 23 had tremors, all had blackouts, and 23 had serious family problems). As has been previously discussed, productivity measures were useless for detecting concurrent alcoholism of top executives. Shirley concluded that the alcoholism prevented "stunning" performance by these individuals, partly on the basis of assumptions about alcoholism and partly based upon the fact that 15 of the 25 subjects immediately advanced their careers after recovery (many of the others had already been at the top, despite their alcoholism). All reported that they believed others viewed their performance as acceptable, despite the feeling that they themselves sensed they were slipping. Bosses tended to cover up or excuse the subjects' drinking.

The most striking findings in the Shirley study dealt with the duration these executives lived with their alcoholism. On average, about 10 years passed between the time that subjects acquired some awareness of alcohol problems and actual seeking out of help. They reported that they would have been open to receiving help seven years before they actually received help (on average), but they did not pursue assistance because they either lacked knowledge of alcoholism or of the types of treatments available. For example, one of the executives said that his condition got so bad that he went to the public library, desperately seeking information on alcoholism. Since he fit every criterion for the disorder, he diagnosed himself as an alcoholic and immediately joined Alcoholics Anonymous. He claimed that he would have sought treatment eight years prior to his library trip if only he would have known about what alcoholism really was. None of the executives found treatment through EAPs, but this is a misleading statistic, since only three worked for companies that had an EAP in place at the time.

Suggestions for Increasing White-collar Penetration

Quite often, white-collar workers help shape the vision of companies. Therefore, it would benefit companies to ensure that visions are not clouded by the bottoms of glasses.

Suggestions for increasing white-collar penetration fall into two general categories: training and prevention. Trice and Beyer (1977) recommend that supervisors of higher-status employees be trained in establishing social distance between themselves and employees. In this way, it would be easier to confront the employees, should drinking become a problem. We would also urge that the training include the process by which higher-status employees attempt to cover up their problems, especially by seeking the assistance of high-status advocates. If all are aware of the seriousness of the alcoholism problem and the difficulties involved in confronting higher-status employees, then various managers and supervisors will be less-likely defenders of alcoholics and more-likely advocates for their recovery.

In terms of prevention, Shain and Groeneveld (1980) suggest that companies institute health and life-style programs. Within the context of such exercise and fitness activities, health-related classes can be introduced in a nonthreatening environment. Emphasis can be placed upon maximizing one's potential rather than minimizing one's losses. This stance is consistent with Virgil's (1986) recommendation of cooperation between EAPs and organizational development programs. Organizational development programs assist companies in anticipated changes in organizational programming and structure. These programs have a natural emphasis on growth and productivity. In a cooperative manner, organizational development programs and EAPs can help one another achieve their goals by increasing productivity through lifting constraints.

SUMMARY

The number of EAPs has been rapidly increasing since 1970. Part of this increase may be attributed to the EAP shift in emphasis from its alcohol roots to a more general mental health emphasis. However, with this broader emphasis comes more complex problems of ethics and implementation. This complexity has added to the difficulties in conducting adequate research. Among the most difficult of research problems is the notion of penetration rates. The limited statistics available indicate that the vast majority of those in need of services do not take advantage of the EAPs. Moreover, white-collar workers are the most elusive of populations into which EAPs penetrate. We suggest two general approaches for increasing white-collar utilization of EAPs. One approach emphasizes training of supervisors to maintain social distance from their supervisees. The other approach emphasizes prevention by encouraging participation in health and life-style programs. In this manner, education and detection can take place in a nonthreatening environment.

FOOTNOTES

1. Sonnenstuhl and Trice also acknowledge this point. Their historical review was designed to broaden the understanding most people have of the momentum of the EAP movement . Nearly every article on EAPs limit the background understanding to the Occupational Alcohol Movement.

2. All supervisory vignettes throughout this chapter are based upon actual supervisory experiences of the authors. To preserve confidentiality, identifying information has been deleted or changed.

3. We will be using "white-collar workers," "executives," and "higher-status individuals" as interchangeable terms in this section.

REFERENCES

Albert, W. C., Smythe, R. C., & Brook, R. C. (1985). Promises to keep:
An evaluator's perspective on employee assistance programs.
Evaluation and Program Planning, 8, 175-182.

Blum, K. (1984). Handbook of abusable drugs. New York: Gardner Press.

Brandes, S. D. (1970). American welfare capitalism. Chicago: University
of Chicago Press.

Briar, K. H., & Vinet, M. (1985). Ethical questions concerning an EAP:
Who is the client? (Company or individual?) In S. H. Klarreich, J. L.
Prancek, & C. E. Moore (Eds.), The human resources management
handbook: Principles and practice of employee assistance programs
(pp. 342-359). New York: Praeger Publishers.

Cermak, T. L. (1986). Diagnostic criteria for codependency. Journal of
Psychoactive Drugs, 18, 15-20.

Edwards, D. W. (1975). The evaluation of troubled-employee and
occupational programs. In R. L. Williams & G. H. Moffat (Eds.),
Occupational alcoholism programs (pp. 40-135). Springfield, IL:
Charles C. Thomas.

Ford, J. D., & Ford, J. C. (1986). A systems theory analysis of employee
assistance programs. Employee Assistance Quarterly, 2, 37-48.

Franz, J. B. (1986). Referral-making: A key EAP skill. Employee
Assistance Quarterly, 2, 1-10.

Gierymski, T., & Williams, T. (1986). Codependency. Journal of
Psychoactive Drugs, 18, 7-13.

Good, R. K. (1986). Employee assistance: A critique of three corporate
drug abuse policies. Personnel Journal, 65, 96-101.

Croeneveld, J., Shain, M., Brayshaw, D., Keaney, J., & Laird, L. (1985).
Cost effectiveness of EAP: Testing assumptions. Employee Assistance
Quarterly, 1, 75-87.

Heyman, M. (1976). Referral to alcoholism programs in industry:
Coercion, confrontation and choice. Journal of Studies on Alcohol,
37, 900-908.

Heyman, M. (1978). Alcoholism programs in industry. New Brunswick, NJ:
Publications Division, Rutgers Center for Alcohol Studies.

Hoffman, E., & Roman, P. L. (1984). Effects of supervisory style and
experientially based frames of reference on organizational alcoholism
programs. Journal of Studies on Alcohol, 45, 260-267.

Jerrell, J. M., & Rightmyer, J. F. (1982). Evaluating employee assistance
programs: A review of methods, outcomes, and future directions.
Evaluation and Program Planning, 5, 255-267.

Korr, W. S., & Ruez, J. F. (1986). How employee assistance programs
determine service utilization: A survey and recommendations.
Evaluation and Program Planning, 9, 367-371.

Lesser, J. G., & Cavaseno, V. H. (1986). Establishing a hospital's employee assistance program. Health & Social Work, 11, 126-132.

Manuso, J. S. J. (1983). (Ed.). Occupational clinical psychology. New York: Praeger Publishers.

Miller, R. E. (1986). EAP research then and now. Employee Assistance Quarterly, 2, 49-86.

Putnam, S. L., & Stout, R. L. (1985). Evaluating employee assistance policy in an HMO-based alcoholism project. Evaluation and Program Planning, 8, 183-194.

Quayle, D. (1985). American productivity: The devastating effect of alcoholism and drug abuse. In J. F. Dickman, W. G. Emener, Jr., & W. S. Hutchison, Jr. (Eds.), Counseling the troubled person in industry: A guide to the organization, implementation, and evaluation of employee assistance programs (pp. 2-29). Springfield, IL: Charles C. Thomas.

Rinella, V. (1986). Ethical issues and psychiatric cost-containment strategies. International Journal of Law and Psychiatry, 9, 125-136.

Roethlisberger, F., & Dickson, W. J. (1939). Management and the worker. Cambridge, MA: Harvard University Press.

Schramm, C. J., Mandell, W., & Archer, J. (1978). Workers who drink: Their treatment in an industrial setting. Lexington, MA: D. C. Heath and Company.

Shain, M., & Groeneveld, J. (1980). Employee assistance programs: Philosophy, theory, and practice. Lexington, MA: D. C. Heath and Company.

Shain, M., Suurvali, H., & Boutilier, M. (1986). Healthier workers: Health promotion and employee assistance programs. Lexington, MA: D. C. Heath and Company.

Shirley, C. E. (1985). TOPEX study: "Hitting bottom in high places." In S. H. Klarreich, J. L. Francek, & C. E. Moore (Eds.), The human resources management handbook: Principles and practice of employee assistance programs (pp. 360-369). New York: Praeger Publishers.

Sonnenstuhl, W. J., & Trice, H. M. (1986). Strategies for employee assistance programs: The crucial balance. Key Issues: Background reports on current topics and trends in labor-managements, No. 30. Ithaca, NY: Cornell University Press.

Trice, H. M. (1962). Alcoholism in industry: Modern procedures. New York: Christopher D. Smithers Foundation.

Trice, H. M., & Beyer, J. M. (1977). Differential use of an alcoholism policy in federal organizations by skill level of employees. In C. J. Schramm (Ed.), Alcoholism and its treatment in industry (pp. 44-68). Baltimore: The Johns Hopkins University Press.

Trice, H. M., & Beyer, J. M. (1984). Work-related outcomes of the constructive-confrontation strategy in a job-based alcoholism program. Journal of Studies on Alcohol, 45, 393-404.

Virgil, L. D. (1986). The EAP movement and organizational development: Working together for mutual benefit. Employee Assistance Quarterly, 1, 35-48.

Wrich, J. T. (1980). The employee assistance program. Minneapolis: Hazelden Foundation.

STRESS AND PERFORMANCE IN NURSING: IMPLICATIONS FOR PRODUCTIVITY

Nora P. Reilly

Washington State University
Pullman, Washington

James P. Clevenger

Colorado State University
Fort Collins, Colorado

Like other white collar professionals, nurses provide a service that is difficult to perform and difficult to evaluate. A nurse's "output" is often intangible, and is wrought with other measurement problems. It varies by hospital or department. It varies by patient. It varies by nurse. To make matters worse, the Department of Labor has identified hospital nursing as one of the more stressful occupations (McLean, 1974). In this chapter, we will illustrate some of the organizatonal variables related to stress in nursing, present some of our own relevant data, and discuss implications of these for the measurement and improvement of productivity in the nursing profession. First, however, a brief review of the empirical work on occupational stress is in order.

Occupational Stress

Although we recognize the lack of consensus in defining stresses and strains (see Holt, 1982; Schuler, 1980), stress may be said to occur when there is an imbalance, either real or perceived, between the environmental demands and the response capability of the individual. Occupational stress, therefore, refers to this imbalance resulting from job-related demands and abilities. Personnel conflicts, administrative problems, emotional overload, inappropriate procedures, frustration with medical limitations, and morbid experiences are just some of the frequently cited stressors reported by hospital nurses (Yancik, 1984). Several studies (Bailey, 1979, 1980; Maloney, 1982; Steffen & Bailey, 1979; Yancik, 1984) have found that a major source of stress arises from working with terminally ill and dying patients. Not surprisingly, this kind of stress is exacerbated when a patient dies after the nurse formed emotional attachments to the patient or family. Price and Bergen (1976) and Hirsch and David (1983) also found that nurses suffered distress from over-identification with the patient or family, as well as irrational feelings of responsibility for patient conditions and feelings of helplessness for patient care. Hirsch and David (1983) contend that the characteristics of a nurse's responsibilities make hospital nursing stressful in distinct ways. For example, nurses may value providing emotional support for patients, but doing so takes time away from performing an overload of required tasks. In addition, administrative policies may actually constrain a nurse's performance and, potentially, prevent the nurse from performing activities that would otherwise enrich his or her job experience. Although there are data that suggest that nurses know what they are getting themselves into when they choose a career in nursing (cf. Green, 1988), we would argue that "knowing" about potential stressors is not the same thing as experiencing them. The following narrative from Hirsch and David (1983) illustrates that the stress in nursing is not only created by the work itself but, also, by organizational processes and policies.

> They were assigned too many patients, making
> the work day a constant whirl of attending to
> routine nursing care, punctuated by the necessity
> to deal with emergency situations. Identification
> with particular work groups or patients was
> hampered in many hospitals by policies which
> required frequent rotating shifts (day, swing,
> nights), floating back and forth between different
> treatment units, and assignments to different
> patients from day to day. Tensions obviously
> existed in physician-nurse relationships and
> at times nurses felt they had to implement
> treatment plans they did not consider in the
> best interests of the patients. (p. 496)

Common Predictors of Occupational Stress

The preceding narrative presents a panorama of research-relevant ideas. In fact, many of the traditional independent variables, dependent measures, and moderators of occupational stress are described. Holt (1982) divides independent variables in stress research into "objectively" defined and "subjectively" defined stressors, with the distinction being whether the researcher defines a stressful stimulus (an objective stressor) or the person being stressed does so (a subjective stressor). A sample of some of objectively defined stressors directly applicable to a hospital nursing environment is presented in the top of Table 1. For the record, we should note that other classifications of stress are also relevant. For example, Brief, Schuler, and Van Sell (1981) have categorized the independent variables typically used in stress research into four types: personal characteristics, interpersonal factors, task properties, and organizational variables. The latter two categories − task properties and organizational variables − correspond well with Holt's (1982) "objective" stressors.

Research on subjectively defined stressors is dominated by a role relations perspective (cf. Hardy & Conway, 1978) and this perspective parallels the "interpersonal factors" category proposed by Brief et al. (1981). Representative subjective stressors are listed in the bottom of Table 1. It is readily argued, of course, that an individuals' perceptions of stress must, by definition, be a subjective matter. Both perceptions of and reactions to stress are highly individualistic and it is the individual's perception of stress, rather than its objective existence, which ultimately serves as the most valid independent variable in stress research. For example, Lazarus and his colleagues (e.g., Folkman & Lazarus, 1980; Lazarus & Opton, 1966) have proposed that it is an individual's primary cognitive appraisal of a potentially stressful stimulus that determines whether a given stimulus is perceived as stressful.

Table 1. Objective and subjective stressors

Objective Stressors	Representative Studies
Nonstandard working hours	Theorell, 1974
Time pressure	Gladstein & Reilly, 1983
Length of time in work position	Freudenberger, 1977
Administrative "red tape"	Cummings & DeCotiis, 1973
Work load and overload	Kahn, 1973
Responsibility	Cobb, 1973
Departmental membership	Parasuraman & Alutto, 1981
Pay and prestige	House, 1972
Lateral job change and promotion	Freudenberger, 1977
Poor labor-management relations	Colligan & Murphy, 1979

Subjective Stressors	Representative Studies
Role ambiguity and role conflict	Kahn, 1973; Kahn, Wolfe, Snoek, & Rosenthal, 1964
Role strain	MacKinnon, 1978
Perceived control over work events	Frankenhauser & Gardell, 1976
Feedback and communication	Moch, Bartunek, & Brass, 1979
Responsibility for people	Caplan et al., 1975
Participation	Caplan et al., 1975
Inadequate supervisor support or performance	Pearse, 1977
Supervisor and coworker relationships	Theorell, 1974

Moderators of Occupational Stress

The majority of the aforementioned studies are correlational in nature, thereby occluding distinctions among independent, moderator, and dependent variables. With this in mind, we chose to classify Brief et al.'s (1981) "personal characteristics" category as a moderator rather than an independent variable. As is often the case with complex relationships, much organizational stress research has focused upon "moderator" variables, those predictors which suggest that people differentially experience stress under some conditions but not others. Moderator variables provide the opportunity to test if the relationship between the perception and experience of stress is curvilinear rather than linear or, perhaps, indirect rather than direct. Thus, moderator variables allow for more realistic and less simplistic explanations. It is reasonable to assume that the "fit" between an individual's personality or abilities and the demands of the job would greatly contribute to explaining the magnitude of experienced stress (Gaines & Jermier, 1983).

Moderator variables can be classified into those emanating from "within the person" (i.e., individual difference and personality variables) and those existing external to the person (situational, environmental, or contextual variables). A representative sample of these is presented in Table 2. Particularly important among the variables listed are attachment to the organization and commitment. In fact, the relationship among stress, commitment, and productivity is as yet undetermined but is theoretically critical for organizational effectiveness (Cherniss, 1980; Farber, 1983). We will discuss this relationship at length in a later section. In addition, moderator variables have often been described as serving as "buffers" against stress

Table 2. Moderators of stress

Intra-Individual Moderators	Representative Studies
Sex (gender)	Maslach & Jackson, 1981b
Marital status	Reilly & Clevenger, 1988
Age	Rosse & Rosse, 1981
Stage of life	Kellam, 1974
Type A behavior pattern	Motowidlo, Packard, & Manning, 1986
Self-esteem	London & Klimoski, 1975
Neuroticism	Gulian, 1974; Kahn, 1973
Depressive tendencies	Mott, et al., 1965
Machiavellianism	Gemmill & Heisler, 1972
Locus of control	Lefcourt, Miller, Ware, & Sherk, 1982
Flexibility-rigidity	Kahn, 1973
Attachment to the organization	Porter & Dubin, 1975
Attachment to work	O'Reilly & Chatman, 1986
Organizational or job commitment	O'Reilly & Chatman, 1986 Mowday, Steers, & Porter, 1977

External Moderators	Representative Studies
Coworker social support	Caplan et al., 1975 Cobb, 1976
Supervisor social support	Caplan et al., 1975 Reilly & Clevenger, 1988
Formal control of work responsibilities	Gemmill & Heisler, 1972
Group cohesiveness	Beehr, 1976
Organizational climate	James & Jones, 1974
Organizational structure	Ivancevich & Donnelly, 1975

(e.g., Beehr & Newman, 1978; Ganster, Fusilier, & Mayes, 1986; LaRocco, House, & French, 1980). However, Holt (1982) reports the use of moderating variables as being unreliable due to many failures to replicate existing effects in the literature (see also Kaufmann & Beehr, 1986). Given the lack of convergent definitions and the dissimilar methods of analysis used in a variety of organizational settings, unreliability is not surprising.

Measures of Occupational Stress

Common dependent variables in occupational stress research may be roughly divided into physiological/physical illness and behavioral/social with behavioral/social measures occurring at each of the individual and group or organizational levels of analysis. Given our interest in organizational variables and service, the physiological/physical illness measures (e.g., blood pressure, electrocardiogram, GSR, cholesterol level, EMG, etc.) are of less utility than those which are behavioral/social in nature and we refer you to Caplan et al. (1975), Cooper and Marshall (1976), and Holt (1982) for an overview of them. Behavioral and social dependent variables are both diverse and extensive, as Table 3 illustrates.

A potential by-product of working in a high stress profession like nursing is "burnout" (Farber, 1983; Maslach & Jackson, 1981a). As one of the buzzwords in occupational stress research for over a decade, the phenomenon is gaining empirical support. The term "burnout" was

Table 3. Measures of stress

Individual Measures	Representative Studies
Rate of smoking; caffeine intake	Caplan et al., 1975
Use of drugs or alcohol or other counterproductive behaviors	Lederer, 1973
	Mangione & Quinn, 1975
Accidents and errors	Theorell, 1974
Depression	Ilfeld, 1977
Burnout	Maslach & Jackson, 1981a & b
Frequency and intensity of stressful events	Motowidlo, Packard, & Manning, 1986
Subjective perceptions of stress	Jayaratne & Chess, 1988
	Maloney, 1982

Group or Organizational Measures	Representative Studies
Absenteeism	Beehr & Newman, 1978
	Cohen, 1980
Turnover	Porter & Steers, 1973
	Price & Mueller, 1981

originated by Freudenberger (1974, 1975) to describe the state of
emotional and physical depletion produced by conditions at work in the
human service professions. Technically, burnout may be better described
as a stress-induced condition rather than as a dependent measure, but we
have chosen to describe it here for pragmatic reasons.

According to Farber (1983), stress is unavoidable in the helping
professions but the constructs of "stress" and "burnout" are not identical
(except, perhaps, for similarities in the fuzziness of domain). Burnout
is the result of unmediated stress, of being stressed over time and having
"no way out," no support systems, no buffers, no escape. The last stage
of Selye's (1956, 1976) classic General Adaptation Syndrome is the
precursor to the modern definition of burnout. Selye's syndrome proceeds
in stages from an alarm reaction, to resistance, and then to exhaustion.
Exhaustion marks the point at which one can no longer cope; the cumulative
effects of negative stressors have become too severe to allow for
adaptation. Maslach and her colleagues (e.g., Maslach & Jackson, 1981a &
b, 1984; Pines & Aronson, 1981) have popularized and extended this
description of exhaustion. Maslach (1976) considers burnout to be a
process rather than a reaction to a single event. She has proposed that
burned out professionals become less idealistic, are more frequently late
or absent for work, demonstrate a deterioration in performance and "lose
all concern, all emotional feelings for the persons they work with and
come to treat them in detached and even dehumanized ways" (Maslach, 1976).
Research on burnout has focused almost exclusively on human service
workers such as educators, nurses, physicians, lawyers, social workers,
and police officers (see Perlman & Hartman, 1982, for a review) because of
the constant demands made upon these professionals to help others in need.

Maslach and Jackson (1981a, 1984) have proposed that burnout has
three loosely related components. The first is emotional exhaustion, the
pivotal burnout dimension. Emotional exhaustion results from the
excessive psychological and emotional demands made of professionals whose
work is very involving. The demands for peak performance never stop,
eventually draining the energy needed to continue interacting with clients
at the same level of intensity. Note that this depth of involvement
implies a high state of arousal which differentiates emotional exhaustion
from a state of fatigue produced in occupations whose demands are better

characterized by tedium. The second component of burnout is
depersonalization, which refers to treating people like objects, and
exhibiting a detachment more similar to callousness and cynicism than to
that of a "professional distance." For example, always referring to
patients by room number or diagnosis (e.g., "the liver in room 337 is
acting up again...") rather than name may indicate too little concern or,
perhaps, an overly mechanized demeanor serving to reduce personal
involvement well beyond the point which professionalism requires.
Feelings of low personal accomplishment, the third component of burnout,
is an empirically derived dimension characterized by feelings of
inefficacy and a greater likelihood to "quit trying." It is a form of
self-devaluation which has serious motivational implications for
performance. It has been suggested that the process of burnout begins
with emotional exhaustion, a chronic feeling resulting from unrelenting
stressors in a highly involving occupation, and the later stages of
depersonalization and lack of personal accomplishment develop both as a
reaction to and coping mechanism for emotional exhaustion (Gaines &
Jermier, 1983).

The Maslach Burnout Inventory, or MBI (Maslach & Jackson, 1981a), is
a psychometric instrument designed to assess each of the three dimensions
of burnout via separate subscales. MBI items typical of emotional
exhaustion, depersonalization, and feelings of low personal accomplishment
include "I feel emotionally drained from my work," "I feel I treat some
patients as if they were impersonal objects," and "I feel I'm positively
influencing other people's lives through my work" (reverse scored),
respectively. Use of the MBI is growing (Farber, 1983; Jackson, Schwab, &
Schuler, 1986) and it has demonstrated adequate evidence of convergent and
discriminant validity, as well as acceptable internal consistency
reliabilities (Maslach & Jackson, 1981a & b).

Organizational Psychology's Contribution to the Study of Nursing Stress

Our brief review of predictors, moderators, and measures of
occupational stress is representative, though certainly not exhaustive, of
general approaches taken in stress research. The majority of variables we
presented could be applicable to any number of white collar occupations.
Indeed, stress research specific to impaired physicians (Mawardi, 1983),
lawyers (Jackson, Turner, & Brief, 1987), and corporate executives (Ahmad
et al., 1985) explored various subsets of these variables. Our next
objective is to highlight empirical evidence of organizational variables
related to stress in nursing professionals.

Price and Mueller (1981) have constructed a tentative causal model of
turnover in nurses. Turnover was defined, as is typical, as voluntarily
leaving the organization or hospital. Their model was based on a
longitudinal study using over 1,000 nurses from seven hospitals as
subjects. Their initial review of the literature suggested that there are
at least 11 variables that have been used to explain turnover in one way
or another. These variables were integration, pay, distributive justice,
routinization, participation, promotional opportunity, professionalism,
general training, kinship responsibility, and opportunity. In addition to
these, job satisfaction and intent to stay served as hypothetical
intervening variables. (Definitions of these terms appear in Price and
Mueller, 1981, pp. 545-546. Operationalizations of each term were survey
items originally presented in Price and Bluedorn, 1979, with Cronbach's
alphas reported as no less than .83 for each subscale, as reported in
Price and Mueller.) The first seven variables listed above were thought
to indirectly affect turnover through job satisfaction, the next three
variables' impact on turnover was supposedly filtered through nurses'

intent to stay, and only the last variable, opportunity (the availability of alternative jobs), was thought to be directly linked to turnover.

Before we discuss which of these variables seemed to actually make a difference, we would like to point out three specific things about the Price and Mueller (1981) study that interested us. First, the authors narrowed the number of variables to those that were potentially explanatory, rather than simply predictive. In other words, various demographic variables, such as those described earlier as commonly used in stress research, were not used in the model because they did not explicate the process through which variations in turnover occurred. Price and Mueller demonstrate this point via a description of "age" as a predictor. Price (1977) cites a strong relationship between turnover and age whereby turnover is greater among younger rather than older nurses. They suggest that perhaps this is because the jobs of younger nurses are typically more routine, the younger nurses have less knowledge about their profession, less participation in decision making, and lower pay. They claim that "it is not age per se that produces variations in turnover but routinization, participation,... (and) pay..., all of which are correlated with age." (p. 548) In short, Price and Mueller promoted greater construct parsimony and reduced problems associated with multicollinearity in an area commonly overrun with interrelated variables. If one wishes to design interventions based on significant predictors of turnover, it is considerably easier to manipulate variables like pay, amount of participation in decisions, and job tedium than it is to change someone's age.

Our second interest was the authors' attempt to integrate existing models, again narrowing the number as opposed to the scope of extant constructs related to variations in turnover. Finally, our third interest revolved around the sheer number of subjects: their sample consisted of 1,091 non-supervisory registered nurses. Any reasonable relationships observed in a sample of such breadth deserve serious regard. Although Price and Mueller were not expressly interested in the effects of perceived stress on turnover, the relationship between some of their variables and stress or negative affect is obvious. Importantly, they introduced "intent to stay" as an intervening variable in their proposed model. "Intent to stay" has been viewed as one dimension of commitment (see Mowday, Porter, & Steers, 1982; Reichers, 1985) and commitment has been shown to be significantly and negatively related to turnover (Mobley, 1977; Mobley, Griffith, Hand, & Meglino, 1979). In fact, of the 13 total variables Price and Mueller chose to study, intent to stay had the largest zero-order correlation with turnover (r = -.404). In addition, Reilly et al., (1988) recently found evidence of significant negative relationships between various measures of perceived stress (notably, emotional exhaustion) and commitment.

After refining their mass of data through path analyses, Price and Mueller concluded that turnover was most affected by four determinants: intent to stay, opportunity, general training, and job satisfaction. The total effects, or sum of both the direct and indirect effects (see Pedhazur, 1982), of each of these four variables on turnover were -.37, .15, .11, and -.09, respectively. In sum: (1) job satisfaction had no significant net influence on turnover but mediated among five of the other variables and turnover, (2) general training and opportunity had both direct and indirect effects on turnover, and (3) intent to stay had the largest total impact on turnover. Their results support previous research involving these variables. For example, Mowday, Porter, and their colleagues (see Mowday et al., 1982, for a summary) suggest that commitment is more important than job satisfaction in explaining turnover. Mobley and his colleagues (1977, 1979) have claimed that job satisfaction indirectly affects turnover through commitment, and Hrebiniak and Alutto (1971) have found that both job tension and job satisfaction are significant static predictors of commitment.

Having established a legitimate interest in the role of commitment, further examination of the literature on satisfaction and commitment revealed somewhat contradictory results. Bateman and Strasser (1984) conducted a longitudinal study and cross-lagged analysis of the antecedents of organizational commitment. They employed some 13 variables as possible predictors of commitment for the 129 nurses from four hospitals who participated. The non-demographic predictors were leader reward and punishment behaviors, job characteristics, centralization, need for achievement, environmental alternatives, job tension, and job satisfaction. The dependent variable was commitment. Each of these variables was assessed at Time 1 and then five months later at Time 2. Job tension, job satisfaction, and environmental alternatives were of greatest interest to us as potential predictors of commitment and each of these was measured by fairly traditional instruments used in industrial and organizational psychology. Job tension was measured by the Job Related Tension Scale developed by Kahn et al. (1964). Satisfaction was measured by Smith, Kendall, and Hulin's (1969) Job Descriptive Index. Environmental alternatives were assessed via a three item subscale on the chances of finding, desirability, and comparison level of acceptable alternative jobs. Commitment was tapped by the Organizational Commitment Questionnaire (Porter et al., 1974; Mowday et al., 1982). We noted that, although the internal consistency of these measures was acceptable (Cronbach's alphas ranged from .58 to .90), the test-retest reliabilities only ranged from .53 to .68.

We examined Bateman and Strasser's (1984) data with an eye toward supporting or refuting the relationships found in Price and Mueller's (1981) study. Although static correlations of job tension at Time 1 were significantly related to satisfaction ($\underline{r}$ = -.46) and commitment ($\underline{r}$ = -.38) at Time 2, the time-lagged multiple regression analyses suggested that none of the predictors emerged as being antecedent to organizational commitment. Instead, Bateman and Strasser's evidence indicates that overall satisfaction is not a cause of commitment but, rather, a result of it. The authors concluded that their set of variables predicted job satisfaction much better than they predicted subsequent commitment, although job satisfaction and employment alternatives accounted for the most variance in their commitment measure. Their results also suggest that commitment may not necessarily result from, nor simultaneously occur with, job satisfaction. Instead, organizational commitment may be just one of the many possible causes of job satisfaction.

Jackson et al. (1986) cite low correlations between the MBI and job dissatisfaction whereas Farber (1983) has reviewed a literature which suggests that, not only do high levels of job satisfaction coexist with high levels of burnout, a high level of commitment may be a required condition for burnout to occur. Indeed, some individuals may be more susceptible to burnout than others. For example, Bloch (1977) claims that teachers who are more idealistic and dedicated to their work are more prone to burnout. In addition, Motowidlo, Packard, and Manning (1986) report that nurses with Type A behavior patterns and nurses with a greater fear of negative evaluation report stronger feelings of stress regardless of actual exposure to stressful events. Our interpretation of the various anecdotal descriptions of burnout in a variety of professions is that it is the most involved, caring, and idealistic individuals who will succumb to it. Although it is unclear whether individuals with burnout-prone personality characteristics tend to select service professions in the first place, involved and idealistic employees "are the ones for whom a discrepancy between effort and results matters the most." (Farber, 1983; p. 9)

Interestingly, a closer examination of the study by Jackson et al. (1986) inadvertently lends a good deal of support for the anecdotes connecting burnout and commitment. Their intention was to examine burnout's relationship with unmet employee expectations and job conditions in a sample of 248 elementary and secondary school teachers. Six consequences of burnout were hypothesized: a change in preference of job type, increased thoughts about leaving the job, increased job search behaviors, training for a new occupation, intentions to leave the job or occupation, and voluntarily leaving the job. Assessment of virtually all of these potential consequences employed measures typically used to indicate changes in job or organizational commitment (Mowday et al., 1982; Scholl, 1981). Using the subscale scores of the MBI as predictors, Jackson et al. reported significant relationships (primarily with emotional exhaustion) with thoughts of leaving the job, actually leaving the job, and receiving training for a new career. Although the design of Jackson et al.'s study limits our ability to draw causal conclusions, the fact that relationships were observed between time-lagged measures taken a year apart provides a great deal of face validity for stress as a motivation for organizational withdrawal behaviors in a human service profession.

What do we know now? We know that stress affects performance, we know that stress can develop into a state of burnout, and we know that burnout proceeds through different stages, which can have strong deleterious effects on work behaviors. We know that constructs reflecting stress and commitment are related. Studies have shown that commitment is related to a number of work behaviors, including turnover, absenteeism, employment alternative and job search behaviors, and even performance effectiveness (Angle & Perry, 1981; Marsh & Mannari, 1977; Porter et al., 1982). Interestingly, commitment is also related to a number of variables previously identified as subjective and objective stressors, such as job characteristics, autonomy, responsibility, role conflict and ambiguity, and personal characteristics of the employee (Hall & Schneider, 1972; Jackson et al., 1986; Koch & Steers, 1978; Morris & Koch, 1979; O'Reilly & Caldwell, 1981). Yet, we do not exactly know what commitment is, just that it has gained strength as an explanatory variable in a number of job stress-related studies. Our next goal, then, is to elaborate on views of commitment so that we may integrate them into a discussion of problems and directions in the study of stress and productivity in nursing.

The Value of Commitment

The past decade has seen a sharp increase in the study of organizational commitment (Mowday et al., 1982; O'Reilly & Chatman, 1986; Reichers, 1985), along with an explosion of commitment related constructs and measures. Morrow (1983) has warned against an unjustifiable proliferation of constructs and measures related to commitment when the theoretical domain of the construct has not been empirically verified. However, there is some consistency in the belief that increased commitment aids organizational effectiveness and, therefore, that developing organizational commitment is a good thing to do.

But what is commitment? One broad perspective is that commitment is an attitude that has both performance and membership implications. Employees identify with and internalize the goals of the organization (O'Reilly & Chatman, 1986); they exert greater effort because of this identification and, likewise, report stronger intentions to remain with the organization. Scholl (1981) identifies the antecedents of these

intentions as personal characteristics, job characteristics, and positive
work experiences. Presumably, positive work experiences create an
affective attachment to the organization; employees work because the
nature of the work itself is rewarding. Steers (1977) reports the
outcomes as increased performance, reduced absenteeism, and reduced
turnover. The best known proponents of this view of commitment are
Mowday, Porter, and Steers (1982, see also Porter, Steers, Mowday, &
Boulian, 1974). An alternative view of commitment is based on the
membership criterion, but not the performance criterion. Initiated by the
work of Becker (1960) and partially validated in studies by Meyer and
Allen (1984) and McGee and Ford (1987), commitment is a force which
motivates membership in a organization due to extraneous interests
provided by continued membership. These "extraneous" interests may
include investments such as the accrual of benefits, higher pay, intact
social circles, longer vacation periods, and, perhaps, an office with a
window. Becker's (1960) "side-bet" theory of commitment promoted this
primarily behavioral orientation toward the continuance of organizational
membership.

Mowday, Porter, and Steers (1982) suggested that commitment develops
and changes over the course of an employee's career. An employee may
first pass through the "pre-entry" stage of commitment, during which the
anticipation and expectations of the future position affect organizational
attachment. Initial determinants of organizational commitment are largely
the characteristics of the person and the job. The former may, perhaps,
be controlled through selection techniques. The next stage of commitment
is the early employment stage. Again, person and job characteristics come
into play, but Salancik (1977) suggests that factors such as work groups,
supervision, and pay will enhance feelings of commitment during this
initiation period by increasing the felt responsibility of the employee to
the organization. Alternatively, the availability of employment
alternatives may detract from positive attitudes toward the organization
and, consequently, commitment. Mowday and McDade (1980) have found that
commitment levels of new hires stabilize rather rapidly, and that the
first few months are likely to be critical for continued attachment. In
fact, Dalme (1983) has found that new nurses change from a professional or
service orientation to a more bureaucratic orientation during the first
few months of employment (see also Corwin & Taves, 1962; Green, 1988).
Wanous (1980) suggests that employees who will terminate are more likely
to do so in the first six to twelve months. We would also like to call
attention to the study previously described by Jackson et al. (1986).
Their proposition was that unmet expectations should lead to feelings of
burnout. Finally, long-term employment appears to be a strong influence
on entrenchment, the third stage of commitment. Length of service
increases the likelihood of higher pay, more interesting assignments, and
greater autonomy and responsibility. The investments the employee has
made over time are likely to maintain commitment. The accrual of
benefits, the sacrifice or potential loss of benefits, intact social
circles, and, perhaps, a decrease in alternative employment opportunities
may all serve to enhance organizational commitment.

As mentioned earlier, the past decade or so has seen over twenty-five
new constructs and measures of commitment (see Morrow, 1983; Reichers,
1985). Porter, Steers, Mowday, and Boulian (1974) developed the most
widely known instrument - the Organizational Commitment Questionnaire.
This fifteen item scale provides a summary index of commitment which taps
identification with the organization and an affective commitment to pursue
the organizations' goals. Unfortunately, it does not distinguish between
stages of commitment, as described above. A lesser known scale with
acceptable psychometric properties has been developed by Meyer and Allen
(1984) and refined by MeGee and Ford (1987). McGee and Ford have

identified "affective" and "continuance" commitment, dimensions more directly reflective of the theoretical development of commitment over a career. Affective commitment was empirically demonstrated to be undimensional but continuance commitment was further divided into two distinct subscales: continuance commitment for low alternatives and continuance commitment for high sacrifice. As the names imply, the first of these is based on the employee's perception of few existing employment alternatives and the second is based on perceptions of personal sacrifice associated with leaving the organization. In fact, Becker's (1960) "side-bet theory" of commitment embodies the latter form of continuance commitment, an attachment to the organization based on extraneous interests.

Let us now clarify our motives. Do the theoretical processes of burnout and commitment covary? Can we observe systematic differences in these relationships over the course of a career? Researchers in the area of stress and burnout in the human service professions have made consistent reference to the particularly harsh effects of stressors on the more "committed" or "involved" employees. Cherniss (1980) argues that there is a publicly held "professional mystique" surrounding service professionals such as nurses, teachers, and social workers. It is believed that they are satisfied with their jobs, having worked so hard to attain them, are compassionate and idealistic, and work with responsive clients. The incoming professionals buy into this mystique and reinforced by it. "Inevitably, though, this mystique clashes with the reality of bureaucratic constraints and work-related stresses, ultimately culminating in disillusionment and burnout." (Farber, 1983, p. 13).

Reilly, Clevenger, and Ikeda (1988) conducted a pilot study to explore the proposed linkages between stress, burnout, and organizational commitment in a sample of practicing hospital nurses. We believed that successfully establishing an empirical link, even if self-report in nature, would justify a more detailed examination of changes in stress and commitment over the career span. Specifically, we hypothesized that the relationship between nursing stress measures and burnout should be visible when examining patterns of correlations between the two in nurses at different stages of their careers. Burnout should be progressively related to stress measures. We also planned to explore patterns of correlations between burnout or stress measures and indices of commitment in nurses at different stages of their careers. Shifts in relationships may not be detectable through static correlations made without regard to career stage. Stress or burnout and commitment may not be correlated across an entire sample but may be evident at different career stages, lending credence to the developmental nature of both.

Fifty-two usable surveys were returned from an initial distribution of 263. Various data were missing in the usable surveys, producing variable Ns for analyses. Demographic information on respondents showed that all respondents were female, eight different departments or units were represented, 67% of the sample worked 35 or more hours per week, and the average tenure (total time working as a nurse at any hospital) was approximately 12 years. Unfortunately, respondents' tenure ranged from 21 months to over 25 years; we were therefore unable to examine the theoretically critical initiation stage of commitment. Nonetheless, we divided our small sample into 5 progressive "career stages" by dividing a cumulative frequency distribution into relatively equal parts. Based on this, Stage 1 subjects averaged just under 5 years working as a nurse, Stage 2 subjects averaged 8 years, Stage 3 averaged 11 years, Stage 4 averaged 16 years, and Stage 5 subjects averaged almost 25 years working as a nurse. These stages were determined solely by the natural clustering and dispersion of the data.

We employed the three subscales of the MBI as indices of
burnout - emotional exhaustion, depersonalization, and low personal
accomplishment - and obtained subscale values comparable to those reported
by Maslach and Jackson (1981a). Subscales were coded such that high
scores are indicative of high emotional exhaustion, greater
depersonalization, and lower personal accomplishment. Forty-five
stressful events specific to hospital nursing (see Motowidlo et al., 1986,
Study 1) were presented to subjects. Subjects provided a frequency rating
(1=never to 5=fairly often (daily)) and an intensity rating (1=not at all
stressful to 5=extremely stressful) for each event. These were summed to
form a "frequency index" and an "intensity" index, respectively. We then
multiplied the frequency and intensity rating for each event and summed
those values, producing a "frequency x intensity" index. Finally, we used
a four item scale of subjective perceptions of stress (called "subjective
stress"), as in Motowidlo et al. (1986) Study 2. A sample item was "I
feel a great deal of stress because of my job." Items were rated on a 5
point agreement/disagreement scale. These items were coded and summed so
that the higher the score, the greater the perceived stress. Our
frequency and subjective stress indices were comparable to those found by
Motowidlo et al. (1986).

We employed the previously mentioned commitment scale developed by
McGee and Ford (1987), which incorporated separate dimensions of affective
and continuance commitment. An affective commitment subscale consisted of
8 items, a form of continuance commitment based on perceptions of low
employment alternatives was tapped by 3 items, and a form of continuance
commitment based on loss of accumulated investments or "high sacrifice"
was assessed by 3 items. Items were rated on a 5 point scale ranging from
(1) strongly agree to (3) unsure to (5) strongly disagree. Items were
coded such that the higher the score, the greater the affective
commitment, the lower the perceived alternatives, and the greater the
personal sacrifice for each of the subscales, respectively.

We also recorded various demographic measures. Notably, length of
time in nursing and number of hours worked per week were recorded for each
subject. Tenure in nursing was assessed to determine if the relationships
between stress, burnout, and commitment changed over time. Hours worked
per week was assessed to explore if perceptions of stress, burnout, and
commitment changed over time in the absence of objective changes in the
amount of work at different career stages.

Pearson product-moment correlations between the four stress measures
(frequency x intensity, frequency, intensity, and subjective stress
indices) and the three subscales of the MBI (emotional exhaustion,
depersonalization, and low personal accomplishment) were conducted on the
full sample. (However, our N per analysis varied between 46 to 52 due to
missing data. In addition, all reported alpha levels are two-tailed.)
Emotional exhaustion was significantly (range of rs: .37 to .57; all
alpha levels < .01) and positively correlated with the four stress indices.
Depersonalization was significantly (range rs: .35 to .50; all alpha
levels < .05) and positively correlated with all stress measures but
frequency, and low personal accomplishment was only marginally (r = .24,
p. <10) correlated with intensity.

As expected, indices of stress were highly related to indices of
burnout. However, the more interesting question was whether the
relationship between stress and burnout seemed to systematically change at
different career stages. We then correlated the stress indices with the
burnout subscales at each of the 5 separate "career stages" described
earlier. Given that each career stage had only about 10 representatives,
we fully recognized that these analyses could only be exploratory and

inconclusive, we wanted to search for patterns, not test if correlations were different. Although only suggestive, the patterns of results support the idea that burnout develops over time. Emotional exhaustion seemed to gain strength in its relation to frequency x intensity and frequency over the different career stages. In fact, tenure in nursing (months as nurse) was differentially related to emotional exhaustion at different career stages. Although the frequency of stressors may remain relatively constant over time, feelings of burnout become increasingly associated with reports of stressors. Depersonalization seemed to be more consistently related to the stress indices over time, though nurses in Stage 5 do not show any relationship between depersonalization and subjective stress (r = .11) and are the only group for whom tenure in nursing and depersonalization significantly and negatively covaried (r = -.67, p <.05). This may be a result of self-selection: only the nurses more able to cope stayed in the field. Correlations between low personal accomplishment and the frequency x intensity and frequency indices of stress suggest a possible shift in relationship between feelings of accomplishment and the frequency of stressors at some point in mid-career. However, intensity seemed to steadily increase the strength of its relationship with feelings of low personal accomplishment over time. Finally, the moderate but nonsignificant relationship (r = -.52) between tenure and low personal accomplishment at Stage 1 may reflect initial stages of changes in feelings of accomplishment when compared to the later stages. Overall, we think these results support the conception of burnout as a developing "process." A lack of method variance may account for some of the significant relationships observed for the total sample. "Method variance" is a technique in which researchers employ a variety of measures (e.g., paper and pencil, observational, physiological) to ensure that systematic relationships were not obtained purely because of similarities in the way in which the different variables were measured. However, we think this is a less plausible explanation because of the observed changes in the patterns of correlations for individuals at different stages in their careers.

Our next set of analyses compared the indices of stress and burnout with the subscales of commitment. Affective commitment was found to be significantly and negatively correlated with subjective stress (r = -.32, p <.05), but not with other stress or burnout indices when examined for the total sample. The correlations between feelings of low personal accomplishment and continuance commitment for low alternatives (r = -.30, p <.05) and between depersonalization and continuance for high sacrifice (r = .35), p .01) were the only other significant relationship observed when correlations were performed on the total sample. We would like to note that each of the commitment subscales was significantly related to a different subscale of the MBI; feelings of burnout and commitment do systematically covary in our sample. Again, lack of method variance is a possible explanation, although the specificity of the correlations with different subscales argues otherwise. Replications and appropriate tests of significance are clearly in order before conclusions should be drawn.

An examination of the correlations performed at each of the career stages again suggested interesting but inconclusive patterns. Most of the correlations associated with affective commitment suggested that stress and burnout were inversely related to affective commitment regardless of career stage. However, the pattern of correlations between affective commitment and feelings of low personal accomplishment appear to change direction and gain strength with career tenure, producing a significant negative relationship (r = -.78, p <.01) between the two at Stage 5. This could not have been detected from the correlation performed on the total sample. Although significant relationships exist with continuance commitment for low alternatives at different career stages, the only possible pattern we can detect is for the correlation with tenure at Stage 1 (r = .57, p < .10). Perhaps nurses at this stage recognize that they will have fewer alternatives the longer they stay in nursing. Different correlations with employment alternatives in the later stages may be a result of an early self-selection out of the profession. Of course, any single significant or near significant correlation can simply occur by chance. Finally, we observed some striking relationships between the frequency measures of stress and continuance commitment based on high sacrifice. Relationships changed from being negative and strongly significant in the earlier career stages to positive and strongly significant in the later stages. These could not have been detected from the correlation on the total sample. We interpret this pattern as follows: a nurse in an early career stage finds that, as the number of stressful events and daily hassles increases, she/he feels less committed because his/her "side-bets" in investments are not yet worth much. The direction of this relationship changes later in a career because of sacrifice of investments would be too costly; an increase in stressful events reminds the long-term employee that he/she must be committed in order to justify putting up with the hassles.

A final and more parsimonious explanation for all reported relationships involving a change in direction from early to late career stages is simple attrition. The more committed nurses "stuck it out." The less committed ones were more susceptible to stressors (see Motowidlo et al., 1986) in the first place and were more likely to leave the profession. This explanation begs the questions of when and how this presumed attrition occurred.

We have presented data which suggests that stress does indeed develop into a state of "burnout." We believe we have demonstrated that stress, burnout, and commitment are related, for whatever reasons. We have found that persons who report being more committed also report feeling less stressed, regardless of career stage. Theoretically, the role of unmet expectations is related both to commitment (Scholl, 1981) and burnout (Jackson et al., 1981). Though there appears to be some imperfect but discernible inverse relationship between commitment and burnout, the studies available to us thusfar have only established that some global construct "X" is associated with another global construct "Y". We would now like to discuss in some detail the set of studies by Motowidlo et al. (1986) which had been conducted to describe the relationship between occupational stress and performance. Fortunately for us, these researchers chose hospital nursing as their "stressful occupation." We will use these studies to initiate a discussion of the measurement of performance in nursing.

Stress and Performance in Nursing

Using samples of nurses, Motowidlo, Packard, and Manning (1986) conducted a set of studies exploring the relationship between occupational stress, its antecedent variables, and job performance in a hospital setting. They proposed that subjective stressors lead to negative affective states which, in turn, decrease job performance and that the stress is caused by specific work events. Their rationale comes from Cohen's (1980) review of the literature on the aftereffects of stress on social behavior. Although the processes through which stress effects occurred were somewhat speculative, Cohen supported the idea that common stressors such as noise, bureaucratic frustration, and workload "sap energy" needed for task performance. This loss of energy creates a performance decrement on tasks which require greater attention or are more readily frustrating. In addition, stressors such as those described above adversely affect interpersonal sensitivity as evidenced by more aggressive and less prosocial behaviors, a description highly suggestive of Maslach and Jackson's (1981) depersonalization stage in the development of burnout. Although Motowidlo et al. were not interested in nurses per se, we believe that their extension of Cohen's model to stress and performance in a nursing population serves as an excellent springboard for new and useful ideas on how to measure threats to productivity in nursing.

Motowidlo et al. sensibly proposed that some stressors - the more frequent and intense ones - are more likely to cause stress than others (see Caspi, Bolger, & Eckenrode, 1987) and that these stressors must be empirically identified for different jobs. Cherniss (1980) has also implored burnout researchers to examine specific stressors for specific jobs held by specific individuals. Although earlier research exploring how some constructs were or were not associated with other constructs was theoretically useful, a direct application of what a given construct means for a particular job may be much more illuminating.

The first of Motowidlo et al.'s two studies went about the task of identifying specific stressors for hospital nurses. One hundred four nurses from different clinical areas and hospitals participated in small group discussions to produce 608 descriptions of stressful incidents on the job. This larger set of descriptions was then reduced to 82 incidents to account for similarities and redundancies. A separate sample of 96 practicing, non-supervisory nurses, again from different hospitals, rated each of these items on their frequency of occurrence using a five-point scale ranging from "never" to "fairly often" along with a variety of other subjective stress measures. The subjective stress measures were combined into a composite and the composite was correlated with each of the 82 stressful events. The component stress index correlated at .20 or better with 45 of the stressful events. Examples of the final items were "You fall behind in your regular duties because you have extra work that is not part of your daily routine," "A patient complains to you about the food or other things not under your control," and "You disagree with the patient care ordered by a doctor." The correlations of each of these with the composite stress index were .42, .37, and .25, respectively, and the average intercorrelation between the 45 stressful events and the composite stress index was approximately .28.

Although individual correlations between stressful events and the composite stress score accounted for less than nine percent of the variance, on the average, and it is likely that the reported frequencies of stressful events are themselves intercorrelated, the approach taken by Motowidlo and his colleagues represents a realistic and potentially diagnostic approach to the measurement of stress for a specific occupation. Research by Folkman and her colleagues (e.g., DeLongis, Coyne, Dakof, Folkman, & Lazarus, 1982) has demonstrated that "daily hassles" are significant predictors of negative affect, more so than major life events. Motowidlo et al. have more objectively created a list of the daily hassles particular to hospital nursing. We (Reilly & Clevenger, 1988; Reilly et al., 1988) have already used the 45 stressors produced by Motowidlo et al. and can attest that at least seven of the stressful events occurred almost daily in two separate samples of nurses.

Motowidlo et al.'s second study pursued the proposition that nurses who experience stressful events more frequently and with greater intensity are more stressed and, consequently, less effective at their jobs. We have good news and bad news about this study. The bad news is that their precision in measurement reverted back to a more global assessment of performance dimensions presumably related to effectiveness. The good news is that they assessed the performance dimensions of the nurses as seen through the eyes of coworkers and supervisors, not through self-report.

More specifically, Study 2 examined the relationships among work conditions, individual characteristics, subjective stress, dispositional affect, and job performance with the specific stressful events identified in Study 1.

Out of approximately twelve hundred possible respondents, 171 nurses from five different hospitals (different from those in the previous study) and at least seven different clinical areas participated in this "self-report plus cohort" survey. Subjects rated the frequency and intensity of stressful events on the job, their subjective perceptions of job stress, and their general affective state (i.e., hostility, anxiety, depression) over the past few months at work. They also provided information which identified their clinical area, years of nursing experience, propensity toward Type A behavior pattern (see Jenkins, Rosenman, & Zyzansky, 1974) and fear of negative evaluation (see Leary, 1983). Motowidlo et al.'s rationale for including this combination of variables was that, first, the frequency of stressful events was related to both individual characteristics and work conditions and, second, people with certain individual characteristics may behave in a way that influences the frequency with which stressful events occur. Performance ratings were provided by a supervisor and/or a coworker selected by the nurse. If both a supervisor and a coworker provided ratings for a given nurse, the average of their ratings was used as the performance measure. We note, however, that the interrater correlations only ranged from .31 to .47. Seven performance dimensions were assessed by the nurse's cohort(s): composure, quality of patient care, tolerance with patients, warmth toward other nurses, tolerance with nurses and doctors, interpersonal effectiveness, and cognitive/motivational effectiveness. The first five dimensions were the result of a factor analysis of a forty item questionnaire. Separate items were rated on a five point likelihood scale following the statement "If the opportunity arose, how likely is it that this nurse would...?" Examples of the items are "Become nervous or tired when working with a difficult or uncooperative patient?", "Explain nursing procedures to a patient before performing them?", "Become angry with an uncooperative patient?", "Try to help and support another nurse?" and "Argue with a doctor about a medical or nursing procedure?" for each of the first five performance dimensions, respectively. Although each of these dimensions had adequate internal consistency ratings (.70 to .92), we would point out that selection of items for subscales was determined "according to judgments about their content, guided by information about their factor loadings." (p. 621) In addition, the subscales have no proven reliability. The last two performance dimensions were determined from a separate factor analysis of nine point "behaviorally illustrated" rating scales. The "interpersonal effectiveness" dimension represented a composite score of items concerning personal warmth, morale, caring for uncooperative patients, teamwork, cooperation, and sensitivity to patients. The final dimension, labelled "cognitive/motivational effectiveness," was composed of items reflecting composure, concentration, perseverance, and adaptability. Not only do these last two dimensions appear highly related to each other, they are primarily composed of behaviors incorporated by the first five performance dimensions. In fact, Motowidlo et al. report intercorrelations between the seven performance dimensions ranging from .27 to .83, with a median of .54.

Motowidlo et al. then pursued a set of complicated path analyses, relating the self-report measures ("independent" variables) completed by the subjects with the performance measures ("dependent" variables) provided by the cohort(s). However, we believe that the low interrater reliabilities between the cohorts and the high intercorrelations among the seven performance dimensions make any such analyses suspect. Instead, a summary of some of the significant zero order correlations will be more useful for our purposes. With respect to the self-report measures, individual difference characteristics (Type A behavior pattern, fear of negative evaluation) were positively related to the perception, frequency, and intensity of stressful events. Measures of dispositional affect (hostility, anxiety, depression) were also related to the stress measures. However, "years of nursing experience" was related to affect (depression, in particular) but not to self-reported measures of stress. The results of Reilly et al. (1988) tentatively suggest that years of nursing experience may, in fact, be associated with perceptions of stress but that this may not become evident unless examined at the different career stages. Nurses' self-selection out of nursing over time may occlude real stress effects when "years of nursing" is not controlled for in some way. There may well be individual differences associated with those nurses who stay in the profession; somehow, they have the "right stuff." Finally, differing work conditions' (i.e., different clinical areas') relationships with the other "independent" variables were not reported.

Did any of these variables predict performance? Or, more appropriately, did any of these variables predict the cohorts' judgment that a given type of behavior was likely to occur? The highlights of these results were that the perception, frequency, and intensity of stressful events do seem to be significantly and negatively related to many of the performance dimensions. However, the range of values was rather small; significant correlations ranged from -.17 to -.30, whereas the nonsignificant correlations ranged from -.04 to -.15. Nonetheless, the direction of the relationships was appropriate, as a sign test would have indicated. The remaining analyses – those employing job and individual characteristics as predictors of performance – revealed scattered and unsystematic results (except for unexpectedly poor evaluations of emergency room nurses.)

Although we question whether true performance is being assessed at all in this study, we will accept that Motowidlo et al.'s data suggest relationships between affective variables and global evaluations of performance. We point to the following series of admittedly selective results. First, nursing experience is inversely related to depressive affect. Second, depressive affect and stress measures are positively related. Third, both stress and affect measures are inversely related to the performance dimensions. In addition, Fischer (1983) has posited that there are developmental similarities between emotional exhaustion and depression, and that the former may be mistaken for the latter because of commonalities in cognitive and behavioral dysfunctions. Therefore, this pattern of results can be interpreted, tentatively and inconclusively, as support of a developmental relationship between burnout and performance.

In support of Motowidlo et al.'s rather arbitrary choice of stress-related performance dimensions, Zedeck and Kafry (1977) report that empathy with and psychological support for patients constituted the most heavily weighted dimension of performance for a sample of nurses who were hypothetically evaluating "overall effectiveness" in their own profession. In addition, Zedeck and Kafry incorporated less affectively-laden dimensions of performance, such as clinical knowledge and performance, organizational ability, teaching ability, and communication skills. Arguably, all the dimensions suggested by Motowidlo et al. and by Zedeck and Kafry do reflect some kind of performance. But do they reflect actual nursing effectiveness? How can we estimate "overall effectiveness" for such an occupation?

At the beginning of this chapter, we stated that the output of nurses is often intangible and difficult to measure. This is where the study of occupational stress dovetails with the study of job or organizational productivity. More precisely, we should say that this is the point at which the difficulties of measurement of both stress and productivity or performance in nursing are most evident and most impactful. Relatively few organizational studies of this kind have been directed at the nursing population, but those which do exist provide evidence and direction for both stress reduction and productivity enhancement in the field. In our next section, we shall discuss the problems of assessing performance and improving productivity in nursing.

Performance and Productivity in Nursing

Although there is an obvious conceptual link between performance effectiveness and ultimate productivity, the complexity of the relationship makes it extremely difficult to operationalize and, therefore, measure. Is performance an input variable or an output variable? What performance dimensions need to be assessed to estimate productivity? In the case of hospital nursing, we can say that productivity itself refers to the value of the services provided (output) minus the cost of producing those services (input). Establishing definitions of the components in this typical productivity equation is particularly difficult for human service professions. Murphy (1988) states that the human influence on input and output variables is rarely equal. Depending on whether the industry under scrutiny is labor intensive or capital intensive, an optimal strategy for improving productivity may involve increasing the amount of goods and services produced or decreasing the overall costs of production. Nursing itself is labor intensive, but it must occur in a highly technological society which requires hospital administrations to be concerned about economic feasibility. Conflict occurs between individual nurse's professional emphasis on labor and the organization's necessary concern for capital.

For example, it may be that the conflict between a professional and a service orientation which newly hired nurses seem to experience (Corwin & Taves, 1962; Dalme, 1983) is readily tied to a struggle between a view of the practice of nursing as the fulfillment of a set of professional ideals versus a view that sees the practice of nursing as just one facet in the operation of a business. This is not to suggest that administrative views of nursing do not consider the value of professional ideals. However, we must acknowledge that professional ideals may be compromised in the service of maintaining the very existence of the overall organization. We do not yet know whether indices of nursing performance differ when comparing traditional non-profit health organizations to the more recent profit-oriented hospitals. The fact that both types of hospitals are still service organizations does not change. However, the implications for motivation and subsequent performance might. Organizational psychology has yet to tell whether any changes in nursing have occurred, and only then whether any such changes will be for better or worse.

Notwithstanding potential differences resulting from health organization ideologies, we have still not determined what performance is. Performance itself is multifaceted, and may be defined differently depending on the context in which an individual works. An adequate assessment of performance dimensions in nursing may require consideration of the tasks required of nurses in different clinical areas, a weighting of the importance of those tasks, a weighting of the difficulty of those tasks, and perhaps even a weighting of the noxiousness of those tasks. Cherniss (1980) has suggested that we need to identify specific stressors for specific jobs. Must we also identify the difficulty and importance of stress-related tasks? As we have discussed at length, Motowidlo et al. (1986) were generally successful with the former (specificity of stressful

events) but not the latter. They examined some of the nursing performance
domain by having hospital cohorts evaluate performance-related tasks and
hypothetical performance situations. General nursing tasks and situations
were grouped together into performance dimensions such as "quality of
patient care" and "interpersonal effectiveness." Unfortunately, not only
were these tasks not specific to different clinical areas, the authors did
not consider how the combination of dimensions could influence performance
and productivity. We are unsure as to whether the specificity of task
assessment or the interaction among performance dimensions is more
important. When we evaluate overall performance, is the whole more than
the sum of its parts?

The performance literature does in fact demonstrate that task
performance is not equivalent to job performance. For example, Murphy
(1988) claims that observations of work behavior suggest that workers
spend relatively little time performing what would be regarded as "tasks."
Campbell, Dunnette, Lawler, and Weick (1970) also report that evaluations
of the daily behaviors of managers are not directly linked to the tasks
they have performed. Such observations have interesting implications for
criterion development of the appropriate dimensions for evaluating nursing
(and other types of job) performance. The job performance domain, which
includes turnover, absenteeism, dependability, and motivation, is
perceived as broader than the task performance domain. We can again ask
whether a nurse's performance should be defined in terms of behaviors or
the results of those behaviors. Clearly, both process and outcome are
important in this job, and both process and outcome need to be assessed
separately and in combination. We cannot systematically improve
performance and productivity if we cannot adequately operationalize them.

Wilson, Prescott, and Aleksandrowicz (1988) claim that there are
three major cost components associated with hospital nursing: nursing
intensity, tangible nursing costs (i.e., supplies, equipment, time) and
hospital organizational factors. It is critical to note that an accurate
appraisal of these components depends upon two obvious conditions. First,
patients must be assigned an optimal choice of therapy and, second,
efficient performance depends upon the compliance of the patient. A nurse
must constantly adapt to meet the demands of changing conditions.
Therefore, an appraisal of nursing performance must reflect this
fluctuation in environmental conditions. We believe that the frequency
and intensity of stressful events, as described in Motowidlo et al.
(1986), constitute a major deterrent to both performance and the appraisal
of performance. At the organizational level, interventions may be
introduced that decrease the objective occurrence of stressful events. At
the individual level, interventions may be introduced that enhance
commitment to the organization and the job. Murphy (1988) states that
employee identification with the organization is one of the keys to higher
productivity and that, in order to design effective interventions, using
ones which increase worker commitment to and identification with the
organization would seem most promising. We agree.

What sort of interventions might improve productivity in nursing?
Katzell and Guzzo (1983) discuss the impact of psychologically based
interventions, many of which, we note, are ultimately motivational
techniques. They reviewed 207 productivity experiments to find that 87%
of them showed improvement in at least one area of productivity after an
intervention program was employed. The programs included recruitment and
selection, training and instruction, appraisal and feedback, goal setting,
financial compensation, work redesign, supervisory methods, organizational
structure, decision-making techniques, work scheduling and sociotechnical
systems redesign. Their outcome measures were classified as "output,"
"withdrawal," and "disruption." Output measures included those of

quantity and quality of production and of cost effectiveness. Withdrawal measures consisted primarily of absenteeism and turnover. "Disruptions" included accidents, strikes, and other costly disturbances. Guzzo, Jette, and Katzell (1985) followed up their own review with a meta-analysis (see Glass, McGaw, & Smith, 1981) of the success of the intervention programs on the three outcome measures. Although the studies described were primarily conducted in non-"service" organizations (e.g., manufacturing industries), 37 of the 330 effects which were analyzed involved non-profit, educational, or health service organizations. Despite the fact that we cannot disentangle effects particular to health service organizations from the overall analyses, we find it promising that the greatest effect sizes (i.e., impacts) on outcome measures were for training, goal setting, and decision-making strategies. In addition, productivity criteria also showed the greatest effect sizes for "disruptions." If we allow a liberal interpretation of how "disruptions" can be operationalized in a hospital setting, we would argue that the deleterious effects of stress and burnout could easily fall into this category of outcomes. If this is the case, we find it very promising that stress-reduction interventions can and will make a difference.

Katzell and Guzzo (1983) and Guzzo et al. (1985) also discuss the various costs associated with productivity improvement programs. Financial costs primarily involve time, at least over the short term. Non-financial costs may include changes in the worker, changes in the work method, and changes in the relationships between organizational levels. We would argue that these three categories of costs simply represent the potential hazards of the three categories which actually represent productivity interventions, i.e., changes in the worker, changes in the work method, and changes in the relationships between organizational levels.

Changing the nature of the worker may be accomplished in a few ways, such as thorough training and continuing education of experienced nurses and the recruitment, selection, and training of new employees. Promoting commitment to and identification with the organization is a critical goal at the time of organizational entry. Continued efforts toward maintaining commitment with experienced nurses can only be accomplished in a reciprocal exchange with the organization. That is, the organization must sincerely demonstrate that it deserves its employees' commitment and must view the expenses associated with such demonstrations as capital investments. In addition, we suspect that there are different characteristics of nurses who "stick it out" and remain in the field for a longer time (Reilly et al., 1988). We need to identify, study, and possibly attempt to manipulate those individual characteristics.

Changing the work method may involve work redesign, work load adjustments, flexible scheduling, participation in decision making, and clarification of work objectives. Indeed, defining a set of attainable goals and the behaviors required to meet those goals should decrease role ambiguity and, consequently, decrease stress. "Attainable" is the key word here. Our review of nursing stressors indicates that nurses often have impossible workloads, with constant interruptions, and that this is the norm for the profession. In addition, we know that the choice of patient therapy and the compliance of the patient are unpredictable. All of these factors involve externally imposed restrictions on the sense of control of the nurse. Cohen's (1980) review of the stress literature suggests that interventions enhancing personal control and stressor predictability were most effective in reducing feelings of stress. As we have stated, identifying and managing controllable stressors should enhance productivity.

Finally, changes in the relationships between organizational levels may be accomplished through adjustments of supervisory methods, appraisal and feedback procedures, organizational structure, and equitable financial compensation. There are organizational procedures which can serve to reduce stress, improve commitment, and alleviate the "reality shock" often experienced by new hires. Nursing managers and supervisors need adequate training in <u>management</u> techniques - good nurses do not necessarily make good managers. Appraisal and feedback systems can be structured in a less threatening, more cooperative format which includes feedback on a job well done. Nursing research and training specialists can facilitate interventions which include changes in the worker and changes in the work method. Finally, health service organizations can establish policies which prioritize investments in their "human service professionals."

General Implications for the Effects of Stress on White Collar Productivity
-----

We have shown that stress adversely affects performance across a number of dimensions, but that estimating productivity - or the loss of productivity - from performance information is a difficult task. Nonetheless, productivity can be improved in a wide variety of organizational settings. Katzell and Guzzo (1983) and Guzzo et al. (1985) provide evidence that psychological interventions designed to enhance productivity have the greatest effect for a class of outcome measures called "disruptions." In turn, we believe that stressful incidents that occur in the workplace can be classified as disruptions and, therefore, that interventions designed to alleviate stress should also improve productivity. Interventions may be directed toward changing the worker, changing the work method, or changing the way in which individuals at different organizational levels interact with each other. The potential to "change the worker" is of particular interest to us in that the nurturance of commitment in an employee has considerable anecdotal evidence - and some growing empirical evidence - to support its positive role in improving performance effectiveness and productivity.

The general principle that the reduction of stress will improve performance assumes some interesting preconditions. First, we are really referring to the reduction of extreme, unnecessary, and harmful arousal produced by stress. Given the well known inverted "U" relationship between arousal and performance, we need to maintain some optimal level of arousal for peak performance. Therefore, we are only trying to control "negative" stressors. Theoretically, stressors may be either negative or positive, and the arousal produced either by arguing with a belligerent patient or successfully treating a cooperative patient with complicated procedures may be the same. The problem with controlling arousal in many white collar professions is the uncontrollable nature of potential stressors, such as getting caught between conflicting organizational roles or dealing with a noncompliant client. Second, we must measure stress and performance in ways which allow for interventions. Reports of <u>specific</u> stressful incidents for <u>specific</u> occupations must serve as the basis for successful intervention. We cannot fix that which we cannot identify. In addition, there are measurement problems associated with performance, in general. Job performance is more than just the sum of the specific tasks in which an individual engages. Both the means of achieving and the end result of job tasks need to be identified, and we must learn how to balance specificity and dimensionality in the assessment of a particular job. It takes time to find the right mix of "objective" criterion-referenced performance data and more "subjective" norm-referenced performance data to accurately evaluate job performance (see Landy & Farr, 1980) and, ultimately, productivity. Given the intangible nature of services provided by many white collar professionals, particularly those in the human services, much research is needed to attain these goals.

SUMMARY

In this chapter, we outlined some of the more common variables involved in the study of occupational stress and discussed how the construct of stress-induced "burnout" has come to characterize the human service professions. We focused on a particular white collar profession - hospital nursing - as a prime example. We then presented evidence for commitment as an organizational variable inextricably linked to stress and burnout in the human services. Finally, we illustrated how specific stressors may affect performance in nursing and discussed how various behavioral science interventions - changes in the worker, changes in the work method, and changes in organizational interaction - could reduce stress and improve productivity in nursing. Improvements in measurement techniques appear to be prerequisite for success.

REFERENCES

Ahmad, et al. (1985). A study of stress among executives. Journal of Personality and Clinical Studies, 1, 47-50.

Angle, H.L., & Perry, J.L. (1981). An empirical assessment of organizational commitment and organizational effectiveness. Administrative Science Quarterly, 26, 1-13.

Bailey, J.T. (1980). Stress management: An overview. Journal of Nursing Education, 191, 5-7.

Bateman, T.S., & Strasser, S. (1984). A longitudinal analysis of the antecedents of organizational commitment. Academy of Management Journal, 27, 95-112.

Becker, H.S. (1960). Notes on the concept of commitment. The American Journal of Sociology, 66, 32-42.

Beehr, T.A. (1976). Perceived situational moderators of the relationship between subjective role ambiguity and role strain. Journal of Applied Psychology, 61, 35-40.

Beehr, T.A., & Newman, J.E. (1978). Job stress, employee health, and organizational effectiveness: A facet analysis, model, and literature review. Personnel Psychology, 31, 665-699.

Bloch, A.M. (1977). The battered teacher. Today's Education, 66, 58-62.

Brief, A., Schuler, R., & VanSell, M. (1981). Managing job stress. Boston: Little, Brown.

Campbell, J.P., Dunnette, M.D., Lawler, E.E., III, & Weick, K.E., Jr. Managerial behavior, performance, and effectiveness. New York: McGraw-Hill.

Caplan, R.D., Cobb, S., French, J.R.P., Jr., Harrison, R.Y., & Pinneau, S.R., Jr. (1975). Job demands and worker health: Main effects and occupational differences. DHEW (NIOSH) publication no. 75-160. Washington D.C.: U.S. Government Printing Office.

Caspi, A., Bolger, N., & Eckenrode, J. (1987). Linking person and context in the daily stress process. Journal of Personality and Social Psychology, 52, 184-195.

Cherniss, C. (1980). Staff burnout: Job stress in the human services. Beverly Hills: Sage.

Cobb, S. (1973). Role responsibility: The differentiation of a concept. Occupational Mental Health, 3, 10-14.

Cobb, S. (1976). Social support as a moderator of life stress. Psychosomatic Medicine, 38, 300-314.

Cohen, S. (1980). Aftereffects of stress on human performance and social behavior: A review of research and theory. Psychological Bulletin, 88, 82-108.

Colligan, M.J., & Murphy, L.R. (1979). Mass psychogenic illness in organizations: An overview. Journal of Occupational Psychology, 52, 77-90.

Cooper, C.L., & Marshall, J. (1976). Occupational sources of stress: A review of the literature relating to coronary heart disease and mental ill health. Journal of Occupational Psychology, 49, 11-28.

Corwin, R.G., & Taves, M.J. (1962). Some concomitants of bureaucratic and professional conceptions of the nurse role. Nursing Research, 11, 223-227.

Cummings, L.L., & DeCotiis, T.A. (1973). Organizational correlates of perceived stress in a professional organization. Public Personnel Management, 2, 275-282.

Daley, M.R. (1979). Burnout: Smoldering problem in protective services. Social Work, 24, 375-379.

Dalme, F.C. (1983). Nursing students and the development of a professional identity. In N.L. Chaska (Ed.), The nursing profession: A time to speak. (pp. 134-145). New York: McGraw-Hill.

Delongis, A., Coyne, J.C., Dakof, G., Folkman, S., & Lazarus, R.S. (1982). Relationship of daily hassles, uplifts, and major life events to health status. Health Psychology, 1, 119-136.

Farber, B.A. (1983). Stress and burnout in the human service professions. New York: Pengamon Press.

Fischer, H.J. (1983). A psychoanalytic view of burnout. In B.A. Farber (Ed.), Stress and burnout in the human service professions. (pp. 40-45) New York: Pergamon Press.

Folkman, S., & Lazarus, R.S. (1980). An analysis of coping in a middle-aged community sample. Journal of Health and Social Behavior, 21, 219-239.

Frankenhauser, M., & Gardell, B. (1976). Underload and overload in working life: Outline of a multidisciplinary approach. Journal of Human Stress, 2, 35-46.

Freudenberger, H.J. (1974). Staff burnout. Journal of Social Issues, 30, 159-165.

Freudenberger, H.J. (1975). The staff burnout syndrome in alternative institutions. Psychotherapy: Theory, research and practice, 12, 73-82.

Freudenberger, H.J. (1977). Burnout: Occupational hazard of the child care worker. Child Care Quarterly, 6, 90-99.

Gaines, J., & Jermier, J.M. (1983). Emotional exhaustion in a high stress organization. Academy of Management Journal, 26, 567-586.

Ganster, D.C., Fusilier, M.R., & Mayes, B.T. (1986). Role of social support in the experience of stress at work. Journal of Applied Psychology, 71, 102-110.

Gemmill, R., & Heisler, W.G. (1972). Machiavellianism as a factor in managerial job strain, job satisfaction, and upward mobility. Academy of Management Journal, 15, 51-62.

Gladstein, D., & Reilly, N.P. (1983). Group decision making under threat: The Tycoon Game. Academy of Management Journal, 28, 613-627.

Glass, G.V., McGaw, B., & Smith, M.L. (1981). Meta-analysis in social research. Beverly Hills, CA: Sage.

Green, G.J. (1988). Relationships between role models and role perceptions of new graduate nurses. Nursing Research, 37, 245-248.

Guzzo, R.A., Jette, R.D., & Katzell, R.A. (1985). The effects of psychologically based intervention programs on worker productivity: A meta-analysis. Personnel Psychology, 38, 275-291.

Hall, D.T., & Schneider, B. (1972). Correlates of organizational identification as a function of career pattern and organizational type. Administrative Science Quarterly, 17, 340-350.

Hardy, M.E., & Conway, M.E. (1978). Role Theory: Perspective for health professionals. New York: Appleton-Century-Crofts.

Hirsch, B., & David, T. (1983). Social networks and work/nonwork life: Action research with nurse managers. American Journal of Community Psychology, 11, 493-507.

Holt, R.R. (1982). Occupational stress. In L. Goldberger & S. Breznitz (Eds.), Handbook of stress: Theoretical and clinical aspects, (pp. 419-444). New York: Free Press.

House, J.S. (1972). The relationship of intrinsic and extrinsic work motivations to occupational stress and coronary heart disease risk. Dissertation Abstracts International, 33(5A), 2514A.

Hrebiniak, L.G., & Alutto, J.G. (1972). Personal and role-related factors in the development of organizational commitment. Administrative Science Quarterly, 17, 555-573.

Ilfeld, F.W., Jr. (1977). Current social stressors and symptoms of depression. American Journal of Psychiatry, 134, 161-166.

Ivancevich, J.M. & Donnelly, J.H. (1975). Relation of organizational structure to job satisfaction, anxiety-stress, and performance. Administrative Science Quarterly, 20, 272-280.

Jackson, S.E., Schwab, R.L., & Schuler, R.S. (1986). Toward an understanding of the burnout phenomenon. Journal of Applied Psychology, 71, 630-640.

Jackson, S.E., Turner, J.A., & Brief, A.P. (1987). Correlates of burnout among public service lawyers. Journal of Occupational Behaviour, 5, 339-349.

James, L.R., & Jones, A.P. (1974). Organizational climate: A review of theory and research. Psychological Bulletin, 81, 1096-1112.

Jayaratne, S., & Chess, W.A. (1984). The effects of emotional support on perceived job stress and strain. The Journal of Applied Behavioral Science, 20, 141-153.

Jenkins, C.D., Rosenman, R.H., & Zyzanski, S.J. (1974). Prediction of clinical coronary heart disease by a test for the coronary-prone behavior pattern. New England Journal of Medicine, 23, 1271-1275.

Kahn, R.L. (1973). Conflict, ambiguity, and overload: Three elements in job stress. Occupational Mental Health, 3, 2-9.

Kahn, R.L., Wolfe, D.M., Quinn, R.P., Snoek, J.D., & Rosenthal, R.A. (1964). Organizational stress: Studies in role conflict and ambiguity. New York: Wiley.

Katzell, R.A., & Guzzo, R.A. (1983). Psychological approaches to productivity improvement. American Psychologist, 38, 468-472.

Kellam, S.G. (1974). Stressful life events and illness: A research area in need of conceptual development. In B.S. Dohrenwend & B.P. Dohrenwend (Eds.), Stressful life events: Their nature and effects. New York: Wiley.

Koch, J.D., & Steers, R.M. (1978). Job attachment, satisfaction, and turnover among public sector employees. Journal of Vocational Behavior, 12, 119-128.

LaRocco, J.M., House, J.S., & French, J.R.P. (1980). Social support, occupational stress and health. Journal of Health and Social Behavior, 21, 202-218.

Lazarus, R.S., & Opton, E.M. (1966). The study of psychological stress: A summary of theoretical formulations and experimental findings. In C.D. Speilberger (Eds.), Anxiety and behavior: Vol. 1. New York: Academic Press.

Leary, M.R. (1983). A brief version of the fear of negative evaluation scale. Personality and Social Psychology Bulletin, 9, 371-375.

Lederer, L.G. (1973). Psychologic and psychopathologic aspects of behavior during airline pilot transition training. Revue de Medicine Aeronatuque et Spatial (Paris), 12, 299-300.

Lefcourt, H.M., Miller, R.S., Ware, E.E. & Sherk, D. (1981). Locus of control as a modifier of the relationship between stressors and moods. Journal of Personality and Social Psychology, 41, 357-369.

MacKinnon, N.J. (1978). Role strain: An assessment of a measure and its invariance of factor structure across studies. Journal of Applied Psychology, 63, 321-328.

Maloney, J.P. (1982). Job stress and its consequences on a group of intensive care and non-intensive care nurses. Advances in Nursing Science, 4, 31-42.

Mangione, T.W., & Quinn, R.P. (1975). Job satisfaction, counterproductive behavior, and drug use at work. Journal of Applied Psychology, 60, 114-116.

Marsh, R.M., & Mannari, H. (1977). Organizational commitment and turnover: A prediction study. Administrative Science Quarterly, 22, 57-75.

Maslach, C. (1976). Burned out, Human Behavior, 5, 16-22.

Maslach, C., & Jackson, S.E. (1981a). The Maslach Burnout Inventory. Palo Alto, CA: Consulting Psychologists Press.

Maslach, C., & Jackson, S.E. (1981b). The measurement of experienced burnout. Journal of Occupational Behavior, 2, 99-113.

Maslach, C., & Jackson, S.E. (1984). Burnout in organizational settings. In S. Oskamp (Ed.), Applied social psychology annual: Vol. 5. Applications in organizational settings (pp. 133-154). Beverly Hills, CA: Sage.

Mawardi, B.H. (1983). Aspects of the impaired physcian. In B.A. Farber (Ed.). Stress and burnout in the human service professions. (pp. 119-128). New York: Pergamon Press

Meyer, J.P., & Allen, N.J. (1984). Testing the "side-bet theory" of organizational commitment: Some methodological considerations. Journal of Applied Psychology, 69, 372-378.

Mobley, W.H. (1977). Intermediate linkages in the relationship between job satisfaction and employee turnover. Journal of Applied Psychology, 62, 237-240.

Mobley, W.H., Griffeth, R.W., Hand, H.H., & Meglino, B.M. (1979). Review and conceptual analysis of the employee turnover process. Psychological Bulletin, 86, 493-522.

Moch, M.K., Bartunek, J., & Brass, D.J. (1979). Structure, task characteristics, and experienced role stress in organizations employing complex technology. Organizational Behavior and Human Performance, 24, 258-268.

Morris, J.H., & Koch, J.L. (1979). Impacts of role perceptions of organizational commitment, job involvement, and psychomatic illness among three vocational groupings. Journal of Vocational Behavior, 14, 88-101.

Morrow, P. (1983). Concept redundancy in organizational research: The case of work commitment. Academy of Management Review, 8, 486-500.

Motowidlo, S.J., Packard, J.S., & Manning, M.R. (1986). Occupational stress: Its causes and consequences for job performance. Journal of Applied Psychology, 71, 618-629.

Mott, P.E., Mann, F.C., McLouglin, Q., Warwick, D.P. (1965). Shift work: The social psychological consequences. Ann Arbor, University of Michigan Press.

Mowday, R., & McDade, T. (1980, August). The development of job attitudes, job perceptions, and withdrawal propensities during the early employment period. Papers presented at the 40th Annual Meeting of the Academy of Management, Detroit.

Mowday, R.T., Porter, L. & Steers, R.M. (1982). Employee-organization linkages: The psychology of commitment, absenteeism, and turnover. New York: Academic Press.

Mowday, R.T., Steers, R.M., & Porter, L.W. (1979). The measurement of organizational commitment. Journal of Vocational Behavior, 14, 224-247.

Murphy, K.R. (in press). Job performance and productivity. In K. Murphy and F. Saal (Eds.), Psychology in organizations: Integrating science and practice. Hillsdale, NJ: Erlbaum.

McGee, G.W., & Ford, R.C. (1987). Two (or more?) dimensions of organizational commitment: Reexamination of the affective and continuance commitment scales. Journal of Applied Psychology, 72, 638-642.

McLean, A. (1974). Occupational stress. Springfield, ILL: Charles C. Thomas, Publishers.

O'Reilly, C.A., & Caldwell, D.F. (1981). The commitment and job tenure of new employees: Some evidence of post-decisional justification. Administrative Science Quarterly, 26, 597-616.

O'Reilly, C., III, & Chatman, J. (1986). Organizational commitment and psychological attachment: The effects of compliance, identification, and internalization on prosocial behavior. Journal of Applied Psychology, 71, 492-499.

Parasuraman, S., & Alutto, J.A. (1981). An examination of the organizational antecedents of stressors at work. Academy of Management Journal, 24, 48-67.

Pearse, R. (1977). What managers think about their managerial careers. New York: American Management Association.

Pedhazur, E.J. (1982). Multiple regression in behavioral research (2nd ed.). New York: Holt, Rinehart, & Winston.

Perlman, B., & Hartman, E.A. (1982). Burnout: Summary and future research. Human Relations, 35, 283-305.

Pines, A., & Aronson, E. (1981). Burnout: From tedium to personal growth. New York: Free Press.

Porter, L.W., & Dubin, R. (1975). The organization and the person: Final report of the individual occupational linkages project. Washington, D.C.: U.S. Office of Naval Research.

Porter, L.W., & Steers, R.M. (1973). Organizational, work, and personal factors in employee turnover and absenteeism. Psychological Bulletin, 80, 151-176.

Porter, L.W., Steers, R.M., Mowday, R.T., & Boulian, P.V. (1974). Organizational commitment, job satisfaction, and turnover among psychiatric technicians. Journal of Applied Psychology, 5, 603-609.

Price, J.L. (1977). The study of turnover. Ames, IA: The Iowa State University Press.

Price, T., & Bergen, B. (1976). The relationship to death as a source of stress for nurses on a coronary care unit. Omega, 8, 229-237.

Price, J.L., & Bluedorn, A.C. (1979). Test of a causal model of turnover from organizations. In D. Dunkerley & G. Salaman (Eds.), The international yearbook of organizational studies (pp. 217-236). London and Boston: Routledge and Kegan Paul, Ltd.

Price, J.L., & Mueller, C.W. (1981). A causal model of turnover for nurses. Academy of Management Journal, 24, 543-565.

Reichers, A.E. (1985). A review and reconceptualization of organizational commitment. Academy of Management Review, 10, 465-476.

Reilly, N.P., & Clevenger, J.P. (1988). Nursing stress, coping, and social support. Unpublished manuscript: Washington State University.

Reilly, N.P., Clevenger, J.P., & Ikeda, M.I. (1988). Toward an understanding of the relationship between commitment and burnout. Unpublished manuscript: Washington State University.

Rentos, P.G., & Shepard, R.D. (Eds.) (1976). Shift work and health: A symposium. DHEW (NIOSH) Publication no. 76-203. Washington, D.C.: U.S. Government Printing Office.

Rosse, J.G., & Rosse, P.H. (1981). Role conflict and ambiguity: An empirical investigation of nursing personnel. Evaluation and the Health Professions, 4, 385-405.

Rousseau, D.M. (1978). Characteristics of departments, positions, and individuals: Contexts for attitudes and behavior. Administrative Science Quarterly, 23, 521-540.

Salancik, G.R. (1977). Commitment and control of organizational behavior and belief. In B. Staw & G. Salancik (Eds.), New directions in organizational behavior. Chicago: St. Clair Press.

Scholl, R. (1981). Differentiating organizational commitment from expectancy as a motivating force. Academy of Management Review, 6, 589-599.

Schuler, R.S. (1980). Definition and conceptualization of stress in organizations. Organizational Behavior and Human Performance, 25, 184-215.

Selye, H. (1956). The Stress of Life. New York: McGraw-Hill.

Selye, H. (1976). The Stress of Life. (Revised ed.). New York: McGraw-Hill.

Smith, P.C., Kendall, L.M., & Hulin, C.L. (1969). The measurement of satisfaction in work and retirement: A strategy for the study of attitudes. Chicago: Rand-McNally.

Steffen, S., & Bailey, J.T. (1979). Sources of stress and satisfaction in ICU nursing. Focus, 6, 26-32.

Steers, R.M. (1977). Antecedents and outcomes of organizational commitment. Administrative Science Quarterly, 22, 46-56.

Theorell, T. (1974). Life events before and after the onset of a premature myocardial infarction. In B.S. Dohrenwend & B.P. Dohrenwend (Eds.), Stressful life events: Their nature and effects. New York: Wiley.

Wanous, J.P. (1980). Organizational entry: Recruitment, selection, and socialization of newcomers. Reading, MA: Addison-Wesley.

Wilson, L., Prescott, P.A., & Aleksandrowicz, L. (1988). Nursing: A major hospital cost component. Health Services Research, 22, 773-796.

Yancik, R. (1984). Sources of work stress for hospice staff. Journal of Psychosocial Oncology, 2, 21-31.

Zedeck, S., & Kafry, D. (1977). Capturing rater policies for processing evaluation data. Organizational Behavior and Human Performance, 18, 269-294.

CAN WE PUT RESEARCH TO WORK?

TASK CYCLE THEORY:

A LEARNING-BASED VIEW OF ORGANIZATION BEHAVIOR

Clark L. Wilson

Emeritus, Graduate School of Management
University of Bridgeport

Those of us who practice Industrial-Organizational Psychology for a living outside of academia don't get--or don't take--the opportunity to interface with our academic colleagues as often as we should. Accordingly, this chance to present my thoughts is especially welcome.

As I see the role of I/O psychologists, we are in the business of change. We try to change individual and organizational behavior so people and groups can function more effectively in achieving relevant goals. However, I am not too sure we fully understand the important fundamental implications of such a statement. In my view, this charge calls for thrusts in areas where the literature is woefully inadequate.

Let me cite three shortfalls which I perceive to be critical:

1. The lack of operational models of organizational behavior. A model should give a total picture of the behaviors required to carry out a given activity or function. A model is a defining structure. It should make clear which behaviors are appropriate and which are inappropriate. I do not see this in the literature. I use the term "operational" in the most basic sense, to imply the spelling out of the actual behavioral steps taken to implement or define a concept. This is not done to anywhere near the degree necessary in our field.

Instead, we have had a plethora of theories that seem to encompass only parts of the whole. Likert (1967), McGregor (1966), McClelland (1961) all focused primarily on interpersonal relations but ignored the actual steps needed to get tasks accomplished. McGregor (1966), finding his notions did not serve him well in practice, concluded that "The boss must boss" and "I could not have been more wrong." I realize much has been written since these earlier proposals, but I see no progress toward operational translation of behaviors.

Nowhere has this lack of good modeling inhibited progress more than in the study of leadership. The literature does little more than take a stab at differentiating between management and leadership. I find this strange. Many writers, especially in the military literature (e.g., Taylor & Rosenback, 1984) insist that management and leadership are two different things. However, most students of industrial organization leadership use managers as subjects. Failing good models and failing effective measurement (which is my third shortfall below) operational concepts of leadership and management have never been adequately differentiated.

My other primary criticisms focus on the failure to take advantage of two theoretical legacies which have developed over the past 100 years.

2. The failure to take advantage of the literature on learning theory. In my view, the basic theoretical framework for understanding how to change behavior rests in learning theory, that which is often today referred to as cognitive theory. I prefer the term "learning" because "cognitive" is now used in so many widely diverse contexts that it has become diverse in meaning. I will expand on this point at length.

3. The failure to apply good measurement techniques. This shortfall seems to have started with the follow-up of the Ohio State Leadership Studies which gave us the Initiating Structure and Consideration constructs. The original studies of the 1940s and 50s appear to have been the last full-scale probe to identify an array of skills and attributes of leaders or managers (Stogdill & Coons, 1957). But, unfortunately, the follow-up studies did not employ the same level of psychometric insight as was displayed in the original series (Stogdill, 1974).

My views do not simply reflect a slavish devotion to quantification. It is of fundamental importance to see that, without measurement, there is no way to field test a hypothesis or model. Anecdotal reporting (e.g., Deal & Kennedy, 1982; Fordyce & Weil, 1979; Kanter, 1983; Leavitt, 1978; Peters & Waterman, 1982; and others) is not at all adequate. It stops at the level of hypothesis, is highly personal, and is not subject to challenge by other researchers. It is a nice "safe" approach for a writer. The author can say that he or she observed a certain dynamic and you or I can't dispute it because we were not there. Consequently, the large numbers of books on organizations, culture, leadership, and related topics make interesting reading and contain interesting hypotheses. But they fail to develop the necessary methodology to contribute to the literature on the mechanisms of change.

RE-ORIENTING THE PERSPECTIVE

I have been working since 1970 toward overcoming these shortfalls and would like to lay some of the results before you.

Let me couch my work and that of my colleagues in terms of trying to change the skills and attributes of managers and leaders. This is especially relevant today because it is reported that over 50% of major corporations have been restructured in recent years. Their aim has been to be more efficient in meeting competitive thrusts, particularly from abroad. However, top managements must make lasting changes, not just structural payroll reductions. To be effective in their strategies, top executives must keep three vital objectives in mind. They must (1) develop sound management skills to meet current goals, (2) develop foresighted leadership to remain competitive tomorrow, and (3) maintain a strong and supportive corporate climate or culture so the necessary changes and adaptations are implemented with minimized resistance. In the remainder of this chapter, I will focus on management skills and leadership and leave cultural considerations to another time.

To begin, it is important to understand how I differentiate management from leadership. Following that I will present the basic model: Task Cycle Theory.

Managers are responsible for achieving the goals and objectives implied by the organization's mission statements, whether implicit or explicit. They must be sure today's job gets done as dictated by appropriate goal allocations. Effective managers must have the balance--a word that crops up often in our studies of managerial skills--to achieve these operational goals and, in the process, bolster the quality of working life. If you hear echoes of the Ohio State Leadership Studies in these words, you are quite right. Structure and Consideration are very much alive, but in expanded form, as you will see.

Leaders function at a higher level--an extension of the manager's role. They, too, are responsible for performance and improved quality of working life, but they must also display the attributes that enable them to change the organization and its systems for the better: vision, competence, resourcefulness, venturesomeness, persuasiveness, and charisma. Such attributes induce others to follow. The key elements in leadership are the foresight and skills to visualize positive changes and to bring them about. These elements are distinct from--but in addition to--the managerial skills of facilitating immediate, short-term, goal-seeking activities.

THE TASK CYCLE MODEL OF ORGANIZATION BEHAVIOR

Table 1 presents the Task Cycle Model and will be the primary reference for the ensuing discussion.

By way of introduction, let me start with the general concept of the task cycle. In the first column of Table 1, I have shown how it relates to a simple generic task. The remaining columns adapt the concept to several key organizational roles.

Note that all of these are roles in which one person or group of people aims to influence others. They try to change or modify the behavior of others, whether they are in the roles of supervisors, peer specialists, sales representatives, or whatever.

Let me walk you through the logic of the task cycle. Every task starts with a purpose; a goal of some sort (Phase I). Once you have a goal, you must develop a plan to get there (Phase II). Then, to carry out your plan, you provide or acquire the necessary resources such as time, training, coaching, materials, etc. (Phase III). As you proceed, you keep track of your progress by obtaining feedback (Phase IV). If your feedback indicates you are off track or behind time, you make adjustments (Phase V). As you reach your goal, you give and gain reinforcement in whatever form is appropriate (Phase VI). Finally, the repeated implementation of this behavioral cycle leaves a residual profile of attributes which round out the personality of the task performer or manager.

I would like to elaborate on the dynamics of the model in general terms. First, I make no brief for there being precisely six phases in a task cycle. You may wish to add more or change it in other ways. The relevant point is that it is a sequence of chained activities, spelled out in sufficient detail as to serve as a source of hypotheses. These hypothesis, in turn, can be used in the creation of scales with which to operationalize the behaviors involved in the model.

Second, to achieve an organization's mission or to make it adapt and change, the work of many people must be coordinated. There are two operative concepts in that statement: Work and coordination. Work is not one uninterrupted stream of effort but a series of tasks, each with a

Table 1. The Task Cycle Model

Generic Task	Executives	Leaders	Managers
I. The goal What do I do?	I. The goal Clarify and direct mission achievement	I. The goal Envision and initiate change for future	I. The goal Clarify and communicate today's goals
II. The plan How do I do it?	II. The plan Develop and communicate strategies	II. The plan Solve novel problems resourcefully	II. The plan Plan and solve problems encountered
III. Resources How do I carry out the plan?	III. Resources Develop supportive culture	III. Resources Modeling, mentoring, and caring	III. Resources Facilitate by coaching, training
IV. Feedback How do I know I am performing?	IV. Feedback Track and share information	IV. Feedback Develop awareness of impact	IV. Feedback Obtain and give feedback on performance
V. Adjustment How do I fix my mistakes?	V. Adjustment Direct/oversee other managers	V. Adjustment Use persuasion to gain/maintain commitment	V. Adjustment Correct time and details to meet goals
VI. Reinforcement Satisfaction from achievement of the task	VI. Reinforcement Share rewards for organization success	VI. Reinforcement Share rewards for supporting change	VI. Reinforcement Recognize/ reinforce performance
Outcome Task achievement	Outcome Mission accomplishment	Outcome Change for the better	Outcome Today's goals achieved
Consequences Learning and growth	Consequences Recognition as industry leader	Consequences Recognition as a leader, innovator	Consequences Recognition, promotion

beginning and an end. Tasks group into projects and projects into missions. In every sense, a task is the unit of work; total performance is the sum of coordinated individual task and project performances.

Third, note that the behavior phases in the task cycle are sufficiently generic to be applicable to the wide range of tasks. At the top of the organization, a goal may be a mission, a plan, a strategy. At the first line level, we think more in terms of an immediate work goal and an operating procedure. But generally, the behaviors of all phases of the cycle can be seen in the work of executives, leaders, managers and supervisors at any level, or in independent contributors and organization representatives who contact clients and prospects.

Fourth, every manager (or leader) goes through the relevant phases of the cycle with every task he or she supervises. This means, with successive tasks and with multiple people, a manager iterates task cycle behaviors many times over. This puts forward two important and basic implications.

First, each task is fully equivalent to a learning trial. Managers learn about the individuals they supervise. But, equally important, if not more so, the relevant others learn a lot about the manager or leader. Especially, they learn what behaviors to expect on the next task so they can adapt to those expectations. This means very clearly that we can lean on the learning literature to get a better understanding of the dynamics of adaptation and change in organizations.

Therefore, let me point out briefly how this model ties into the cognitive learning paradigm of E.C. Tolman. Examination of Tolman's (1932) thinking has yielded especially useful insights. Two more recent, but excellent, sources provided the understanding necessary for this research. Bolles' (1972) updating of Tolman's cognitive theory contributed greatly to the original formulation of the task cycle model. Then, Hilgard's (1956; Hilgard & Bower, 1966) elaborations helped materially in putting task cycle theory into the Tolman perspective.

Hilgard observed that stimulus-response theories (for example, those of Hull, Skinner, and others) ". . . imply that an individual is goaded along a path by internal and external stimuli, learning the correct movement sequences [emphasis added] so that they are released under appropriate circumstances of drive and environmental stimulation" (Hilgard, 1956, p. 191; Hilgard & Bower, 1966, p. 196).

By contrast, Hilgard referred to Tolman's theory as sign learning in that ". . . the learner is following signs to a goal, is learning his way about, is following sort of a map . . . learning not movements but meanings [emphasis added]." The individual learns "sign-significate relations [emphasis added], . . . a behavior route, not a movement pattern." Further, Tolman's theory included the concept of expectancy: that with repeated experiences, an individual learns to discriminate a probability that a given behavior will lead to the expected end result. Hilgard added that these expectancies are confirmed or modified by the level of success in repeated trials.

To summarize Hilgard's observations, stimulus response theory put the emphasis on reinforcement. Reinforcement leads the individual to learn the appropriate steps to bring about that reinforcement. On the other hand, Tolman, placing less emphasis on reinforcement, took a broader view which included three elements that are important to us in understanding task management behaviors: (1) the individual learns the broader meaning of the task, (2) what is learned are the significant signs, and (3) the individual learns probabilities or expectancies that a given response pattern will lead to a goal and satisfy the need at hand.

Task cycle theory relates readily to Tolman's formulations. In the terminology of the managerial task cycle, the early phases of the cycle--especially Goal Clarification, Planning, Facilitation, and Feedback--are conceived of as equivalent to Tolman's signs. These "up-front" phases of the cycle signal direction and support to co-workers in the process of task execution. The level of these behaviors and their interaction with control behaviors are instrumental in generating levels of expectancy of success. Similarly, the final phase of the task cycle (Phase VI--Reinforcing Good Performance) is instrumental in generating expectancies of reward.

To view this point clearly, see the role of the manager in the Tolman context: <u>To raise the expectation of successfully reaching a work goal that satisfies a need of the worker and the organization</u>.

How are these expectancies generated? By providing the meaning and the signs--clear goals, effective planning, good coaching, continuous feedback, supportive control, and positive reinforcement--so that co-workers can have high levels of expectation of reaching worthwhile personal goals. If we pay inadequate attention to the early signs in the sequence and to the skills of sign givers--managers and leaders--we have, in effect, a leaderless leadership literature. We are not attending to how expectancies are developed in the first place (cf. Vroom, 1967; Vroom & Yetton, 1973).

So, in the Tolman context, the aim of task cycle theory is to provide a practical and meaningful conceptual framework to study the skills by which managers communicate appropriate behavioral signs to their co-workers.

One further observation should be made about how task cycle theory relates to learning theory. Seldom in writings on leadership or organizations does one see an emphasis on the sequential chaining of behaviors (Gagne, 1970; Skinner, 1938). Instead, investigators seem to have focused on single attributes or static arrays of descriptors. They have not probed the underlying sequences of behaviors that make up participative management, decision making, goal setting, interpersonal relations, etc. This has occurred despite the frequent references to management and leadership being "processes." A notable exception would be Simon's (1960) work on decision making. Looking at Tolman's concept as a sequence or chain of signs and resulting expectancies was the key to formulating task cycle theory.

The notion of chaining plays an important role not only in research strategies but also in teaching and training for change. Presenting desirable role behaviors as sequentially chained models gives participants a more completely integrated picture of the process one is trying to impart. It thus provides a conceptual strategy of what Gagne (1984, Chapter 7) and others would call a "learning strategy." Tying basic skills together into a meaningful sequence enables learners to integrate them more readily. This has been shown repeatedly in workshops. Participants have been taught goal setting, planning, coaching, etc. but without the awareness that they are interdependent and fit into a single practical sequence for more effective application.

The second inference to be drawn from the repeated cycling through task behaviors is that, with iteration, opportunities for reliable observations are readily present. The proof of this will be in the data, of course. And that is where we go next.

MEASURING MANAGERIAL SKILLS

With time, trial, and error, the concept finalized itself into the six phases of the <u>Managerial Task Cycle</u> (Wilson, 1975, 1978). Concurrently, analysis of field data led to specific scales to operationalize these phases. The following paragraphs list the scales that underpin the six phases. Following that, we will look at how the scales differentiate good from not-so-good managers. Then, we will do the same for the <u>Leadership Cycle</u> which is just beginning to produce data from field studies.

The <u>Survey of Management Practices</u> (SMP) assesses 11 operational dimensions representing the six phases of the Task Cycle and four relating to Interpersonal Relations. They are presented in the phased task cycle framework.

Task Cycle Phase I: Making Goals Clear and Important

1. Clarification of Goals and Objectives. The extent to which a manager discusses goals to be sure they are clear.

Task Cycle Phase II: Planning and Problem Solving

2. Upward Communications and Participation. The degree to which managers ask for suggestions and take action on them. This concept will be quickly recognized as springing from Likert's (1961, 1967) writings.

3. Orderly Work Planning. How well organized or systematic a manager is seen in the supervision of daily work.

4. Expertise. The degree of generalized knowledge of the organization and how to get things done; also contains items on general functional expertise, but not specific occupations.

Task Cycle Phase III: Facilitating the Work of Others

5. Work Facilitation. The extent to which a manager provides coaching, training, and other support for co-workers.

Task Cycle Phase IV: Obtaining and Providing Feedback

6. Feedback. This assesses downward feedback from manager to co-workers in the group. Upward Communications (No. 2 in Phase II) assesses the upward flow. The two together indicate the general health of the communications circuitry.

Task Cycle Phase V: Making Control Adjustments

7. Time Emphasis. The extent to which a manager makes sure that deadlines are met and things get done on time.

8. Control of Details. The extent to which a manager stays on top of the details and makes sure they are taken care of.

9. Goal Pressure. This assesses the exercise of pressure and push. In the extreme, it can mean punishing people and yelling at them for mistakes. However, in moderation and in balance with the up-front scales, it can be positive.

10. Delegation (Permissiveness). These items deal with letting people do things their own way, showing confidence in their ability to do their own planning, etc. High scores here are interpreted as good delegation if up-front behaviors in the task cycle are at or above norms. But they approach permissiveness when those up-front behaviors, excepting Upward Communications, fall below norms. If goals are unclear, plans not formulated, etc., then giving freedom amounts to laissez faire management.

Task Cycle Phase VI: Reinforcing Good Performance

11. Recognizing Good Performance. Providing pats on the back, compliments, and other rewards at the disposal of the manager; money is not mentioned.

Interpersonal Relations

Task Cycle rationale positions Interpersonal Relations as impact variables, the consequence of basic skills. The notion is that, surely, a good personality stands one in good stead to start. But to develop lasting favorable relations on a personal level, one must demonstrate that his or her managerial skills help subordinates reach higher levels of job satisfaction through meaningful contributions to organization goal achievement.

12. Approachability. Simple friendliness; ease of access and approach.

13. Teambuilding. Reflects efforts to get people to work together and cooperate. Also reflects effectiveness at making it happen. It is not unusual to see higher scores on the items reflecting effort than on those indicating effectiveness.

14. Interest in Subordinate Growth. Adaptations of McGregor's "Theory Y" and "Herzberg's Job Enrichment," which clustered together in an all item-level factor analyses (Wilson, 1978). Participants may be strong on Upward Communications and Approachability but be soft here on Subordinate Growth. This happens when other up-front scores (in the first four phases of the task cycle) are low. Subordinates see their bosses as easy to get along with but do not feel challenged.

15. Building Trust. This reflects two elements: the extent to which one's words and promises are kept and the extent to which the manager is seen as trusted by upper levels of management.

TESTING FOR VALIDITY: HOSPITAL WEIGHTED EQUIVALENT WORK UNITS (WEWUs)

The first requirement of any proposed model--and scaling instrument derived from it--is to demonstrate that it makes a difference and that you can make valid operational inferences from the data produced.

Over the past 15 years, we have tested the Survey of Management Practices (SMP) against hard performance data such as sales, budget variances, and other goal achievement measures (MbO) and against softer criteria such as performance evaluations and on-the-spot ratings. Almost without exception, higher level performers have scored better on most scales than their less successful counterparts. The largest and most stable differences have come from ratings by subordinates who usually differentiate more clearly between highs and lows. Superiors are next, except when performance evaluations and survey ratings are given by the same individuals. Then the superior ratings are more valid because of the confounding. Self-ratings are usually not significantly valid. In fact, it is not unusual to see self-ratings relate negatively, with high performers rating themselves lower on SMP than their counterparts. Interview data often reveal that high performers are often striving individuals who feel they can do better.

The most recent study, and one of the most relevant to the theme of "white collar" productivity was conducted by Professor Frank Shipper of Arizona State University with the cooperation of the Director and Staff of the Veterans Administration Medical Center in Phoenix. I think your interest will be heightened by the Weighted Equivalent Work Units (WEWU) criterion.

The Veterans Administration (VA) evaluates productivity by a measure of WEWUs, an approach adapted from industrial engineering. The basic quantity is an estimate of the number of personnel hours it should take to perform each task or "work unit." Various laboratory tests carry various WEWUs or "earned hours." Operations on patients carry a WEWU value depending on complexity, etc. Administrative departments also earn WEWUs. With repeated measures over successive periods, standards or norms are established to evaluate performance in later periods.

In practice, the sum of WEWUs at the end of a period is divided by the number of staff hours charged to the department. The resulting ratio of earned WEWUs divided by actual hours charged is a direct engineering-type measure of productivity on which an operating unit can be evaluated.

In Shipper's study, the SMP was administered for 68 managers. Then WEWU ratios were calculated for each one over a period of five quarters to use as a criterion in a concurrent validity study. The results are reported in Table 2 as an analysis of variance of direct reports ratings. The subordinate ratings on the SMP discriminated much more significantly than either supervisor or self ratings. In fact, no F-values were meaningfully significant for either of the latter two groups. Those that approached or reached statistical significance were based on curvelinear relationships with the Middle group (see Table 2) usually lower than the other two and thus providing the discriminating variance.

As in many such field studies, certain anomalies arose in the data gathering process. First, because several managers from a single department participated, it was not possible to sort out direct WEWU values for each one separately. Therefore, all managers within such departments were credited with the same number of WEWUs though it was apparent that their SMP scores varied from one to the other. In addition, some participants did not answer surveys about themselves; others did not receive ratings from supervisors. Four participants did not receive ratings from subordinates. Therefore, only 64 of the original 68 managers are accounted for in the ANOVA of subordinate ratings in Table 2.

Further, and of special significance in this study, the distribution of WEWUs was highly leptokurtic (g_2 = 14.2 when 0 fits the normal curve; SMP scales typically were between plus or minus 1.0). In fact, WEWU scores ranged from .845 to 2.23, but 22 of the 68 were squeezed between 1.040 and 1.125, bunched about the median of the distribution. This may not be too surprising because the center has evolved WEWU standards over time and the departments have become adjusted to working to meet those levels.

The pattern of significant scales is of interest: Clarification of Goals, Orderly Work Planning, Expertise, Work Facilitation, Feedback, Time Emphasis, and Building Trust. If we consider that a one-tailed test is appropriate, then Teambuilding and Interest in Subordinate Growth join the significant group.

The omissions are especially interesting. The four dimensions usually associated with the tone of personal relations--good or bad--are all non-significant: Encouraging Upward Communications and Participation, Delegation (Permissiveness), and Approachability that indicate positive tone while Goal Pressure marks the negative.

In short, the significant dimensions pertain to structuring the work in a positive supportive way. While they do not imply strong positive tone, neither do they lend a negative note. For example, Work Facilitation, Feedback, Expertise, and Trust are all very favorable supportive scales in their primary thrust. They imply coaching and communicating in helpful, meaningful ways.

Table 2. Difference in Subordinate Ratings of High, Middle, and Low WEWU Unit Managers

Dimension	High[1] Mean	SD	Middle[1] Mean	SD	Low[1] Mean	SD	High-Low[2] Diff	F	p-value
Task Cycle Phase I: Making Goals Clear and Important									
1. Clarification of Goals	63[3]	16	53	18	49	16	+14	4.00	.023*
Task Cycle Phase II: Planning and Problem Solving									
2. Upward Communications	64	17	57	18	56	18	+ 8	1.23	.300
3. Orderly Planning	65	16	55	21	50	18	+15	3.75	.029*
4. Expertise	73	14	63	17	57	14	+16	5.74	.005*
Task Cycle Phase III: Facilitating the Work of Others									
5. Work Facilitation	66	16	57	19	51	18	+15	3.78	.028*
Task Cycle Phase IV: Obtaining and Providing Feedback									
6. Feedback	64	16	53	18	52	15	+12	3.86	.026*
Task Cycle Phase V: Making Control Adjustments									
7. Time Emphasis	71	12	62	16	57	12	+14	6.19	.004*
8. Control of Details	52	13	45	14	40	9	+12	4.93	.010*
9. Goal Pressure	39	14	38	11	36	16	+ 3	0.30	.743
10. Delegation (Permissiveness)	65	13	59	13	61	13	+ 4	1.29	.284
Task Cycle Phase VI: Reinforcing Performance									
11. Recognition	66	17	57	18	54	21	+12	2.38	.102
Interpersonal Relations									
12. Approachability	69	17	61	19	62	18	+ 7	1.12	.334
13. Teambuilding	65	16	58	19	52	20	+13	2.87	.064
14. Interest in Subs	63	18	55	19	52	19	+11	2.37	.102
15. Building Trust	72	17	62	20	58	18	+14	3.22	.047*

[1] N = 20 High, 21 Middle, 23 Low.
[2] Diff: + = High is above Low; - = vice versa; degrees of freedom: 2.61.
[3] All scores are percentages of maximum possible, rounded.
* = significance approaching or bettering .05.

Once we could show that the SMP detects differences between high and low performers--as we have done many times--the next question was whether or not we could induce participants to change their behaviors in the indicated direction by feedback and whatever training or development opportunities we could offer them. The SMP has been used in several studies of change, one of which is exemplified in Table 3.

This study was conducted in another white-collar environment, a multinational bank. The SMP was administered as prework for a management training course. Participants got feedback from their superiors and two

Table 3. Changes in Measured Management Practices Following Training

Dimension	Pre[1] Mean	SD	Post[1] Mean	SD	Pre-Post Diff	F	p-value[2]
Task Cycle Phase I: Making Goals Clear and Important							
1. Clarifying Goals	59.7[3]	13	63.2[3]	11	+3.5[4]	2.86	.102
Task Cycle Phase II: Planning and Problem Solving							
2. Upward Communications	64.7	14	70.3	11	+5.6	6.25	.019*
3. Orderly Planning	59.9	15	62.1	13	+2.2	0.88	.357
4. Expertise	61.6	12	65.6	10	+4.0	4.32	.047*
Task Cycle Phase III: Facilitating the Work of Others							
5. Work Facilitation	57.5	13	60.9	10	+3.4	2.96	.096
Task Cycle Phase IV: Obtaining and Providing Feedback							
6. Feedback	58.5	13	63.7	11	+5.2	6.67	.015*
Task Cycle Phase V: Making Control Adjustments							
7. Time Emphasis	66.8	13	64.4	13	-2.4	1.46	.237
8. Control of Details	50.7	12	51.6	10	+0.9	0.28	.602
9. Goal Pressure	36.4	13	31.2	14	-5.2	10.37	.003*
10. Delegation (Permissive)	58.7	11	61.9	9	+3.2	3.59	.069
Task Cycle Phase VI: Reinforcing Good Performance							
11. Recognition	64.7	14	70.1	12	+5.4	7.13	.013*
Interpersonal Relations							
12. Approachability	68.2	16	74.3	16	+6.1	6.36	.018*
13. Teambuilding	60.8	13	65.8	11	+5.0	6.08	.020*
14. Interest/Sub-Growth	59.4	13	66.7	11	+7.3	10.52	.003*
15. Building Trust	66.2	13	70.7	12	+4.5	4.79	.037*

[1] N of managers = 29
[2] p-value is two-tailed
[3] Scores are percentage of maximum possible, based on averages of four subordinates for each manager.
[4] Positive signs (+) indicate postscores higher than pre and vice versa.
* = significance approaching or bettering .05.

groups of subordinates which they could compare with their self-assessments. One subordinate group included four support or clerical staff, while the other included four professional staff members.

The course was administered in three sessions of one week each, conducted at six-month intervals. The SMP was administered before the first and again before the second session, six months later. Thus, any measurable change might be ascribed to the feedback and training in the first session plus counselling between sessions.

Table 3 shows the results for 29 managers who participated in both sessions. It shows the changes in ratings from their professional staff subordinates. Ratings by their support/clerical staffs did not change significantly. It was acknowledged that the participants were more concerned with their relations with their higher level staff members who were, to all intents and purposes, their professional peers.

Note that in this study the variables showing the most significant change were those of a more interpersonal nature, which reflect Ohio State's Consideration construct: Upward Communications, Feedback, Goal Pressure (negative), Recognition, Approachability, Teambuilding, Interest in Subordinate Growth, and Trust. The positive change in Expertise may well be attributed to closer personal communications. These changes reflect the emphasis of the initial training session and the orientation of the management development program toward the needs of the institution.

The number of change studies is accumulating (Wilson, in press). We have shown positive change from feedback alone in as little as five weeks. However, in that case, the differences did not persist, leading to the conclusion that feedback needs to be accompanied by training or, at least, periodic reinforcement. In another study, in a private health-care facility, very significant and enduring changes were reported over a year's time. In this instance, the workshops focused on the skills of the Managerial Task Cycle. The course consisted of eight half-day seminars spaced a week apart and reinforced by application exercises on the job.

THE LEADERSHIP CYCLE

Having demonstrated to our satisfaction that we could differentiate between high and not-so-high performing managers and shown that we could change their practices over time, the next challenge was to try to do the same for leadership. Our work in this area is only about a year along, so the results I can share with you are very preliminary. But they are promising.

The instrument was the Survey of Leadership Qualities, Form D. It covers 16 dimensions, allocated to the phases of the Leadership Cycle as follows:

Leadership Cycle Phase I. Initiative

This involves the vision to see possible changes for the better and the confidence to make the thrust. The dimensions are:

1. Vision. Foresightedness; the ability to see around the corner. A key ability in bringing about change.

2. Risk Taking/Autonomy/Venturesomeness. The willingness to try new things for the good of the organization; to show an entrepreneurial spirit; to stick one's neck out.

170

3. Self Confidence. Self-assuredness of progress; confidence to step out and take the lead.

Leadership Cycle Phase II. Resourcefulness

This phase covers skills at finding new and novel ways to carry out initiatives; the ability to overcome obstacles.

4. Creativity. The ability to come up with original, new solutions to problems; inventiveness, ingeniousness.

5. Resourcefulness. Here the emphasis is on the ability to overcome obstacles; to get things done against odds; to reach a goal even when the going gets tough.

6. Judgement/Competence. The judgement and ability to make sound decisions; getting around in the organization's environment and operations.

Leadership Cycle Phase III. Exemplary Behavior

The essence of this phase is getting others to follow by setting examples; coaching and showing an interest in their well being.

7. Modeling or Symbolic Behavior. Reflects a leader's behaviors that are intended to be seen as examples for others.

8. Mentoring/Support. This pertains to lending a hand to support co-workers; coaching as necessary; enabling others to contribute to the accomplishment of a vision.

9. Caring. The extent to which the leader projects a concern about the personal well-being and growth of co-workers; reaching out.

Leadership Cycle Phase IV. Monitoring

People achieve higher goals and are willing to make changes if high standards are set for them and they know the leader is interested.

10. Expectations of Excellence. Letting people know that shoddy performance is not acceptable but to do this in a leaderlike way, not with a heavy hand (See 12. Push/Pressure, below).

Leadership Cycle Phase V. Follow-Through

A leader must exercise control and motivate others, but not in an overbearing way. There is nothing wrong with exercising push or shove, but it mustn't turn to pressure.

11. Persuasiveness in Gaining Commitment. The ability to get people to work with enthusiasm by influence and persuasion.

12. Push/Pressure. If this is high by itself, one can be a boorish individual, one whose behavior gets results through fear. But leaders can score high on PUSH if they have strong scores in the preceding phases. In that case, it may reflect energy and a healthy push, not pressure.

Leadership Cycle Phase VI. Recognition/Reinforcement

All people work for recognition. Effective leaders make sure that those who follow their lead are recognized for loyalty and support.

13. Recognition. The extent to which a leader makes people aware that their support and teamwork are worthwhile; that they gain something by the changes the leader is trying to achieve.

Residual Impact

The focus here pertains to direct measures of impact on, and relations with, co-workers.

14. Integrity. The degree to which a leader demonstrates high moral values. Trying to change things for the benefit of the organization and the well being of co-workers, particularly not making changes purely for personal, selfish ends.

15. Charisma. The degree to which co-workers are attracted by an individual to the point of following.

16. Leadership Potential. This is a capstone scale which serves both internal and external validation purposes. As you would recognize, it is extremely difficult to obtain a sound performance-based leadership criterion if we define it as bringing about change for the better. It is nearly impossible to demonstrate that specific changes--or the quality or number of changes--are attributable to a given individual. Therefore I inserted this dimension, which amounts to an adaptation of the literature on peer nominations. We use it to test the correlations with other scales to identify which of the measured attributes are most closely related to perceived potential. Whenever possible, as you will see in a moment, we also correlate it with an external criterion to see if that assessment does, indeed, measure something the survey respondents might agree is "leadership."

In practice, by the way, we find that this dimension carries considerable impact. Thus, it must be used with caution in feedback sessions. We usually report it separately from the results on the other 15 dimensions.

PRELIMINARY FINDINGS

Following are the results of a pilot study of bank managers in a chain of medium- to small-sized banks in Wisconsin. The CEO and President selected 17 managers, all of whom they considered to be good managers, but they rated ten as good leaders and the other seven with lesser leadership characteristics. The Survey of Leadership Qualities (Form D) was answered by the 17 participants about themselves and, in turn, they were each rated by the CEO and President and by five to eight subordinates. The data in Table 4 come from the subordinate ratings, but the criterion separation into high and low groups was made jointly by the CEO and President.

In Table 4, it is clear that the CEO and President made their criterion evaluations on the basis of the managers' ability to get things done; a reflection and expansion of Ohio State's Initiating Structure. The subordinates' ratings bear this out in that the most significant differences are on such dimensions as Modeling, Expectations of Excellence, Self-confidence, and Push/Pressure. Risk-taking almost came through but the scales on Vision Creativity, Resourcefulness, Competence, Mentoring, Caring, Recognition, and Integrity missed significance, in some cases by a substantial margin.

The capstone dimension, Leadership Potential, also differentiates, so the instrument appears to enable subordinate raters to tap dimensions which

Table 4. The Leadership Qualities of High and Low Rated Bank Managers on SLQ

Dimension	High[1] Rated Mean	SD	Low[1] Rated Mean	SD	Diff	Hi-Low t-val	p-val[2]
Phase I. Initiative							
1. Vision	73.5[3]	14	70.5[3]	15	+ 3.0[4]	1.02	.309
2. Risk-Taking	75.0	13	79.7	14	+ 5.3	1.88	.062
3. Self-Confidence	84.5	12	77.6	15	+ 6.9	2.52	.013*
Phase II. Resourcefulness							
4. Creativity	65.0	15	67.8	15	- 2.8	0.88	.383
5. Resourcefulness	68.1	15	67.0	15	+ 1.1	0.35	.730
6. Competence	75.8	15	75.0	17	+ 0.8	0.23	.819
Phase III. Exemplary Behavior							
7. Modeling	67.3	14	57.2	11	+10.1	3.62	.000*
8. Mentoring	64.3	16	60.7	19	+ 3.6	1.00	.318
9. Caring	61.4	22	59.3	22	+ 2.2	0.93	.353
Phase IV. Monitoring							
10. Expectations of Excellence	79.4	12	70.4	16	+ 9.0	3.18	.002*
Phase V. Follow-Through							
11. Persuasion	64.5	15	60.2	15	+ 4.3	1.38	.172
12. Push/Pressure	54.9	19	45.4	17	+ 9.5	2.50	.014*
Phase VI. Recognition/Reinforcement							
13. Recognition	61.8	21	59.3	22	+ 2.5	0.55	.584
Residual Impact							
14. Integrity	74.5	18	75.8	16	- 1.3	0.35	.728
15. Charisma	68.0	17	63.5	18	+ 4.5	1.23	.220
Potential	73.9	18	65.0	22	+ 8.9	2.12	.031*

[1] 76 ratings of 10 highly regarded leaders; 33 raters of lower 7
[2] p-values are for a two-tailed test
[3] Scores are in percentage of maximum possible
[4] Differences are + if high-rated managers received higher scores on a dimension and vice versa.
* = significance reaches or betters .05

the CEO and President had, by inference, used to separate good from not-so-good leaders in the first place.

By no means should one study of this magnitude be given too much weight. At best, it is only indicative of what may be done. In that vein, a previous experience may be of interest. On an earlier form of this instrument, I had respondents from two distinct populations. One was the multinational bank. The other was a group of people working in charitable and educational organizations. They all rated their managers and supervisors on leadership qualities, including Leadership Potential. In the educational-charitable population, the dimensions of Caring and Charisma both correlated very positively with Potential. However, this was not the case with the bank population. There, the highest correlations with Potential were on Self-Confidence, Expectations of Excellence, and so forth, findings not greatly different from the small bank population reported here.

THE MANAGEMENT-LEADERSHIP INTERFACE

Having asserted at the outset that there had been too little effort to differentiate between management and leadership and having presented data on both domains, I feel compelled to discuss what I think we are learning about that differentiation.

So far, only one sample of managers (N = 38) has been administered both the Survey of Management Practices (SMP) and the Survey of Leadership Qualities (SLQ). These 38 managers were rated by just under 200 subordinates on each instrument. Several more samples are in the offing.

Of the 240 correlation coefficients that account for the overlap between the 15 SMP and the 16 SLQ variables, only 15 exceeded .40 and 210 were less than .30.

Since 12 coefficients would have achieved significance by chance alone, one can say with reasonable confidence that the two instruments are tapping different domains. The internal consistency coefficients on both instruments ranged from .75 to over .90, so lack of reliability did not restrict the level of the intercorelations.

STRUCTURE AND CONSIDERATION REVISITED

As a matter of course, I frequently run second-order factor analyses of scale scores. Invariably, if I clamp down on the number of factors extracted and rotated, I end up with super factors which resemble the original Ohio State variables quite clearly. For example, with SMP, the following three-factor solution is typical. I cite only the top structure coefficients, or loadings, to give you a flavor:

Factor I: Facilitation + .87; Approachability +.85; Participation +.84; Recognition +.82; Feedback +.76.

Factor II: Control of Details +.79; Time Emphasis +.65; Orderly Planning +.54; Clarification of Goals +.40.

Factor III: Goal Pressure -.85; Facilitation +.38.

I interpret Factor I as an expansion of Consideration; Factor II as Structure; and Factor III as a more extreme structuring to the point of overcontrol.

With SLQ, the picture is similar with this comparable solution:

Factor I: Caring +.89; Charisma +.71; Mentoring +.69; and Integrity +.58. Leadership Potential, the capstone variable, loads +.52.

Factor II: Vision +.89; Self-Confidence +.88; Expectations of Excellence +.76; Risk-Taking +.74; Modeling +.69; Resourcefulness +.69; and Potential, the capstone variable, loads +.76.

Factor III: Push/Pressure -.80; Persuasiveness +.84; and Recognition +.79.

In this instrument, insofar as these data are representative of what is to come, Factor I is clearly reflective of <u>Consideration</u>. Factor II takes on a similar cast for leaders as for managers. Here, we see a <u>Forward Thrust</u> in addition to straight structuring, as was intended. Factor III is much the same as its counterpart in SMP with the negative implications of Pressure polarized by positive implications of Persuasiveness and Recognition; the totality reflecting something akin to an urgency which can go too far. Thus, it duplicates Factor III in SMP with the negative sign on Goal Pressure and the positive on Facilitation.

CONCLUSIONS

What are we learning? The main points are these:

Yes, you can assess meaningful skills and attributes if you work at operational levels and abide by some basic measurement rules. You can show that assessments are meaningful in that scores correlate with external measures of performance, whether they be hard or soft measures of productivity.

Further, you can change behavior in meaningful ways with feedback and training. We have demonstrated this with managerial-level skills and attributes (Wilson, in press).

We have also learned that we can differentiate between good and not-so-good leaders and, most importantly, that the dimensions of leadership, as we define them, are different from those of basic management.

Changes in measured leadership skills and attributes from feedback and training or other interventions are still to be demonstrated.

Finally, one cannot work in the area of managerial, leadership, and organization behavior without developing a keen awareness of the original Ohio State dimensions of <u>Initiating Structure</u> and <u>Consideration</u>.

Every time we do a validity of change study, we find that the variables tend to differentiate or move in sets which can be identified with those original Ohio State dimensions. There is little doubt in my own mind that these two venerable dimensions must be seen as second-order or, even, third-order factors which encompass more specific scales. They turn out to be the super factors from which most all others are derivatives. Many of my higher-level factor analyses bear this out just as can be seen in these studies of managerial and leadership attributes and practices.

REFERENCES

Bolles, R. C. (1972). Reinforcement, expectancy, and learning. <u>Psychological Review</u>, <u>79</u>, 394-409.

Deal, T. E., & Kennedy, A. A. (1982). <u>Corporate cultures</u>. Reading: Addison-Wesley.

Fordyce, J. K., & Weil, R. (1979). <u>Managing with people</u> (2nd ed.). Reading: Addison-Wesley.

Gagne, R. M. (1970). Conditions of learning (2nd ed.). New York: Holt, Rinehart, and Winston.

Gagne, R. M. (1985). Conditions of learning (4th ed.). New York: Holt, Rinehart, and Winston.

Hilgard, E. R. (1956). Theories of learning (2nd ed.). New York: Appleton Century.

Hilgard, E. R., & Bower, G. H. (1966). Theories of learning (3rd ed.). New York: Appleton Century.

Kanter, R. M. (1983). The change masters. New York: Simon and Schuster.

Leavitt, H. J. (1978). Managerial psychology (4th ed.). Chicago: University of Chicago Press.

Likert, R. (1961). New patterns of management. New York: McGraw-Hill.

Likert, R. (1967). The human organization. New York: McGraw-Hill.

McClelland, D. C. (1961). The achieving society. Princeton: Van Nostrand.

McGregor, D. (1966). Leadership and motivation. Cambridge: Massachusetts Institute of Technology. (First published in Adventure in thought and action, Proceedings of the Fifth Anniversary Convocation of the School of Industrial Management, M.I.T., 1957.)

Peters, T. J., & Waterman, R. H. (1982). In search of excellence. New York: Harper and Row.

Simon, H. A. (1960). The new science of management decision. New York: Harper and Row.

Skinner, B. F. (1938). The behavior of organisms; an experimental approach. Englewood Cliffs: Prentice-Hall.

Stogdill, R. M. (1974). Handbook of leadership. New York: Free Press.

Stogdill, R. M., & Coons, A. E. (1957). Leader behavior: Its description and measurement. Columbus: Research Monograph No. 88, Ohio State University.

Taylor, R. L., & Rosenbach, W. G. (eds.). (1984). Military leadership. Boulder: Westview Press.

Tolman, E. C. (1932). Purposive behavior in animals and men. New York: Appleton Century Crofts.

Vroom, V. H. (1964). Work and motivation. New York: Wiley.

Vroom, V. H., & Yetton, P. W. (1973). Leadership and decision making. Pittsburg: Pittsburg University Press.

Wilson, C. L. (1975). Multi-level management surveys: Feasibility studies and initial applications. JSAS Catalog of Selected Documents in Psychology, 5 (Manuscript No. 1137). Washington: American Psychological Association.

Wilson, C. L. (1978). The Wilson multi-level management surveys: Refinement and replication of the scales. JSAS Catalog of Selected Documents in Psychology, 8 (Manuscript No. 1707). Washington: American Psychological Association.

Wilson, C. L. (in press). Improving management practices through feedback and training. In J. W. Jones, B. D. Steffy, & D. W. Bray (Eds.), Applying Psychology in Business: The Manager's Handbook. New York: Lexington Books.

A SYSTEMS ANALYSIS OF WHITE COLLAR TRAINING

Robert B. Ochsman

University of Arkansas at Little Rock
Little Rock, Arkansas

Roger A. Webb

University of Arkansas at Little Rock
Little Rock, Arkansas

IMPACT OF TECHNOLOGY ON TRAINING NEEDS

There is a TV ad for a computer company that is very instructive. The actor who we know as Radar from MASH answers the phone of a business at what appears to be closing time. An unseen customer apparently asks about prices since, after a few key strokes on a console, the actor answers about a price being in effect until a particular date. When the phone rings again the former Radar transfers himself with another few key strokes and effects a working class voice to answer a question about a shipping date. To a third call, the actor switches himself to research, effects a stuffy accent and answers yet another question. Finally, he puts on his hat and leaves after a grateful salute to the machine. This ad is ostensibly about the power of technology and is designed to sell a particular brand of computer. Appropriately configured, of course, any number of machines could function in this manner, so we see another feature of this situation as much more interesting. Here is an employee, who is actually utilizing the power of his company's technology and who can function within a complex, multifaceted, organization in a comfortable and efficient manner. As psychologists we have two questions: where did they get this guy, and more important, where could they get some more?

Our ad example actually introduces an interacting set of serious and complex questions. The major problems for organizations in the information age becomes more and more a question of human performance--the machines to an increasing degree can do anything we ask of them. But how do we staff our machinery to get anything approaching full utilization of their power. The ability to use the machinery, moreover, is only one source of the new pressure on employees. The nature of jobs and current management theory are also pushing toward the necessity for employees that are competent in new ways.

The Small Business Development Center at our university tried to project the job market ten years into the future and came to some striking conclusions (Opitz, 1986). For example, their projections suggest that many of the new jobs created (and virtually all the good ones) will require specialized knowledge in at least one area, and that the best jobs will require the ability to integrate complex data from different sources in order to make decisions (i.e. will involve management functions). Most of the new jobs--from clerical to management--will be oriented heavily toward technology. Both the available technology and modern theories of management are pushing decision making down to lower levels of organizations. Thus, more is being expected of entry level employees.

At the crudest level, the initial question may be what general strategy to pursue: selection or training. In the process of finding more people who can function like the hero of our ad, does the company need to concentrate on actually finding a person to do this (selection) or can they teach these skills to existing or newly hired employees (training)? In this chapter we will look primarily at training aspects of improving white collar productivity. However, we will return to the issue of selection later.

An initial stress on training can be justified on pragmatic grounds. We can predict with great accuracy how many individuals will reach their 21st birthday or retire in the next twenty years. It is clear that the "baby trough" that has been moving through the population and causing havoc in the educational community is reaching the entry level job market, and we presently have a dearth of potential entry level employees. People born in 1965, the first post-Baby Boom year, turn 23 this year. At least until the "baby boomlet" hits the job market, businesses are going to have to upgrade positions by retraining old employees. Other sources suggest that the single biggest investment cost facing American business in the remaining years of the 20th century will be the costs associated with training workers to use the technology that is available. These projections suggest that the cost of training may be ten times greater than the investments in the hardware and software of information systems, and--for those of us who are college professors--relatively little of the money is likely to go to colleges and universities.

CURRENT STATE AND THEORY OF TRAINING

A cursory review of the training literature in the late 1980's is something of a good news/bad news joke. The good news is that technological innovations now available offer a true revolution in the efficiency of training. As a quick example: Hidden away in a subdirectory of the system on which this line is being written is a typing tutor that cost about $35. This marvelous piece of software will give each new user a typing test to assess the speed level and errors of that user, keep track of the records of that individual user by name, help plan training goals, and create lessons that challenge, but do not overwhelm, on an individual basis. These are teaching skills that we associate with master teachers, but which are available to anyone with a home computer and a few dollars. What we will be able to do with laser disk, and other advanced technology, is only beginning to be recognized. The possibilities are truly amazing.

About ten miles north of our university's campus, at the Jacksonville Air Force Base, the U. S. Air Force is building its main training facility for its largest cargo plane. At that facility, it is, or soon will be, possible to fly a C-130 into most airports or Air Force facilities in the world under a variety of conditions and to perform a number of standard missions without leaving the ground. A state of the art simulator will provide visual, auditory, and even correct vestibular input, and will respond to controls exactly as the real air craft would--except that you cannot hurt yourself or destroy the plane. A home computer version of a less sophisticated flight simulator has been available for some time. The flight simulator--particularly in its more sophisticated from--is a near perfect training device. It provides an opportunity to practice a virtual analog of a real task with completely appropriate sensory input and feed back in real time.

There is more good news. Not only do we have better and better toys, but psychology has a reasonably well developed theory of training that specifies to a high degree what constitutes good and bad training exercises and directs the construction of new training activities. It is hard to think of an area in any behavioral science that has such a strong theoretical base. The theory is admittedly not one of the great monuments to the human intellect, being borrowed in pieces from learning studies, but it is serviceable, and has been in place with remarkably little fundamental change for almost thirty years. If we compare the 1965 edition of Gagne's Conditions of Learning with the 1985 version, we find a good deal more similar than different. The language is still that of stimulus-response conditioning and learning. Analyzing tasks into learnable units is still critical. Clear response definition--usually of a functional type--is borrowed from laboratory operant conditioning studies. Periods of information intake need to be interspersed with periods of practice. Reinforcement appears to be more of an informational than motivational concept, and the immediacy of reinforcement is still probably the most important aid to learning that can be delivered by technology. The basic relationships captured many years ago in Osgood's transfer surface are still valid. Incompatible responses to an near identical stimulus situation produce maximal proactive interference. Why else would we keep the inefficient QWERTY keyboard as the standard despite the ready availability of much better designed alternatives (e.g. the Dvorak.)?

This is not to say that there have not been theoretical changes. People still tend to refer to displays of new tasks to be learned as stimuli. However, a filmed demonstration of the operation of a computer driven lathe is not a stimulus either in the classical sense of an event that elicits a response or in the operant sense of an event that signals the occasion to emit a response. The taped demonstration is a complex display. The processing of the display is probably best understood in terms of a cognitive model with translation of that model into action. It is not surprising that the main differences in old and new versions of work on instructional psychology is an acknowledgment of cognitive strategies. Still, calling the demonstration a stimulus is a convenient short-hand.

And now for the bad news. The bad news is that many of the problems of training, particularly in industry, seem to be the same as those cited by Hinrichs (1974) in his review of the literature for the Handbook of I/O Psychology. Training in industry is still largely in the hands of people who are not psychologists, and in the worst cases, seem little better than old fashioned snake oil peddlers. Most training packages or modules that are sold to business are probably marketed without task analysis or training needs analysis. For many practitioners and managers, training implies mainly motivational or interpersonal concepts that are slightly modified from the group techniques of the 1960's. It is much more likely that a accompany will throw a training program at a problem than do a systematic analysis of their training needs and develop a problem solving approach that might include some training. Most training, like most education, is probably never evaluated in any systematic fashion. Much of the best training is done by companies who have no desire to share their data with competitors, and who thus maintain their training records on a proprietary basis. The United States military is probably the largest and most competent user of training technology in the world (and probably has been for 25 years) but much of their work is not accessible.

Possibly, a more serious problem is that what we really know how to train is not relevant any more. The technology and theory of training as it has developed out of the psychology of learning is very good at teaching skills. If you want to train a person to operate a lathe, both good theory and snappy techniques are available, as we argued above, and it will work. We can handle things like word processors pretty well. Simulations of even very difficult and complex skills, such as our C-130 example above, can be used with significant improvements in performance at low cost. But what do we really know about the skills of the man depicted in the ad we described in our opening paragraph. How do you train people to think in systems terms? How do you get a person to develop a functional cognitive model of a corporation? How do you train people to translate figures on a CRT to a living dynamic reality? Most important of all, how do you train people who have grown up in an industrial climate that discourages thinking and responsibility to change their fundamental outlook on their job. We are not at all sure that psychology, at this stage of the game, has much to say about these problems, but are fairly certain that increases in productivity lay in such adaptations to the information age.

Before we despair, let us first outline what we think is the proper way to examine training needs and to plan training investments. Beyond a theory of training and set of techniques, psychology has developed sound heuristics for the analysis of training needs and the measurement of effectiveness. It appears to us that the use of a systems approach to training is, at least, a beginning and goes some way toward clarifying our problem.

A SYSTEMS APPROACH

In the broadest sense, a system is merely a hierarchical assembly of things that are coordinated in action and aimed toward some goal. A business, governmental body, or factory are all examples of systems. In most cases, however, these institutions do not reflect the best in systems planning or implementation and therefore in many situations they have lost the intrinsic advantages that this fundamental structural model affords.

The overriding mentality in developing a systems strategy for development and evaluation is to assess the functioning of combinations of organizational units. The more traditional unit-by-unit analysis defies the rational day to day give-and-take functions within an organization.

There are two key features of systems which are particularly important and bear heavily on the problem of white collar training: interdependencies of subsystems and the specific interactions of those subsystems. A complete analysis of all of the organizational variables is beyond the scope of this chapter. However, the general issues raised by an appreciation of their impact within a training systems framework is presented.

Personnel specialists can increase significantly the effectiveness of managers in an organization by employing a wide range of training and development techniques. There are many potential trade-offs possible in an organization when considering how to increase the output quality of a work force. Indeed, after careful analysis, the strategies for improving the performance among some employees may not even include a training program. The potential trade-offs and a conceptual framework for a particular situational evaluation are best addressed through a systems strategy.

182

LESSONS LEARNED FROM A SYSTEMS ANALYSIS

A primary lesson to be learned from systems analysis is that we must focus on the most significant sources of variance in order to control or change that system. A revealing anecdote told by Al Chapanis (personal communication, 1971) will amplify the point. Some years ago, the U.S. Army was concerned with improving the overall accuracy of their artillery units by decreasing the random variability of the fall of the shells. A less than thorough analysis identified the problem as a hardware difficulty. The officers in charge of dealing with the problem apparently felt that the variance in the performance was in significant part due to variance in the manufacture of the shells. The manufacture of the ammunition was therefore closely scrutinized and there was, indeed, some unacceptable variance in the manufacture of this equipment. With a substantial cost increase, steps were taken to tighten specifications and to increase the quality control in manufacture.

The results were predictable. The total system gain realized by the improvement in the shells was disappointing. There was some very small increase in accuracy, but the time and expense involved could never justify the effort. At that point, the tasks of the soldiers themselves were considered as a potential major source of variance in the system. Specifically, the task of the spotter was examined. Part of the spotter's task is to give a distance estimate to the target. Examination of the accuracy of those estimates revealed a substantial amount of random variance. Indeed, this source of variance was by far the major contributor to the total variance of the performance of the unit and affected its total performance far more than any other source. Remedies for the problem then became more obvious. A combination of job aids, training, and refined selection was aimed at reducing the greatest contributor of variance--the spotter. The results were a substantial increase in accuracy.The moral of the story is clear. If at one point in our system there is an operation which has low inherent error, and if, further, in another location there is an operation which is relatively more inaccurate, it is not economical to attack the operation which has the low source of error, since its contribution to the total error is much smaller than at first we might suppose. It can be statistically shown that it is not the simple addition of error variance but the addition of squares of the error variance which make up the total system variance (Chapanis, 1951).

There are a number of significant insights for the more general case of training and performance in this anecdote. First, when one attempts to refine or improve a system, the first key step is to identify both the sources of variance and the relative contributions of those sources. The greatest and easiest gains will be made here. Second, one will often find that there will be a managerial bias toward dealing with the more mechanical, easily observable elements of the system rather than the human resources in that system. This is most likely due to the familiarity that managers have in trouble shooting a process with observable, easily discernible elements. The third point involves the actual solution to the problem. When the source of the problem was identified, some combination of training, job redesign, or selection seemed to be the solution. The precise combination of those elements cannot be determined, however, until some specific attention has been paid to the systems environment and the trade-offs involved. This chapter will provide some insight into this process through systems criteria and strategies germane to understanding white collar training in organizations.

Table 1. Main Sources of Variance in Performance of White Collar Employees

---

general intelligence
experience
selection
training
placement
relevant personality attributes
technical skills
social skills and social environment
communication skills
drive
job design
the interaction of the above with the corporate environment
all double, triple, etc. interactions

THE SYSTEMS APPROACH APPLIED TO WHITE COLLAR TRAINING

In order to come to a full understanding of the promise and inherent limitations of training white collar employees, a reasonable appreciation of those sources of variance that contribute to the quality of performance of these employees is needed. Table 1 represents probably the great bulk of the sources of variance in white collar productivity. This list is not intended to advance any sort of grand model. The intent is only to serve as a framework for further discussion.

Clearly, these variables are not mutually exclusive and are only listed explicitly in order to try to capture the richness and diversity of skills and aptitudes probably relevant to white collar performance. Although, this is only a coarse analysis, it does serve to illustrate several points.

Many Variables Contribute to Managerial Performance

The strong general tendency for simplistic explanations of behavioral phenomena germane to white collar productivity stems both from a lack of formal training in the determinants of human behavior and a desire for quick and inexpensive solutions to problems. While there are situations in which the "quick fix" mentality may be appropriate it seldom applies to jobs as complex as those of the typical white collar worker.

The list of variables in Table 1 is not exhaustive but does reflect what probably accounts for most of the variance found among white collar employees. To the extent that this is valid, then the magnitude of the problem is clear. There are so many primary variables and interactions among those variables that the amount of variance that any one of those effects taken alone accounts for is most likely not substantial enough to make a profound difference in the total variance mix.

A significant and quite sobering realization about this situation is that only a small subset of these effects can be controlled or manipulated by management. The bottom line is that the amount of variance available for control is limited. The outcomes of superb management in the selection, placement, and training functions may in fact be drowned by the overwhelming effects of all the other variables.

Of even greater significance is the profound impact of interactions. Indeed, it often happens that while the primary variables themselves have little impact, the interactions of those same variables are significant and have important implications. Because the nature and existence of interactions are so easily overlooked in an organization, some detailed consideration of the more significant ones involving training are addressed below.

Some Interactions Involving Training

Training x General Intelligence. This is maybe the most powerful of all the interactions affecting training. Cascio (1987) describes the situation well: "Selection of high caliber employees will enable these individuals to learn more and to learn faster from subsequent training programs than will the selection of lower caliber employees....It's well established that those individuals with greater intellectual competence benefit far more from education than those of lesser aptitude" (p. 48). Cascio also points out that training programs for upper level personnel must be designed to develop competence in meeting a great variety of situations. While the implications of this truism reach far into our social and cultural values, the meaning is clear in a business setting. The realized gains for a business from a white collar training program will be systematically related to the intellectual capacity of its employees.

The one consistently valid prediction that the score on a "paper and pencil" tests can reliably produce is that of one's trainability. It is no accident that tests such as the Graduate Record Exam and the SAT that are used to predict the success in school are really nothing more than lightly disguised intelligence tests. Indeed, the performance of individuals on these standardized tests and intelligence tests correlate highly.

One obvious outcome of this interaction is the burden placed on recruitment, selection and placement to produce individuals who have the greatest potential to maximally benefit from training. Also, this means that the the training program will be fairly sophisticate and therefore more expensive. Also, the number of trainees will be lower under this kind of regime and consequently the per trainee cost will be considerably higher than one aimed at many, less sophisticated students. A careful analysis of the utility of such a strategy should, therefore, be conducted by examining closely the dollar trade-offs.

Let us note briefly that the selection and placement (promotion) of employees on the basis of tests that are primarily intelligence tests is fraught with difficulty. While we will return to this point, we wish to note that a careful documentation of Training X Intelligence interactions may be a critical step in establishing the "business necessity" required by guidelines and court rulings for the use of aptitude tests.

Training x Experience. Both the relevance and the extent of experience are important factors in modifying the effects of training. Positive transfer may occur if the job experience is relevant to the new responsibilities. However, to the extent that the new job may call for a different set of behaviors, negative transfer could easily hinder the effectiveness of a worker. In this situation, training, or at least some kind of re-orientation, would be of value.

If prior experience is extensive and relevant, probably no training program could prove of even marginal benefit unless there is some focused skill or behavior that is being targeted by that training program and for which there is a clear deficit in the job incumbent. Experience in the sense of longevity alone is probably a negative factor in most situations.

The longer people stay in the same job the more likely they are to be less capable or to have learned many bad habits.

Training x Selection & Placement. Selection and placement are two, often distinct processes. However, the two functions are commonly performed concurrently and it becomes impossible to distinguish the two. Also, for purposes here, the two behave similarly in this interaction.

This interaction is of major significance, particularly for a systems analysis of the human resource mission of an organization. The general nature of the interaction is inverse. As the training mission increases in breadth and depth, selection and placement constraints typically fall away, although the character of the relationship is probably far from linear. Conversely, as selection and placement efforts produce a more qualitative outcome, training needs decrease. Placing some exact parameters on the precise nature of these trades-off in the general case would be next to impossible. There is, however, some real merit in attempting to calculate a financial utility prediction for particular business settings.

A brief example will illustrate a possible outcome. This example is patterned after Chapanis (1971) and assumes that there are 10 job applicants for one position. The hypothetical organization is considering two alternative strategies in order to end up with one successful candidate. Alternative "A" has a less elaborate and extensive selection process, which would only eliminate two of the candidates. This scheme would therefore allow a lower per student cost for the training procedure because training costs would be amortised over a greater number of students. Alternative "B" would institute a more complete and rigorous--and therefore more expensive--selection process which would eliminate all but two individuals. The more efficient training program would then have only a two student load. However, since only two individuals are going through training, the per student cost would undoubtedly be higher. Hypothetical costs are estimated as shown in Table 2.

A sizable cost saving is realized under strategy "B". Of course, a decision to commit to either strategy would have to factor in other significant considerations such as the differences in legal jeopardy between the two schemes and the bottom line quality of the applicant who is ultimately placed in the position.

Training x Social Skills and Training x Communication. As social and communication skills ("SCS") commonly interact in a similar fashion with training, we treat them together. The SCS that are most germane to effective management are typically easily trainable. Unless there are some unusual personality characteristics or organic speech difficulties, most individuals can acquire the appropriate skills through appropriate training programs.

Training x Job Design. A poorly designed job will usually produce poor or at least reduced performance whatever training regimen is instituted. If a job makes demands on an individual that are patently unreasonable, a job incumbent may potentially respond in any one of a large number of counterproductive ways. Examples of such situations would be conflicting demands, inadequate or inappropriate resources, defective corporate organization leading to overlapping areas of authority, etc. Certain kinds of training may prepare an individual for this kind of situation and perhaps instill some coping techniques for short term accommodation. In the long term however, no amount or quality of training can overcome a job that is poorly designed.

Table 2. Hiring costs under two selection and training strategies

Cost Item	Strategy A	Strategy B
Selecting one applicant	$ 100	$ 300
Ten applicants	X10	X10
Total for screening	$1000	$3000
Training $ per student	$1000	$1500
Size of class	X8	X2
Total for Training	$8000	$3000
TOTAL	$9000	$6000

Another example of poor job design is illustrated by the <u>functional foremen</u>. Once proposed by Frederick W. Taylor (Taylor, 1903) as an ideal management model, the scheme proposed to have job incumbents supervised by a number of foremen, each of whom specialized in a different part of the task to be performed by a subordinate. The obvious problem of a worker having multiple bosses who may place conflicting demands on the employee apparently was not well considered by Taylor. Examples of managers having to meet a number of conflicting job demands simultaneously are certainly legion.

All Triple, Etc. Interactions. Marvin Dunnette, in his seminal 1963 article presented a model that portrays the complexities of real prediction situations. The major distinguishing feature of his model is the emphasis on the identification of all the relevant variables which contribute some significant variance to the process of selection as well as to identify, or at least understand the nature of, all the possible interactions between those variables.

As Chapanis and Lockhead (1965) pointed out, there may be hidden interactions which serve to negate or even reverse the effects of the major variables. Thus, it may be necessary to focus and customize a training program for a particular individual, who will be in a particular position, with specific resources available, working with a specific kind of workforce in a specific setting.

It is not entirely unthinkable to consider how one might implement a program that reflects this kind of model. Larger organizations with some discretion in their placement decisions may be in a position to implement such a strategy. Also, automated computer assisted instruction systems might be able to tailor a training program from a set of options in a data base.

This list of interactions is probably far from complete. It has been presented only to illustrate a possible strategy for a more complete understanding of the role of a training program for white collar employees in an organization. There are a variety of other systems strategies, some of which are discussed below.

OTHER SYSTEMS CRITERIA

There are several systems methodologies for evaluating white collar training programs. While not addressed in detail here, they all provide an analytical framework that is illustrative of a systems approach:

Closing the loop. It is surprising how often training programs are evaluated by a process that somehow avoids addressing the major question: What is the difference in performance on the job, pre and post training? While there are clearly methodological problems with pre-test and post-test designs, the data collected would still provide a rich resource for evaluating the training program. (Cascio, 1987, offers a brief discussion of experimental designs well suited to the evaluation of training outcomes.) This feedback process would also ensure that the training program remains flexible and would adjust to a changing corporate environment as necessary. The more typical open loop approach for evaluating training programs is far less effective. Usually, only a gross measure of failure or success rate is obtained, revealing nothing about the particular strengths or weaknesses of the training process.

Evaluating the training in terms of goals or mission statements of other units. This can be a difficult standard against which to measure training. Mission statements may be vague or nonexistent. Indeed, at best, this kind of input into the program may provide only a philosophical orientation. Even that, however, can temper the training with a pervasive guiding strategy that will facilitate the integration of the training into the total corporate philosophy.

User characteristics. Demographic and personal characteristics can sometimes be an important component in designing a training program. Qualities such as age, sex, cultural background, health, and adaptive limits for example, may act as moderators in designing a tailored training program for individuals.

Multiple contingencies. White collar personnel are often faced with unanticipated, unique problems and situations for which no amount of training can prepare one in a specific way. History is full of dramatic stories of large scale system failures exacerbated by the inability of managers of that system to deal with problems that have multiple causes and solutions. Such examples are the great northeast power failure of 1965, the crisis at Three Mile Island, and the management decisions leading to the Space Shuttle disaster. White collar employees must be taught how to be effective in less structured situations. They must know how to creatively develop a strategy to deal with a problem for which there is no ready made or obvious solution. They must practice being effective in situations with potentials for multiple foul-ups and break-downs. Their training should include exposure to a breadth of situations in which they must respond with specific, creative interventions.

Human-machine allocation. This is one of those questions that will not go away as technology becomes increasingly advanced. Indeed, the issue is more pressing than ever. The major component of this problem is constantly evaluating the trade-off function inherent in the decision to swap people for machines in an environment of evolving technology. AI and intelligent systems are a potent competitor for many of the tasks per-formed by some white collar employees. Part of that trade-off function may be the cost and time to train individuals to complement and support the machine's functions. For example, systems programmers, and techni-cians may have to be brought on line to support the new technology.

Another consideration in the allocation problem originates from the changing quality of jobs. Computers, for example, clearly have some strengths that are not shared by humans and the reverse is also true. Job dimensions such as environmental constraints, sensory isolation, speed and accuracy, information overload, storage capacity, decision making, learn-ing, etc. should all be factored into these decisions (Woodson, 1981). The outcomes of the allocation decisions have an important bearing on what

kinds of jobs an increasing concentration of white collar personnel will
do. For example, an increasing number of lower-level management positions
are being lost to computers sitting on the desks of middle managers.
These middle- level managers now have the ability to directly access and
integrate large volumes of data and make decisions accordingly without
requiring the services of lower-level managers who formerly filled this
function. The training implications are two-fold. The lower-level
managers will require training in those domains that have not yet experienced displacement by automation and the middle- and upper-level managers
will require training to be able to effectively utilize the new machines.

IMPLICATIONS OF A SYSTEMS APPROACH

The systems analysis outlined above is a framework for locating the
greatest potential sources of variance in job performance, planning
interventions, and assessing outcomes in the context of an organizational
framework. The most important implications are probably the stress on
needs analysis, a heuristic for prioritizing potential impact, and the
stress on evaluation. It is no small wonder, then, that industrial
psychologists, particularly those of an academic bent, have not fared well
in the competition to sell training to industry. How can a rigorous
analytic approach compete with a three-color brochure? Moreover, virtually
all the important sources of variance in outcomes are interactive and
inherently difficult to explain to laymen. Still, we stand by our position
that this is the right and proper way to approach training analysis and
that, in the long run, it will pay off.

The problem that worries us more is the question of what we are
trying to train employees for. The early sections of this presentation
outlined the pressure that new technology and new managerial practice are
putting on employees. To hold even a good entry-level job, people are
going to have to be conversant with the available technology and are going
to have to accept responsibility for a wider range of tasks. Many of
those tasks are ones that we have usually associated with managerial
responsibility. We also suggested that the demographics of the American
work force are going to require companies to up-grade existing employees
rather than hire new ones for new jobs.

A reexamination of our initial example (Radar as the triune employee)
underscores the needs. A few needs are obvious. There is a small skill
component involved and a person X machine interaction: Radar has to know
how to use the computer keyboard. The more important abilities are less
obvious. Our character must have a broad view of the organization as a
whole and know how the components are connected as well as how to access
the information. Finally, he must be motivated to take responsibility for
tasks that certainly transcend a narrow job description. His view of the
organization, his view of his job and his view of himself are critical
elements of this performance. How do we train these things? The answer
is that traditionally we have not. We have considered these features of a
person's performance under the heading of education and class outlook. If
we take the abilities required by our character, they sound very similar
to the list of attributes of a college educated person suggest by the
Association of American Colleges (1985).

If our analysis is correct, some fairly uncomfortable possibilities
are raised. First, we must assume that the intelligence X training and
selection X training interactions are going to be critical. Our ability
to place people in the new, enriched, jobs may be severely limited by
education and social class outlook. Some workers will resist wider
responsibility. Many people may not be bright enough to perform the new

jobs. We concur with Gottfredson (1986) who argues that jobs break into a natural status hierarchy based to a great degree on their complexity and the degree of intelligence required to perform them. What are the implications of discovering that a large percentage of the population are simply incapable of performing the tasks we need them to perform.

Whether the limitations of human performance are inherent to the person or a function of training and job design are obviously based on some very fundamental questions. In its extreme form, we are talking about the nature—nurture problem which is at the heart of many of our theoretical disagreements as well as our theories of society, politics and justice. We are not likely to solve these questions in any simple fashion or any time soon. Still, watching how our work force adapts to the demands of new technology and the relative roles of capacity, education, job design and training in that process may offer data for more fundamental questions than the pragmatic short-run question of white collar productivity.

REFERENCES

Association of American Colleges. (1985). Integrity in the college curriculum: A report to the academic community.

Cascio, C. F. (1987). Applied psychology in personnel management. Englewood Cliffs, NJ: Prentice-Hall. Inc.

Chapanis, A. (1951). Theory and methods for analyzing errors in man—machine systems. Annals of the New York Academy of Sciences, 51, Art. 7.

Chapanis, A. (1970). Systems Staffing. In K. DeGreene (Ed.), Systems psychology (pp. 357-382). New York: McGraw-Hill.

Chapanis, A., & Lockhead, G. R. (1965). A test of the effectiveness of sensor lines showing linkages between displays and controls. Human Factors, 7, 219-229.

Dunnette, M. D. (1963). A modified model for test validation and selection research. Journal of Applied Psychology, 47, 317-323.

Opitz, J. H. (1986). Planning Arkansas' economic future: The new manufactures. Center for research and public policy, University of Arkansas at Little Rock.

Taylor, F. W. (1903). Shop management. New York: American Society of Mechanical Engineers.

Woodson, W. E. (1981). Human factors design handbook (pp. 3-5). New York: McGraw-Hill.

RESEARCH: WHAT GETS IMPLEMENTED, AND WHY

Virginia R. Boehm

Assessment & Development Associates
Portland, Maine

The application of behavioral science research can contribute greatly
to organizational and personal productivity. Our belief in that assertion
is what motivated this conference. But, while there have been some very
successful behavioral science applications including some presented at this
conference (Cascio, this volume) there have been nowhere near as many as
there could have been and should have been, largely because there is a gap,
and a sizable one, between research and implementation.

What I'm going to do is sketch some principles, based on my experience
and the experience of others that seem to predict the likelihood of research
getting implemented, and illustrate them with some examples, some successes,
and some failures.

The first and absolutely essential element that must be present if
implementation is to take place is this:

Principle 1. The subject of the research must be clearly and directly
related to the solution of an organizational problem perceived by the
decision makers in the organization.

Simple, yes, and it has been said many times before. I don't care how
elegant your theory is, how striking your research results, or how
inexpensive they would be to implement. If those in the organization who
make the decisions don't perceive a problem in the area that your research
addresses, the chances of implementation are absolutely zero. Why should
there be implementation if there is, in the eyes of the organization, no
problem to solve. As the old saying goes "If it ain't broke, why fix it?"

In fact, in the eyes of the organization, there is no reason why there
should even be research conducted in the first place in the absence of a
perceived problem. Science for its own sake is simply not viewed by most
organizational decision makers as being an acceptable reason for conducting
behavioral science research in an organizational setting. Research has to
be sold, a fact of life that makes some academic researchers quite
uncomfortable.

When it comes to selling research, there are some very clear, but all
too often ignored "How to" guidelines such as those spelled out in Making it
happen: Designing research with implementation in mind (Hakel, Sorcher,
Beer, & Moses, 1982):

1. Concisely describe in nontechnical terms the primary and secondary objectives of the project and the advantages of conducting it with the methodology you suggest.

2. Ask for and listen to management's reaction.

3. Explain how the project findings will benefit the sponsoring managers and their organization, and contrast these benefits with the consequences or implications of not completing the project (p. 105).

Selling research is much the same as selling anything else. First you qualify your prospect, then you establish a need for your product, then you deal with resistance, explaining what is in it for the buyer, and finally you close the deal. The same steps also apply to getting research results implemented: establish the need, then establish the benefit.

Assuming that the research does address a perceived problem, the next principle to consider is:

Principle 2. The solution provided by the research must cost less to implement than it costs to live with the problem.

Not all organizational problems are worth solving, and "costs" are social, psychological, and political, as well as financial. For example, let us say that your research clearly demonstrates that restructuring a training program will result in productivity improvement. The costs of the new training are the same as for the old. Yet, your revised training program does not get implemented. Why? There could be many reasons. Maybe the person who developed the current program has a psychological investment in it and is in a position to block change. Or the person who delivers the training is seen, rightly or wrongly, as unlikely to be effective in delivering the revised training. Perhaps the new training uses techniques that do not mesh well with the organizational culture. As a general rule, if you cannot figure out why your good, solid, problem solving research does not get implemented, it is a pretty good bet that a cost factor, one that you are totally unaware of, is behind the failure. The paper presented by the Sedelows at this conference (Sedelow, & Sedelow, this volume) provided an excellent illustration of this. Automation was not fully implemented in spite of a very high benefit/cost ratio. The manufacturer was looking down the road at future costs, e.g., if a computer built the cars, who could afford to buy them.

When implementation is considered, Kellas, Simpson, & Ferraro's (this volume) extremely interesting and potentially far reaching research on aging is very likely to run into the same problem. While it does cost organizations substantial amounts of money to entice people to retire and to replace the lost expertise, and while Kellas and his colleagues' work indicates that this is often an unnecessary expense, change in the near future is unlikely because of the demographics of the work force. Behind the relatively small generation approaching early retirement age are the babyboomers, millions of them, and the organizational cost of not providing fast-track opportunities for the high performers in the babyboom generation is viewed as higher than that of funding expensive early retirement programs. However, I predict that a generation from now, when the babyboomers themselves begin to near retirement age, findings such as those noted above will be "rediscovered" and used as a vehicle to justify incentives to keep people in the workplace longer, as the following generation of workers is substantially less numerous.

Costs and benefits of research implementation change, as times change, as society changes, and perhaps most of all as the people in the organization the researcher deals with change. This brings us to Principle 3:

Principle 3. Research is more likely to be implemented if "buy in" is obtained BOTH from those who can effectively block implementation AND those who must approve it.

While nearly all researchers recognize that implementation of research requires the approval of someone with the authority to make a decision to go ahead with it (the "yeasayers"), all too often, potential "naysayers" are overlooked.

Identifying the "yeasayers" is easier. This is what qualifying your prospect is all about. Is your contact point the actual decision maker? How is your contact viewed by the organization? How much political clout does your contact have in the organization? In other words, make sure you understand who the client actually is and make sure that you are working with the right people in the organization. And contrary to a commonly held view, it does not have to be the CEO. The larger the organization, the less likely you are to be dealing with the CEO unless the problem you are investigating is one of earth shaking importance to the organization. But do make sure that the person you are dealing with can make the decision to implement research results. This is usually not difficult to determine. A rule of thumb that I use is that, if the person I am dealing with controls the budget used to fund the research, I conclude that I am dealing with the right person.

Identifying the "naysayers" is more difficult. The "naysayers" are those in the organization that can quash implementation even though they cannot approve it in the first place. One logical "naysayer" in an implementation effort that involves unionized employees is, of course, the union. Either actively, or simply by passive resistance, the union can doom virtually any research based intervention to certain failure if its buy-in is not obtained early in the process. This is especially likely to happen if the goal of the intervention is a productivity improvement that might be viewed as a threat to job security.

It is also possible, although rare, for an intervention to be so acceptable to the union as to lead to the intervention's ultimate failure. One example, and there have been several similar ones in the absence control field, is presented in a study by Pedalino and Gamboa (1977). They implemented a lottery-type incentive to modify attendance behavior. It worked very well and the "game" became so popular with the workers that the organization had to discontinue it or else it would have wound up as part of the union contact.

Another "naysayer" that should be considered is the user of the research product, the person whose job is changed as the result of implementation. The work reported at the conference by Cocklin (this volume) provides illustrations of this. Even if there is no threat to job security brought about by increased use of computers in the work place, there are vast changes in the social fabric of the work environment. If resistance is to be overcome, using computers must not only be easier than not using them, it must be more rewarding as well.

A more subtle and harder to recognize category of "naysayer" is the informational gatekeeper. In order to keep an implemented intervention up and going and functioning properly, there must be monitoring of progress by someone in the organization. And to perform that monitoring function, the monitor must have access to information. The higher the organizational level of the monitor, the more likely that information is withheld or edited, simply because its importance and relevance are not recognized by the gatekeeper.

Business executives simply cannot read every piece of mail they receive or return every phone call. Even if the monitor in charge of keeping an implementation on tract is very much committed to the success of the program, it may fail if the information gatekeeper does not regard "minor" problems as being important enough to get through the screen. By the time the problems are major enough to pass the screen, it may be too late to salvage the program.

Of course, gatekeepers can deliberately as well as inadvertently withhold or distort information. Information is power. Manipulating information is a very common form of organizational politics and frequently interferes with the implementation of research. One reason information manipulation takes place is that the implementation of research is nearly always a threat to someone. Why? Because the research was undertaken to solve a problem, and its implementation represents a "better way" of doing something. This, of course, implies that the old way didn't work or was inefficient. If the implementation has not been sold to whomever was responsible for the old way and that person is put in the position of informational gatekeeper or monitor, the program is likely to be in serious trouble.

The above implies Principle 4:

Principle 4. If implementation is to be successful over the long run, there must be someone in the organization given specific responsibility for making it happen.

A recent article in The Industrial Organizational Psychology (Connolly, 1986) refers to this as the fourth level of delivering consulting services-- providing the answer to the question "How can we make sure this doesn't happen again?" The answer is that somebody has to be in charge, someone in the organization who knows what is going on. If you are an external consul- tant or an academic researcher, this cannot be you. But making sure that the monitoring and control function is established is part of your job. As Connolly states, "Giving something we have created a final 'slam' towards correct implementation as we exit can go a long way towards making those things we design and deliver that 'should' be effective, truly effective" (p. 39).

Making sure that monitoring takes place also makes it much more likely that the consultant will be called in to do further work with that organiza- tion. "Hit and run" is not a good consulting tactic. This is a reason why academic researchers tend to have "bad press" with some organizational decision makers. The researcher obtains the data, gives the organization whatever sort of feedback or report was agreed upon, and, having obtained what is needed for the research program, disappears. The researcher's needs have been met; but as far as the organization is concerned, the effort is far from complete.

Continuing implementation and assuring good, quality implementation requires as much effort, sometimes more, than initiating implementation, particularly if the program is costly or time consuming. After the initial wave of organizational enthusiasm wears off and other priorities emerge, interventions tend to decay. Someone decides a particular step could be left out or the cost of certain aspects reduced, etc. When feedback ceases, productivity begins to decay. If an intervention is not monitored, it will in time undergo change and this change is usually in the direction of increased entropy. Nobody has ever exempted behavioral science phenomena from the second law of thermodynamics!

There is a reverse side to this, however—monitoring can become an end unto itself. If the monitor is so sold on the intervention as to become a "true believer," the intervention may become so entrenched in an organization that it remains long after the need for it has vanished or after the state of the art advances to the point where the task could be done better. The monitor may feel that his/her career advancement, and perhaps even job security, is firmly rooted in the maintenance of what was once a valuable intervention but is now an organizational dinosaur.

In addition to organizational dinosaurs that result from interventions that have outlasted their usefulness, there are organizational unicorns and other mythical beasts that occur when the next principle is violated:

Principle 5. If successful implementation is to occur, the research upon which it is based must be feasible, given the current state of the art.

The reverse of organizational decision makers who do not think that behavioral scientists can contribute anything worthwhile are those who think we can do anything—those who ask for the moon. And sometimes, we are dumb enough to promise it.

I recently received a Request for Proposal (RFP) for a test development project that sought a paper and pencil test that would be demonstrably fair for 13 different applicant groups. Apparently what is being sought is an aptitude test that is content valid and a scientific challenge that would discourage most of us. I am not going to bid on that one, but somebody will, and will spend the next several years in court.

When we promise or acquiesce to do what we know is not presently within our capabilities, we contribute to a perception of behavioral scientists as charlatans. Yes, as I said earlier, we must sell our research, but we must sell it on its merits, not on the basis of promising to do things we cannot.

Sometimes, this is a fine line to walk. It is, of course, flattering that a client or potential client has such confidence in our abilities that we are charged with an impossible mission. We know that if we do not take it on, someone else will. However, over the long run, bad research just does not pay; which brings me to the last principle.

Principle 6. In the long run, good research will be more widely implemented than bad research.

Yes, I have days when I wonder if quality means anything, when I look around and see poor research and even pseudo research being picked up by organizations and implemented.

But while various behavioral science fads get picked up by organizations, they soon fade away. Why? Because interventions based on bad research simply do not work. They do not provide lasting solutions for the problems they are intended to deal with.

Do you know any organizations who are "doing Hertzberg" these days? No. Why? Because a motivation theory that was developed based on studying accountants and engineers (professional people who generally derive intrinsic satisfaction from their work as well as a livelihood) just does not work for groups in the workplace less internally motivated. It was very limited research. It did not last.

How about all those nice theoretical models for predicting turnover? Anybody using them? No. Time has demonstrated that the best way (and the cheapest) of determining likely turnover is to simply ask the question directly.

On the other hand, well researched and developed aptitude tests have been in widespread use in organizations since World War II. And, in spite of many external pressures, they are still there. Why? Because they work, i.e., they are valid and their proper use increases productivity.

Behavioral modeling techniques based on social learning theory are increasingly replacing more lecture-oriented approaches to supervisory training in organizations. Why? Because they produce measurable change in job behavior that can be directly tied to positive organizational outcomes such as decreased absence and improved productivity.

Research on goal setting is beginning to provide a solid basis for performance evaluation and improvement systems that can actually be demon- strated as being linked to improved productivity. Yes, we have had and will have our successes. The reason for success is an underlying basis of good research.

Good research drives out bad. The goals of academic researchers and organizational problem solvers are the same--they want to find out what works, why, and see it used. The difference is simply one of focus. Research scientists focus more on the process. Organizational problem solvers focus more on the outcome. These interests are complementary. Good process is very unlikely to yield a poor product. Bad process is unlikely to yield a good one.

The theme of this conference is "Psychology and Productivity: Bringing Together Research and Practice." In my view, it is nearly impossible to separate them. Practice that is not based on factual underpinnings is "wheel spinning", and research that is not problem based goes nowhere and is soon forgotten.

In the monograph, "What to study: Generating and developing research questions" (Campbell, Daft, & Hulin, 1982), the authors looked at the origins and process of research that has proven to be significant. One of their conclusions was, "In almost every case, the force driving the effort was a specific and important problem to be solved. It was not a method or technique (independent variable) in search of a problem (dependent variable). It was very definitely the other way around" (p. 113).

The business community can benefit greatly from behavioral science research in solving organizational problems, but the academic community can and should benefit equally, by using organizations as a source of meaningful problems to solve. If behavioral science research findings are to be implemented to the greatest extent feasible in the real world, the methods used and the conclusions drawn must be viewed as applicable and relevant by those with problems to solve.

REFERENCES

Campbell, J. P., Daft, R. L. & Hulin, C. L. (1982). What to study: Generating and developing research questions. Beverly Hills: Sage.

Connolly, P. M. (1986). Implementing solutions as a consultant. The Industrial Organizational Psychologist, 23(4), 35-39.

Hakel, M. D., Sorcher, M., Beer, M., & Moses, J. L. (1982). Making it happen: Designing research with implementation in mind. Beverly Hills: Sage.

Pedalino, E. & Gamboa, V. U. (1977). Behavior modification and absenteeism: Intervention in one industrial setting. Journal of Applied Psychology, 62, 529-540.

CONTRIBUTORS

Virginia R. Boehm, Assessment and Development Associates, Portland, Maine.

Wayne F. Cascio, Graduate School of Business Administration, University of Colorado at Denver.

James P. Clevenger, Department of Psychology, Colorado State University, Ft. Collins, Colorado.

Thomas G. Cocklin, Human Interface Group, Hewlett Packard, Ft. Collins, Colorado.

James E. Driskell, Eagle Technology, Orlando, Florida.

Craig K. Goishi, Institute for Motivational Development, Newport Beach, California.

Richard A. Guzzo, Department of Industrial-Organizational Psychology, New York University.

Robert Hogan, Department of Psychology, University of Tulsa.

George Kellas, Department of Psychology, University of Kansas.

Jeffery Scott Mio, Department of Psychology, Washington State University.

Robert B. Ochsman, Department of Psychology, University of Arkansas at Little Rock.

Susan Raza, Department of Psychology, University of Tulsa.

Nora P. Reilly, Department of Psychology, Washington State University

Sally Y. Sedelow, Department of Computer Sciences, University of Arkansas at Little Rock.

Walter A. Sedelow, Department of Computer Sciences, University of Arkansas at Little Rock.

Diana L. W. Whitney, Department of Psychology, Washington State University.

Paul Whitney, Department of Psychology, Washington State University.

Clark L. Wilson, Graduate School of Management, University of Bridgeport.

Survey of Management Practices, 166

Task cycle theory, 160, 164–168
  chaining, role of, 161, 164
  leadership cycle, 164
  management cycle, 164
Technology, 1, 188–189 (see also
        Artificial intelligence;
        Computer systems)
  documentation for, 23–24
Team effectiveness, 3, 82–83, 93–102
  and organizational context,
        100–102
  and personality, 96–100
  in technical tasks, 97, 98
Training, 4, 179–190 (see also
        Selection and training
        programs)
  theory of, 180
  and communication, 184, 186–187
  and experience, 184, 185
  and general intelligence, 184, 185
  and job design, 184, 186
  open loop approach to, 188
  and placement, 184, 186

Word recognition, 37
Writing, 2, 23–31
  computer aids to 24, 27–30
    Invent, 27
    Writer's Workbench, 27
    Writer's Helper, 27
  processes involved in, 25–27
  and productivity, 23–24